14th July

DEREK JACOBI

As Luck Would Have It

MY SEVEN AGES

as told to

Garry O'Connor

HarperCollins*Publishers*

HarperCollins*Publishers*
77–85 Fulham Palace Road,
Hammersmith, London W6 8JB

www.harpercollins.co.uk

First published by HarperCollins*Publishers* 2013

1 3 5 7 9 10 8 6 4 2

© 2013 Derek Jacobi

Derek Jacobi asserts the moral right to be
identified as the author of this work.

A catalogue record of this book is
available from the British Library

HB ISBN 978-0-00-745887-5
PB ISBN 978-0-00-745888-2

Printed and bound in Great Britain by
Clays Ltd, St Ives plc

MIX
Paper from
responsible sources
FSC www.fsc.org **FSC™ C007454**

FSC™ is a non-profit international organisation established to
promote the responsible management of the world's forests.
Products carrying the FSC label are independently certified to
assure consumers that they come from forests that are managed
to meet the social, economic and ecological needs of present
and future generations, and other controlled sources.

Find out more about HarperCollins and the environment at
www.harpercollins.co.uk/green

*I dedicate this book to Mum and Dad,
and to my teacher, Bobby Brown.*

THE SEVEN AGES

All the world's a stage,
And all the men and women merely players:
They have their exits and their entrances;
And one man in his time plays many parts,
His acts being seven ages. At first, the infant,
Mewling and puking in the nurse's arms.
And then the whining school-boy, with his satchel
And shining morning face, creeping like snail
Unwillingly to school. And then the lover,
Sighing like furnace, with a woeful ballad
Made to his mistress' eyebrow. Then a soldier,
Full of strange oaths and bearded like the pard,
Jealous in honour, sudden and quick in quarrel,
Seeking the bubble reputation
Even in the cannon's mouth. And then the justice,
In fair round belly with good capon lined,
With eyes severe and beard of formal cut,
Full of wise saws and modern instances;
And so he plays his part. The sixth age shifts
Into the lean and slipper'd pantaloon,
With spectacles on nose and pouch on side,
His youthful hose, well saved, a world too wide
For his shrunk shank; and his big manly voice,
Turning again toward childish treble, pipes
And whistles in his sound. Last scene of all,
That ends this strange eventful history,
Is second childishness and mere oblivion,
Sans teeth, sans eyes, sans taste, sans everything.

Shakespeare, *As You Like It*, II, vii.

CONTENTS

PROLOGUE

The boy with the veil

It shimmers and enchants; it belongs to a secret, magical, forbidden world, and I have always wanted it.

She keeps her glorious white silk wedding veil – part of her wedding trousseau – in her wardrobe, and I sometimes sneak into my parents' bedroom and gaze at it. And then one day in 1945, when I am six years old and they are both out at work, I creep into their room, open the wardrobe and carefully lift out the veil. I drape the gorgeous white material round my shoulders and over my head, and, swishing it around and puffing myself up like mad, I go out of the house and parade up and down Essex Road.

We East London kids like to play out in the Essex Road and the adjoining streets, and do so in complete safety. The streets of England are our playground. We make dens in the front gardens, and dream and imagine we are other people and characters. From as early as I can remember I have been excited by the idea of dressing up, and this is my first recollection of being in costume.

Perhaps it is to impress Ivy Mills that I have worn Mum's wedding veil, though my first girlfriend is Winnie Spurgeon. We play hopscotch, and doctors and nurses, with two other girls

1

in the street and we chalk our initials on the pavement. Yet it is Ivy, the prettiest of the three, who has now become my favourite. The boys in my class start to chalk on the pavement, 'DJ LOVES IM', and I will do anything to please her.

But on this day I know I'm not just pleasing Ivy. I know in some instinctive way that I am *performing*, perhaps for the first time in my life, and suddenly all the world – or at least Essex Road – is my stage. And in transforming myself, and entertaining Ivy, I have a sudden insight – a sense of who I am, and who I could be, when I'm not just being myself.

I can become other people in my imagination – but can't we all? I can be a hero or villain, strong, weak, timid, arrogant, crafty, trusting, passionate, destructive, nurturing ... I can be anything I want to be. After all, I'm a human being, full of everything you can possibly imagine.

Of course Ivy, Winnie and my friends laugh at me and are most impressed. I play up to it for all it's worth – strutting, waltzing, skipping, galloping around the pavement until my veil is finally shredded to bits on the front garden privets.

———❦———

Mum was back home when I returned. She was waiting.

'Well, this is it,' I thought. 'She's going to go completely bananas at me when she finds her precious wedding veil torn into tatters!'

I was starting to cry as I stood there ready for her to tear me to shreds – just as I had torn her wedding veil.

But her reaction wasn't anger: she hardly told me off at all.

From that moment I continued to fancy myself in the veil. The idea of the veil stuck in my mind as a garment that, whoever wore it, both concealed and revealed the person. Yet the actor in me, the dressing-up part of me, was a mystery which I never could understand, right from the beginning – and that still remains the case today. I can only describe it as a magical process.

Later I would say that the actor must somehow have got in there right from the start, at the moment of conception, but God knows where he came from. Was I simply born an actor, as grandly titled by Edmund Kean – 'A prince and an actor' – a part which I was to play later in Jean-Paul Sartre's play? Even then, in that earlier time as a child, the first part I ever acted was a prince, and this prince was by no means to be the last.

We take it for granted that actors can act; the skill or craft – or the trick – is to make people believe they are seeing somebody real on stage, not an actor acting. Ideally they should leave the theatre talking about the person they've seen and the emotions they've felt, not saying, 'Gosh, isn't he a good actor?' That suggests that it has been merely a spectator sport, and the actor has been showing off. Audiences or viewers want to believe they have been in the presence of a real person.

But theatre, film and television are trickery; a bit of a performance works, and I glow to myself. I know I've managed to carry it off, and it is a moment of pure, private pleasure. As every actor does, I have felt the power and the glory of trickery and mystification.

Yet who would ever have suspected that that little boy who was so excited at putting on his mum's wedding veil would in time come to play real and fictional people – Hamlet, Lear, Hitler or Alan Turing, and a great host of others? Who could ever have known that he would come to live in the palaces or grand locations of his games and imagination, or re-inhabit in stories the real places, such as Bletchley, or the suburbia-like lower-middle-class Leytonstone, which had an importance in his early life?

It was the fate and destiny established way back in my past, in my childhood or before, that there would be many, many parts, well over the 200 mark through my seven ages, behind which I would hide my true self, conceal myself as behind a veil, yet at the same time be able to reveal some of who and what I was.

AGE I
INFANT,
MEWLING

1

THE FRONT ROOM

It was all a ghastly mistake. The state of the world at that time was such that no one thought of having a family. Hitler was already advancing fast and the world was on the brink of war when I was born in East London on 22 October 1938.

This was in our front room in Leytonstone. My mum – Daisy – struggled in labour for forty long hours to give birth. *Forty hours!* Has anyone ever taken so long to be born? It must be a record. Mum was completely worn out, and when at last I'd been delivered she sank back and groaned, 'Never again!'

'Is this what it's all been about?' said our doctor, as he held me up with just his right hand to show Mum and Dad. Mum and I were then placed in an improvised oxygen tent to recover. She had no more children.

The labour may have been endlessly protracted and I was probably the most appallingly mewling, puking infant, but from that moment on I was the sole object of my parents' love and attention. They lived for me, exclusively and without reservation. Each Christmas Day, for instance, I would wake, rub my eyes and gaze in utter wonder at my presents at the end of the bed: not one but two pillowcases stuffed full of presents of every kind – games, toy trains, Meccano, jigsaws – all just for me!

There would never be anyone else in the house besides the three of us: my parents and me. It encouraged me to have the highest ideals and aspirations, and it may well be that the romanticism stemmed from this extraordinary good fortune of being favoured as an only child, with devoted and loving parents, while they, too, grew steadfastly more romantic about me. They always believed in the best of me – and wanted the best for me – in spite of anything that might not prove them right.

So from the start I had no rival; at times I might have missed the presence of a brother or sister, but actually, I had to remember, not only did I get all the pocket money and all the presents, but I carried all their fears, love and aspirations. As my mum Daisy and my dad Alfred both worked, I thought at first we were favoured with wealth and good fortune, but when I found out we weren't, it didn't really matter.

There were few disadvantages in being so well favoured from the start. I might certainly claim that I've been 'dogged' by good luck, so maybe that's my misfortune, and the huge obstacles to overcome that most people have to face to make their way in the world – I've had very few of these. Heartbreaks yes, but that seriously – as we shall see – is another matter. For I was born a romantic, however much I might want to wrestle with it and deny it. Seventy-five years later I am still as much a romantic as I ever was, and still as unromantic in appearance as ever I was.

Yet I have an abiding sense of never having been taken quite seriously enough – that is, it goes without saying, as I take myself! I've always felt there was something about me which doesn't give off that radiation, that sense of power – either it is my look, or the life journey I've been through – which doesn't have suffering crying out at every twist and turn. It is true that few have taken me as seriously as I'd like to have been taken.

Nor have I championed anything, nor been a martyr to anything – no, and I've never been much of a mover or a shaker either, always a follower. If I haven't suffered enough – *mea culpa*, I pray I might be forgiven, for isn't it the dogma of today that to be taken really seriously you have to have suffered? But I haven't and I can't help it!

8

Our terraced house in Essex Road was built in red and brown brick, with an iron gate and tiny paved area in front, bay windows, yellow and red brick features and some fancy stuccoed panels: an average, lower-middle-class property. There were three bedrooms upstairs, Mum and Dad's, mine, and a spare room. At the back was a modest garden where, as I grew into childhood, I used to run around with friends and knock tennis balls about.

Mum and Dad bought the house before my birth, when George VI was on the throne. They paid £800 for the freehold and it took them twenty-five years to pay off the mortgage. They told me later that when they moved in there were green fields and cows opposite, but these were soon replaced by the inevitable blocks of flats. I don't remember any green fields or herds of cows, so for me these flats were always there.

The front room was where we went into on Sundays, the special day, the day of rest, although Mum and Dad rarely if ever went to church. It was the room where the best furniture was kept, well dusted and tidy. Where we played and listened to the gramophone records. Where the cocktail cabinet, the central feature of the front room, was stationed, and where Mum and Dad would display the drinks − which would never be drunk most of the year. The expectations of booze, of parents with their gin and tonics or their nightly glasses of wine, not to mention six pints downed at the pub, were never there for any of us − so different from the way it is for many children born today.

The exception was of course at Christmas, when the cherry brandy would be poured, and then imbibed to celebrate the tree lights being switched on. The radiogram cabinet was huge, almost as big as a sideboard. It housed the sole piece of broadcasting equipment − the sacred wireless, with white buttons and dials to twirl and press, and rasps and crackles of static and a muddle and jumble of strange tongues, like Pentecost, to which we all listened dutifully, even religiously. There were just three channels – the Home Service, the Third Programme and the Light Programme – and that was all there was, well before television came along. The notion of constant choice and switching channels just didn't enter into it.

And so it stayed like that for many years, until I was ten – and to begin with, and for life ever after, the first outlet of my romantic feelings and love was for Mum and Dad, whose whole focus was on me.

Being a happy child and belonging to a small, close-knit family as I did, my memories of childhood mostly centre around the other members of my family who lived locally. There was Grandpa and Grandma, Dad's parents; Dad's brother – Uncle Henry; his wife – Auntie Hilda; and their son Raymond. All five of them lived on two floors in Poplars Road, off Baker's Arms, which was twenty minutes' walk away in Leyton. Grandpa and Grandma lived upstairs, the others on the ground floor. Grandma Sarah was tiny. She and Grandpa Henry were very sweet, kind and gentle.

In the wider family circle my cousin Michael (son of my mother's brother Alfred) and Vicky, his sister, lived just down the road, too. Alf Two was very close to Dad. Tall and gangling with dark hair, he was a builder and later built the lean-to or conservatory on the back of our house. He was Mum's favourite brother, a joker who would have us in fits, but he liked to gamble, and on more than one occasion – as I found out later – got himself into 'a spot of bovver'. One day after the war he suddenly took off with his wife and two children without telling a soul, and sailed for Australia. Mum was heartbroken. On discovering they had gone she came back from their house furious and upset.

We went round and found the house empty. They really had gone. I think this must have been another 'spot of bother' – he'd got himself into a state over money. Even before they left my parents had the feeling that there was something 'not quite right', and were suspicious about what was going on in Uncle Alf's immediate family. Mum wasn't too keen on the Beardmores, as the family her brother married into were called, and we were all a bit doubtful about them. I grew up wary of the Beardmores: not because they were unfriendly or uncommunicative, but because they were a little odd and eccentric.

There was a brother of my maternal grandmother – a great-uncle who was known as Gaga. He sat around in Hackney and did nothing, but on Dad's side Grandpa had six brothers, one of whom was a well-known architect called Julius Jacobi who built some of the first skyscrapers in London, although we never knew him or the other Jacobis.

A remarkable feature of Aunt Hilda's household was the one outside toilet to which I'd head to answer the call of nature. When I was ready I'd call out, 'I'm ready, Aunt Hilda!' – the call I made for Auntie to come and wipe my bottom. Grandpa, who was a cobbler and worked for Dolcis all his life, had a shed in the garden to ply his trade and mend our shoes; this was his holy of holies, where he kept all his cobbling tools – I treasure to this day a metal last as a doorstop.

Not only was there no toilet in the house, but also no bathroom. We took our immersions in a tin bath, filled it up with hot water once a week, with a fire blazing in the hearth to keep us warm. But did we feel deprived? Did we feel others had more than we did? Never – it never once crossed our minds.

Mum's maiden name was Daisy Gertrude Masters. I knew nothing about her paternal background, but her grandmother had the unlikely name of Salomé Lapland, so heaven knows

11

where she came from – most likely from the frozen north – and for all I knew the family could have been gypsies. She had some French relations somewhere, and there were two adored brothers. There were no actors or anyone remotely like artists in her family. She would later claim that my artistic temperament came from her side, for an aunt of hers played the piano!

Mum was pretty, she had a round face, while her hair had turned white when she was in her twenties. She was very conscious of her hair and would go to the hairdressers once a week in Leyton. Dad and I had an old-fashioned barber who lived next door and who would come in once a week to cut our hair. We would lay out newspapers in our front room to collect the cuttings.

I never remember what people look like, but I do remember their voices. The barber had a voice like my uncle Henry, which I learned later had been the result of diphtheria when he was young. It was adenoidal, strained, and he spoke very high, at the top of his throat. His throat had been burned away, or cauterised.

Both my parents were born in Hackney in the same year, 1910. Mum and Dad met first as teenagers, while very much later, in their forties, they both worked at Garnham's department store in Walthamstow High Street, where Dad managed the crockery and hardware department and Mum was the boss's secretary and a department supervisor.

'It was the scout uniform,' she would say. 'To woo me your dad had a motorbike with a sidecar. He would come and collect me, and we would go out together.'

They had a modest wooing, with her on the pillion or sidecar. Sometimes my Auntie Hilda and Uncle Henry joined them.

———— >∘∘∘< ————

War was declared in September 1939, a month before my first birthday. My memories go back to sitting in a pram when we first heard the air-raid sirens. Mum grabbed hold of me, swaddled and wrapped me up, then rushed me down the steps into the Anderson shelter.

I liked the wail of the sirens and never felt fear. Although we didn't live in the area of dense, blanket bombing or the fire bombs that set the whole of Docklands on fire, there were explosions enough – flashes, sirens, wailing searchlights crossing the sky and picking out planes and barrage balloons. Somehow I was never affected. I was too young to feel or understand violent death and destruction as a presence.

Dozens of kids from where I lived were sent away in the early months of war with labels round their necks and a single change of clothing, accompanied by teachers, to board with strangers, but with no guarantee they could stay even with brothers and sisters, and not knowing when they would next see their fathers and mothers.

This never happened to me. I never stood on a station platform looking lost and forlorn with a label round my neck.

During the Blitz in 1940–41 I was still in Leytonstone. Dad, being over thirty, wasn't called up for a while and, like millions of others, dug out and built an Anderson shelter in the back garden. It was purpose-made from sheets of corrugated iron bent into a semi-circular shape. Dad set it over a concrete base embedded two or three feet in the ground. It had no soak-away, but it had bunk beds on either side making four beds in total. Like others, Dad covered it with earth and a little rock garden: planting aubretia, roses, Canterbury bells and geraniums.

I'm not sure if this camouflage decoration put off the Boche from dropping bombs on us. During the raids we were hunched up with sopping feet in the Anderson, which every now and then shook and quaked in the depths from after-shock. I heard later that when I was three one huge bomb fell just hundreds of yards down our road at the junction of Essex Road with Crieg Road in front of the Leyton High School for Boys, gouging out a vast crater.

Grandpa and Grandma were mainly with us during the Blitz. Grandpa stood outside the shelter and stationed himself as if on guard. I can't say what he thought he would be able to do if a bomb fell on us. I do remember later that if anyone farted in the shelter they were made to stand outside – expelled as a punishment. Perhaps this was what Grandpa kept doing!

Soon I would go away, too; that was inevitable. But to where, and with whom?

2

OUR WAR

Dad was called up into the army and left us in 1941, but as he had bunions so badly (at one time he was in Croft's Hospital with them, where they cared for him in the maternity ward!) he was never sent abroad to a war zone. As a humble private he served in the Royal Army Service Corps at postings in Scotland, Wales and the South.

When Hitler threatened to invade England Dad was stationed on Clapham Common, pasting up and setting out dummy tanks and guns of painted cardboard on the Common. They used lorries and dug tracks in the ground to make it all look real, so the Luftwaffe flying above would think we were heavily fortified.

Uncle Henry joined the Catering Corps. He was stationed at Reykjavik in Iceland. Later he was posted to a barracks in Buckinghamshire, so eventually – after the Blitz and not necessarily for my safety – Hilda took Raymond and me to stay with her not far from him in Little Brick Hill, a village outside Bletchley, near Cosgrave. We lived upstairs in the village pub. Mum stayed behind in Essex Road working, so she was very lonely and of all of us most exposed to danger. She'd come out to see us at Little Brick Hill whenever she could, and this was always a treat.

But my life with cousin Raymond was quite the opposite.

<hr />

Raymond and I were billeted together in the pub, sharing a room. My cousin Raymond was six or seven years older than me and I spent a lot of my childhood years with him. Auntie Hilda treated me with kid gloves – she would love the Jesus out of me – while Raymond got the rough end of her tongue. It was he, not me, the golden boy, who always seemed to come in for it.

Not long before we were evacuated there was one hell of a ruction which I will never forget. I was round at Poplars Road and Auntie Hilda asked Raymond to take a jar of precious jam through to the front room and put it in the cabinet where she stored the best pieces. He picked up the jar and pranced up the passageway, puffed up with airs and graces as he went, possibly the more so as I was watching, but as he came through into the front room the lid spun off the jam, and the jam shot out of the jar all over and up the wall. Hilda was so furious that she completely lost her rag and knocked him to kingdom come.

'Auntie, Auntie, stop it, stop it!' I screamed, as I stood by terrified.

Now that we were living together in Little Brick Hill, Raymond at last had me in his power and at night under the bedclothes he had the chance to take his revenge. He would scare and terrorise me, tickling me, pummelling me, playing at 'tortures' under the sheets.

'Why can't he stop trying to frighten me all the time?' I remember thinking. 'I am so much younger than him, so why is he tormenting me so much?'

It was pretty obvious to someone a bit older. With hindsight I could quite understand him wanting revenge on me. I was treated as the special one, the one apart from the rest of the family, while Raymond was the 'bloke', the laddish one. Later I realised that I was always accepted as the one who didn't quite fit in, who wasn't going to take an ordinary route through life.

One day we went apple scrumping together in the orchard of a big house where a grand lady lived – a highly dangerous thing to do, for it was trespassing and illegal. I didn't feel part of it, but

I followed where Raymond led. The school I attended gave a picnic party for the local children, but they wouldn't allow evacuated kids like Raymond and me to join in. Learning of this, Hilda went ballistic, stormed off to the headmistress, and made such a fuss that in the end, while we were still not included, we were taken back to the pub and had our own picnic. At that tender age I'd never heard language like Hilda's – it was quite some gab she had the gift of!

All was clear from bombing raids when I returned home to Essex Road in late 1944. Like the thousands of young children sent out of London to avoid the Blitz and the destruction of much of the East End, I was restored to Mum – and Dad when on leave. We were reunited, Hilda and Raymond, too. Grandma and Grandpa were full of joy to see us again. Dad was still away, but hardly very far away: in Clapham.

Victory was in sight. But unknown to us there was a new and even deadlier threat. We came back to what was the most terrifying ordeal of all, the destruction caused by the pilotless planes; first the V1 flying bombs, then the deadly V2 rockets launched on London from mobile trailers.

The flying bombs were like a dark shadow, chugging, rattling and droning across the sky, with their 1,000 pounds of explosive which always seemed to be released at a point just above your head. We would sense that, because the noise would suddenly cut out, and we never knew if they'd glide onwards or fall straight down. During the cold, miserable winter of 1944 we got to know these new weapons: all at once, without any warning, there would just be this eerie silence. They were fired straight into sub-orbital space and came down so fast that if we heard them we had been lucky and had escaped.

One day this happened to us. 'Face down on the floor everyone!' shouted the white-coated fishmonger. I was round at

Poplars Road. Raymond and I had been sent out to buy fish for Kitty, our cat.

There was a flash and then a huge explosion as the rocket hit the Baker's Arms bus shelter about 150 yards away. Everyone threw themselves on the floor of the shop. Buildings were blown up or simply collapsed. Debris flew everywhere. Bodies, blood and severed limbs were scattered across the street; ambulances screamed and sirens wailed as fire engines and rescue squads arrived.

Raymond and I had flattened ourselves on the fishmonger's floor. We'd had a very lucky escape. There was dust and debris everywhere. A woman came up to where we lay flat on our bellies, quivering with terror.

'Where do you live?' she asked. 'Do you live locally?'

This kind woman then took each of us by the hand and brought us back to Auntie's place in Poplars Road. Here a couple of front windows had been blown out and we found Hilda in a petrified state, sitting on top of the kitchen table. She was perched there as if there was a swirling flood rising around her.

'You must take shelter under the table,' she'd been told before the air-raid warning and the rocket struck. Definitely the safest place was to shelter under it.

'But I can't, no I can't!' she shrieked. 'There's a mouse there!'

The Pathé or Movietone newsreels at the cinema where we viewed the horrifying footage of these new terror weapons were miles away from the reality of their destruction. The rockets had a double demoralising effect on a tired and war-weary East London, where destruction had been diabolical. Over 6,000 people died, many in our area, and tens of thousands more were wounded – a huge toll. My evacuation to Bletchley had then proved to be effective because my worst moment of the war was back at home on my return.

Even so, these years, when so many suffered death, destruction and misery, were for me a happy and secure time when only at rare moments was my sense of good fortune disrupted or broken. We were fighting the Germans, but that was all I knew.

I didn't see much of Dad, so I was hardly aware of him, but in the laundry he sent home to Mum he would include sheets of Bakelite (which he used in his war work in the army to wrap up the imitation planes and soldiers) for me to play with. Aside from the separations, there was such a great spirit with everybody pulling together, and we kids had a great time.

Later when I was a bit older on my return to Leytonstone in late 1944 I remember rushing down the steps in daylight to the shelter, but without Dad. He had gone away and was now a stranger, a shadowy figure who occasionally visited on leave. He played very little part in my life in those early infant years.

Yet even without having my dad there to look after me I was never worried, never scared, and never had any decision to make: I was supremely well cared for by everyone. I never felt lonely and on my own.

I accepted life, I accepted what I was doing, the world around me, and what was happening to me without ever questioning it.

3

THE RETURN OF
ALFRED JACOBI

The war in Europe was over. I had seen virtually nothing of
Dad now since 1941 and was excited at the thought of his
homecoming.

On Victory in Europe (VE) Day in May 1945 we held a
fancy-dress party in Poplars Road. Everyone carried out chairs
and tables into the middle of the road and covered the tables
in tablecloths of all different shapes and colours.

With basic foodstuffs rationed, we had been fed on spam –
plentiful tinned spam – and cheese-and-potato pie was my
favourite, which Hilda used to bake. Vegetables were even
scarcer than fresh meat, but I was too young to know what they
were, so I hardly missed them. Powdered milk and powdered
eggs were part of the staple diet, and there was hardly any fruit
to eat. Everyone has their first banana story. I had no idea what
to do with the first banana I held in my hand, how to peel it
and get at the inside, but it was exotic – extraordinary.

Foods which had been scarce were brought out of hiding and
piled high: sausages, eggs, cakes, cold chicken, mince pies, cup
cakes. Fizzy drinks, too: ginger beer, lemonade, Dandelion and
Burdock, and the new import, Coca-Cola.

There were races and stalls, as well as the sumptuous spread,
and everyone was merry, danced and sang and had the time of
their life. I wore a costume made by Mum out of wartime ration

cards and books, all of which she had carefully sewn together. I had a painted sign pinned to the front of my costume – 'Mother's Worries' – and with this I won first prize. They even took a professional photograph of me wearing it as 'Wartime Ration Boy'.

When Mum took part in the egg and spoon race, she fell over just as she was winning and nearly broke her nose. She was covered in blood and I was screaming. I was terrified by what had happened and suddenly had a terrible premonition and fear that she would die.

———— ⬥ ————

I was too young, not yet seven, to take in the speeches on the radio, the thanksgiving service, the Prime Minister, Winston Churchill, voicing his relief and exultation, and everyone paying their tribute to the King as the Head of our Great Family. All this was going on, yet I missed my chance to listen to the Archbishop of Canterbury who spoke in such a dignified and unselfconscious manner, without an inkling that one day I would be playing his predecessor, Cosmo Lang, who was something of a villain, in The King's Speech.

When we were back home fireworks lit up the sky, which made me for a moment start up with fear, as not long before flashes and explosions had told a different story.

Uncle Henry could pick up any tune on the piano and play it. Just as victory was declared and we were celebrating at home, he got very drunk. He was the one who had cooked for victory all through the war, and been in Iceland, but now he was very inebriated and started hammering out something on the piano. Turning to us with a big grin he said something in a kind of roaring voice which really upset me, really terrified me.

'I'm going to set the house on fire tonight!' he roared.

I instantly burst into tears. I took Uncle Henry's jovial remark quite literally, instantly remembering the V2 rocket that had hit the Baker's Arms bus shelter. It seemed the most dangerous thing anyone could say, and even though I knew he was very jolly and drunk I really believed he was about to set our house on fire with a box of matches.

I looked around at everyone and they didn't seem to mind – but I minded!

———

The VE Day celebrations in 1945 had been and gone and still no Dad had appeared. But then in 1946 there was a national holiday commemorating Victory in Japan (VJ) Day and suddenly Dad was back, still in uniform. Immense crowds gathered in central London, and the rejoicing was universal. The lights were switched on in Piccadilly Circus and the Coca-Cola sign illuminated. We caught the Tube and joined the great congregation of people. Dad hoisted me up on his shoulders above the crowd to give me 'a flying angel'.

I loved it. I was with him at last.

This was the first time I reckoned my father as a presence. Would I rush at him, throw my arms around him as Mum did with me? I had a sense of 'Was I going to like him? Would I take to him?' It was from both of us, Mum too, this feeling of reticence. Mum and he had to get their lives together after the war. There were to be no more babies – and what about sex? Neither ever spoke about it, and I guess probably never did even with each other. I had no insight into where babies came from: I must have lived in cloud cuckoo land. But I never thought about it. Why should I? We never lived in a sexed-up universe.

I'd love to have talked more to both of them, heard more about their experiences, for what had happened during the war would be with them for the rest of their lives. I never discussed with my mother how it had been for her, never questioned her, which I regret. But everyone, in spite of the extreme deprivation, had helped one another, and we knew what it really meant to be a neighbour.

So many people around us lived life without complaining, not fearing death or injury, and accepting one or the other when it came. Life generally was dedicated to a higher role, and it was rare for those around us to exaggerate their sorrows or miseries, or their survival.

But soon people retreated into themselves again and became self-centred, so that feeling of camaraderie after the war didn't last long.

4

THE CHRISTMAS
CONNED 'EM

At the end of the same year, Christmas 1945, there were twelve of us at home, and I was now seven years old.

The Poplars Road crowd came to our house every Christmas. After Christmas dinner, for which Mum cooked the turkey – the first I'd ever seen – and after we'd heard the King's Christmas Day speech on the Home Service – the first since VE Day, 1945 – we settled down to play games. One was called 'Conned 'em' (slang for 'conned them' and not to be confused with something that sounds identical!). Conned 'em had become a family ritual, and we played for money.

We divided into two teams, and to start someone would find a sixpence. The captain of one team placed the tiny coin of silver under the table, and then each one in turn held their hands under until the captain put the sixpence into one of their hands. Then, watched by the other team, they brought up both clenched fists. The other team took it in turns to guess, plump for a hand, and call out 'Peace' if they thought the sixpence was there. It sounds simple, but there were tricks and different calls, which was why it was called 'Conned 'em'.

On this occasion the betting built up into quite a big pile of money. I disappeared under the table and started to pray I would win everything. They watched as I made my retreat, and as usual Raymond, my cousin, was looking very suspicious. I had a flash of instinct and knew who had the sixpence, so I came out from my hiding place and called out 'Peace!' at Raymond.

And that was it. I'd judged correctly: he had the silver sixpence and I'd won the pot. He was furious and stormed out of the room.

It was only much later that I discovered that Raymond was not Uncle Henry and Auntie Hilda's natural son, but had been adopted. Even at a very early age I had a sense of my own entitlement in the way I was treated by Mum and Dad, and Hilda. I could see that Raymond was sort of humiliated in, or by, my presence. Even so, and despite the fact that he terrorised me somewhat – although not too seriously and certainly not traumatically – we spent a lot of time together.

Looking back I can see how there was a slight conspiracy in the family to protect me as someone different, not quite run-of-the-mill, something that in a way cosseted me as special, as if somehow they knew I was going to break the mould, but were not sure how this would happen.

5

MUM

Throughout my childhood, Mum would often be sitting at her Jones sewing machine, extending the life of worn sheets and towels by cutting and re-sewing the less worn outsides to form the middle. Until rationing was stopped in 1952 our allowance of clothing coupons, just over a hundred a year, made people thrifty and careful to re-knit jumpers which had been unpicked for the wool, and to save and cut down old suits.

Kids wore smaller versions of what their parents wore. Mum kept and stored everything that could be re-sewed or adapted for other use, and as a child I had just three sets of clothes, one for school, one for play, and one best suit. I ached for more grown-up clothes. Tea, meat, butter, sugar and footwear: all, too, were rationed.

No dishwasher, no washing machine: Mum did every-thing on her own. She never had a big wardrobe, and didn't have many clothes. Yet as she worked in a store drapery depart-ment, and was the boss's secretary, we always had these lovely materials around the home which she'd make into costumes for me, tasteful wallpaper or decorations, and plenty of knick-knacks, although these were rather kitsch. Otherwise there were net curtains in the front room to stop people looking in, and rich drapes. Very house proud, very clean, and while she was out at work during the day Mum worked hard in the home, but now when I look back I can see she was a terrible cook.

Dad and I would never complain, but her best shot was cooking a joint for Sunday lunch. Her Sunday roast was passable, although well done – and it would always be *very* well done. Later I would be able to say that she couldn't 'nuance' a rare steak. For her it was just meat, and whatever the meat was – lamb, beef, pork – it came out the same. I remember her omelettes were always open, like Spanish ones, large and on the leathery side. Sunday afternoon teas were of tinned salmon, spam, cucumber, radishes, bread and butter; altogether our food was plain and wholesome. She wasn't interested in cooking; she didn't have time to be interested.

Mum spoke, like Dad, with an East End accent, but was slightly more educated than he was. She had been to Hackney Cassland Road School, quite a good school near where my other grandmother lived, and she'd even learned to speak a bit of French.

I had only ever visited this granny once, as a very young child, when I had some flowers – a bunch of anemones – pressed into my hand to give her, and I was waiting outside the door.

'Can I take my flowers in to Granny?' I asked.

Mum said yes and I marched boldly in with them, and laid them beside Granny on the bed where she lay asleep.

I looked at Granny Lapland as she lay there. She seemed so peaceful and I did hope she would like my anemones.

There was a strange atmosphere in Granny's room, as if time were standing still.

It was only later that I found out she was dead.

I knew from the age of six, when I dressed myself up in Mum's wedding veil, that I was going to be an actor.

'Do you know what you want to be when you grow up, Derek?' I remember Mum asking me one day when I was older.

'Oh yes, Mum, I know – I've always known. An actor.'

Would Mum and Dad mind, would they oppose me? It was a world they knew nothing about, nor did I.

'Don't you worry, dear, we'll see you right. I'm sure you'll land on your feet whatever you do.'

'Oh well, it will be something different from your Dad and Uncle Henry – less boring perhaps – although as a chef Henry always fancies he's a bit different from the run of the mill, don't he?'

Henry was short and stocky, sandy-haired and freckled. He had a great sense of fun, and sometimes took risks, putting big money on horses and dogs. Later he'd take me with him to Walthamstow dog stadium, which was very exciting.

For a short time I joined the cubs and scouts, and once went to an annual camp. I remember with no affection sleeping in a tent in a famous scout park, being endlessly soaking wet, and loathing the communal life when we lived off things called 'twists' and 'dampers'. We ate a sort of soup, which I suppose was chicken soup with barley, and which we made ourselves.

In the evening we sat around the campfire singing the usual 'Ging Gang Goolie' – 'Ging gang goolie, goolie goolie goolie, watcha!' – and being very silly. We played awful games like 'British Bulldog', when ten boys would be pitted against one, which was an excuse for a roughhouse. I am physically not very brave, so it didn't suit me at all.

When I acted in plays as a child, I was always dressed up in all the 'best frocks', because Mum made or provided the costumes. It soon became apparent that, with Mum's involvement, school was an extension of home and home an extension of school. She was outgoing, gregarious, chatty and quite extrovert, sometimes even flamboyant, and would speak her mind without inhibition. She could be very demonstrative. I was quite shocked later on when she met the famous actress Diana Wynyard in a car park opposite the Old Vic. She threw herself at her, and kissed her.

But there were other times when I heard her crying out in pain and anguish – though never directly in front of me, for she didn't want me to know she was suffering from an illness I wasn't supposed to be aware of. She would never complain how terrible the pain was. She tried to hide it, and sometimes she'd just go upstairs to be on her own. I was never taken up to see her.

Dad would ring up the doctor at once. Mum was careering round the room like a wounded animal, trying not to show pain, bumping into furniture, and never able to find relief, while Dad would prevail on her to sit down.

She'd had a mastoid operation before I was born, and the middle ear problems she suffered were recurrent. Our doctor visited us every week to examine her. He came every Wednesday and would give her medicine for them. During these terrible attacks she couldn't stand, couldn't lie down and lost all sense of balance. It was agonising for Dad to see and hear her when she was undergoing one of these attacks. I always feared she would die, for basically she was my rock, my comfort.

These problems became a nightmare: I couldn't stand the idea of her attacks, nor could I help them. I had a complete lack of wanting to confront anything, and also a lack of responsibility, which was possibly a sign of how I was protected by Mum and Dad from some of the harsher realities of survival. It was all too evident with my childhood pets.

My first was a rabbit called Floppy; its cage was never cleaned unless my grandfather did it; likewise with my tropical fish aquarium. Then there was the tortoise which hibernated and never woke up. Finding this was horrible, for with a girl friend

I went out into the garden to search, and when we did find it, its body had decomposed. The girl laughed, grabbed it and pushed it in my face to tease me – and that hurt me very much.

Dad grew vegetables and kept chickens, about a dozen. I loved to climb through the hatch into the dark henhouse, and savour being there all on my own, finding it oddly comforting to rest among the clucking of the hens. Certain aspects of life were quite rustic, but I was no good at looking after anything.

I have often since wondered why this was so, and I think it was because I was never very good at making decisions. For I was already the Boy with the Veil – this is what I fancied I was. The actor. And it remained so.

Actors have to keep one foot in the cradle. We must be open, like a child, and retain *naïveté*. I have plenty of the latter – or so my friends tell me – and have kept some of it, I think, from those early years.

I was born on the cusp of Libra, and as a result I am apparently a 'triple Libran'. On the one hand I'm very well balanced, but on the other hand, hopeless at making up my mind. I tend to see both sides of everything and weigh everything equally, so choosing is difficult – and making my mind up is damn hard.

This means I dither, I'm always uncertain.

As a child, I don't believe I thought about anything very much, and never philosophised, so some might say I was just shallow. Or you could say, which I suppose is truer, that I have always set more store by my intuition and imagination than by analytical thinking.

The only creative avenue I have ever walked down is acting.

6

DAD

One day I went back to Aunt Hilda's house after school. Quite often I would go there for lunch in Poplars Road while both of my parents were still out at work. I was a bit ruffled by what I'd heard, for I had just been told something at school and was deeply intrigued.

Hilda was out, and I was met by Grandpa who was downstairs with Grandma.

'Make the boy a cup of tea, girl,' he said. He always called Grandma 'girl'. They were devoted to one another and she used to call him 'mate'.

'Don't do that, mate.'

'All right, girl.'

He, like Dad, was undemonstrative and very mild mannered.

'Grandpa, a boy in my class came up to me in the playground and said, "My Dad says you've got a Jewish name."'

Grandpa's face grew stern, creased and angry. I had never seen him like this before. 'What? What does he know about it?' He became very upset, and it was an ugly moment. 'Let's not mention it again, boy!'

I had recovered by now. 'But it's only a name, Grandpa. It's nothing. Anyway who cares if it's a Jewish name or not, or if we are Jewish? I don't care.'

It was my turn to calm him down. That was all that was

said on the thorny subject. But I knew there was a little more to it.

⎯⎯⎯◦◦◦◦⎯⎯⎯

Sometimes it used to be mentioned in the family that my great-grandfather Jacobi came from East Prussia. I could never be sure. Jacobi is generally a Jewish name, while in America they pronounce it Jacóbi, as opposed to Jácobi here, but some maintain it is not exclusively so. Jacoby with a 'y' is almost always Jewish. I can find no trace of Jewish blood or religious practice in my family; but then my family was undemonstrative. They didn't want to be anything in particular, but quiet, unseen, placid and accepting, just getting on with the job in hand.

When my ancestors left Germany in the middle or late nineteenth century they were probably fleeing from pogroms or persecution of some kind. Like many Jewish and non-Jewish immigrants they settled in the East End of London. Neither Dad nor Grandpa discussed this or delved into the past, and it made Grandpa, a mild man, uneasy to be questioned. Our doctor, the one who brought me into the world, was Jewish. But Dad and Grandpa didn't like to be probed about whether they were Jewish, or where they came from. They were reserved anyway, not only about whether or not they were Jewish, but about their politics and just about everything.

It was a time when no one complained – or rather, those who did stood out like sore thumbs. I'm the same. I should have asked more questions, but never did. I shy away from analysts or faith healers even when I've been in crisis or deeply unhappy, although I went once to a hypnotist in 1979 to cure me of smoking. Successfully!

But, Jewish or not, I do have a touch of the Boche, this is for sure. It came in handy when later I played Dietrich Hessling, a Teutonic louse – my first big television part in *Man of Straw*, from the novel by Heinrich Mann, Thomas Mann's brother.

It must have helped when I played Hitler, another Teutonic louse, in one of the many films made about the Führer: my take on Hitler was to show him as an actor and performer – Hitler as written up in that multifaceted portrait of him by Albert Speer. So you could say the German blood would in the future some-times come into its own!

My father never read books and wouldn't have known who Thomas Mann was. I wasn't surrounded by any of that, while my mother never used to say to me, 'I think you ought to read.' I never had stories at bedtime. I never missed them because there was nothing around to suggest that I should've been read to. They didn't love me the less for not doing it. To read to me, to open my mind, wasn't in their method of bringing me up.

My grandparents never used to read either. As a result, I lived much more in a pretend world, where I fantasised according to my own dreams, and did so when playing with my friends. Where did that world come from? I don't know, it's a mystery, and perhaps ironic when I recall how many 'Books at Bedtime' I've read on the radio.

Was it nurture, or was it nature? I was born an actor, so where did that gene originate? There were no laptop screens, iPhones or television sets to influence my early years. There was, of course, the cinema, and radio was the main influence, for I could sing all the old chestnuts. In that sense I was just like an old man, for I knew all the words to the songs.

When on holiday in Devon, on the coach for an outing, our routine was always the same. We'd play a round of miniature golf on the putting green after breakfast, and have morning coffee with a doughnut. Next down to the beach, then on a trip out – it was always settled, predictable, no hassle. There was the beautiful abbey at Buckfast, and then the wonderful coastline up through Teignmouth and Dawlish, with the red cliffs. On the coach I'd organise a singsong, and they'd all be amazed that I, this kid, knew all the words. I was a bit of a show-off, cocky, and even bossy.

―――――∞∞∞――――――

Dad's passion was his garden. Nothing made him happier than tending his flowers in the garden with love while smoking a cigarette (always Players No. 1). He wouldn't talk much, but when the subject was flowers I could see that this was where his heart was.

He was medium in build – a bit like me – and was shy, rather sharp-featured, not aggressive in any way, quite good-looking and with the sandy hair I had when I was a child – although mine was more ginger. His eyes were strong, with an element of fear or uncertainty in them. He kept his good looks all through life. He was very backward in coming forward, so to speak. Like me, he'd never argue, and as a reticent sort of man he never took offence. We got on fantastically well, and I did rely on him. If I'm honest I'd say I used him, for if anything went wrong I would immediately call him. The habit was there even as a small child.

The garden was not very big, and much later as a teenager I used to play tennis in it with my friends. We would knock over the flowers, but even with his precious tulips flattened, ruined by the tennis balls, Dad never lost his temper: the most he would ever say was, 'Don't do that, son.' In his later years he would come out to France where I had bought a country house near Toulouse. He was very proud of France. He would call it 'Derek's villa in the South of France', and he'd just sit there in the garden, staring for hours and hours. One thing is for sure: he was composed in his own head.

But one night when I was very young there was an incident with Dad, which made me feel very ashamed.

―――――∞∞∞――――――

I was going through a stage of waking in the middle of the night and coming downstairs – to Mum and Dad's great annoyance. There was no apparent reason, but it had been going on for some time.

On this particular night I woke up all of a sudden, left my bed, and then descended the stairs. When I arrived at the bottom my father was standing there with a ruler in his hand; he had never hit me before – ever. But now he brandished it, threatening me with this ruler.

'Do that again, son, and I'll have to use this on you!'

I fled upstairs immediately. I couldn't believe it – nothing like this with Dad had ever happened before. I was so shocked with this threat of Dad hitting me with the ruler that I went upstairs and, to my everlasting shame, shat on the floor of my bedroom. I kept this all to myself, cleaned it up as best I could. They would never know it happened – and I never went downstairs in the middle of the night again!

They did find out next morning, inevitably, and again nothing happened. I think Mum told me off in the gentlest way. This was such an isolated episode of Dad becoming strict, and he never mentioned it again.

AGE II
SHINING
MORNING FACE

7

'WITH ONE LITTLE
TOUCH OF HER HAND'

At the age of seven – as a schoolboy with my satchel and shining morning face – I discovered acting in front of others; or it discovered me. Here, I knew, at once instinctively, was the reality of playing a part that brought me alive.

I had the lead in *The Prince and the Swineherd*, a pantomime staged at our local library. I played both roles, something I loved doing later on when I could bring out the differences between two characters, or both sides of a dual personality. My favourites among these were in the film of *The Fool*, when I played a nineteenth-century poverty-stricken clerk, 'the fool' who sells tickets for the vaudeville, and Frederick, a City of London speculator, whose fortunes tumble when a great financial bubble bursts.

I was bullied at this time by a boy at Capworth School, because I wasn't aggressive, nor was I a toughie. He knew I would not retaliate. I asked Mum and Dad to save me, so after school they'd come to pick me up. I was probably seen as soft, girlish and a bit fey, and I much preferred the company of girls, and they mine, again because there was nothing confrontational about being with them.

———

Karen, a teacher at Capworth School, who was young and unmarried, took me out to the West End to see my first professional show. It was her personal choice to ask me, so I have no idea how it came about, except that she must have asked Mum. The show was the musical *Oh Marguerita*, which had the famous song 'Bella Marguerita':

Her lips have made me her prisoner
A slave to every command
She captivates and intoxicates me
With one little touch of her hand.

It stimulated the romantic lover – the dreamer inside me – but also a nagging awareness of how I appeared to others. I'm not sure which came first, but the other side of show business, the glitz, exerted its pull on me when Mum and Dad bought tickets for the London Palladium Christmas panto, which was *Cinderella*.

'I'm coming down there to pick one or two of you to come on the stage,' Evelyn Laye royally announced to the audience. She was Prince Charming, with Noëlle Gordon as Dandini, the other Principal Boy. Miss Laye tripped down the stairs into the stalls and selected me, so here I was up on stage with the world-famous music hall star: my first professional appearance clocked up at the Palladium! Thrilled to bits, I was given sweets and a balloon.

Fast forward to Westminster Abbey in the 1990s. A plaque is being laid to Noël Coward and at the ceremony I read out an extract from his *War Diaries*. There in the front row I spot Evelyn Laye, a great friend of Coward's, now eighty-six. I go over to her.

'You won't remember, but we have worked together before – at the London Palladium.' Naturally she didn't remember me at all, only the panto!

After this I felt proprietorial about the Palladium, so sometimes for visits to the West End I'd save up pocket money, take the Tube west to Argyle Street, summon the maître d' outside to hail me a taxi to drive me to a theatre nearby: just for the sheer joy of the taxi-ride.

At the age of nine I wrote to Sir Michael Balcon, the Ealing Films boss, asking him outright if I could be in a film of his, and received back a very sweet letter.

If you are that keen, you should pursue your dream and get in touch with us again in a few years' time.

8

CONFINEMENT

One of the basic things I knew at a tender age was that I was attracted to other boys, in particular to a boy in kindergarten whose name was Julian. I would also try to be near him, to join his team, or play with him in the playground or be his partner. I was physically drawn to him – I wanted to touch him, but I never did.

But actually, towards none of the boy friends that I was close to later at school did I feel any kind of physical attraction; neither to Mark Allen, nor Graham Smith, two friends I went around with. I was much closer to girls.

Of all the girls Ivy Mills was the one I became closest to. I remember Ivy and I were at home once while Mum and Dad had gone out for the evening. We deliberately sat side-by-side on the sofa, staring ahead, barely daring to touch, but aware what this might lead to.

'Let's try it,' said Ivy.

So we 'did it' – in those days this meant only kissing like grown-ups 'properly', not quite sure what we were doing.

My friendship with Ivy led to a turning point in my life, for I was invited to her ninth birthday party, where something unforeseen and quite disastrous happened.

Mum and Dad were out at work, so I was without them. But a lot of mums and dads were at the party with their children, and we were all having great fun, when the hosts introduced a game with a name I can't recall; perhaps for the reason that we never got round to playing it – and I was the reason. For this game the boys, who were wearing long trousers, had to roll them up. I duly rolled up mine and was ready to start.

'Derek, what on earth's happened to you?' cried out Ivy's mum, turning completely white and aghast at what she saw. My rolled-up trousers revealed a gruesome spectacle: my legs were covered in spots, reddish spots where the blood vessels had broken. All the mothers instantly panicked, grabbed their off-spring and fled.

And that was the end of the party. It was the time of the much-dreaded polio epidemic. Ivy's parents had to contact Mum and Dad at work to come and pick me up, and they whisked me off to see Dr Byrne, the doctor who'd brought me into the world after Mum's forty-hour labour.

For as long as I can remember, Dr Byrne was always on hand as our doctor, a good Jewish boy who lived with his mum in Snaresbrook. He diagnosed me with puerpera, a form of rheumatic fever, and sent me straight to bed.

Virtually paralysed, I remained bedridden for nearly a year.

═══◦◦◦═══

For the first six months my legs were encased in cotton wool, and a nurse came daily to tend to my bedsores. Such an illness put me into myself and made me brood. For what seemed like an unending sentence it was just me, four walls, Mum and Dad, and the Home, Light and Third Programmes which I listened to day in, day out. Television had not yet made its appearance. We depended on the wireless, and there were wonderful children's programmes – *Toytown* had been my favourite when I was younger, and now it was *Dick Barton*, the detective series.

I was always a listener; sounds and words rather than sights or images featured for me as more truthful and important. This may be one reason why I never grew up with a Cockney accent. And when I eventually climbed out of bed after eleven months my legs almost refused to obey me and I clung to Mum as I shuffled across the floor. My legs were so thin I could practically fit my thumb and forefinger round them. My legs would have shamed a grasshopper: I had to move about on crutches like Tiny Tim.

On the upside, my friends could now come and see me, while Mum brought me work home from school. I became an ace at crossword puzzles, knitting and embroidery. After Dad died aged ninety in 2000, and when I was going through his things at the house, I found a stash of pillowcases all cross-stitched by my ten-year-old self.

Still in convalescence, I took the Eleven Plus exam by correspondence course, with Mum timing me and giving me a bit of unofficial help on the side, and then I joined what they called 'The Pool', which gave me an entrée into Leyton County High School for an interview. Here was my big opportunity, for to go to grammar school if I managed to pass the Eleven Plus was a great privilege and honour.

9

EAST LONDON BOY

When the day came, I set off shakily along Essex Road, for the school was midway down this long road.

The houses expanded in size as I walked along, the grander ones near the middle, and there was a big Gothic church on the right-hand side, known as the Cornerstone Church. Outside the school, which was an impressive, even monolithic, dark brick building of great expanse, there were raw vestiges of that block-buster bomb dropped on the crossroads five years before, which wiped out two or three houses either side, blew out every school window, and took a large slice off the roof. There were lawns and flowerbeds at the front and to the side.

Although I had lived all my life in the same street, I had never been in the building. Built some years earlier than our end-of-terrace house, the portico had Corinthian columns in yellow stone either side; inside, the entrance hall had a grand staircase with two sides, with columns and wrought-iron banisters, and on the wall copper panelling listed the World War One dead of Leytonstone. Running along the building at the back, to the left of the wooden flooring, was a courtyard with *Chariots of Fire* columns, while outside was space enough for three football pitches and tennis courts: but best of all, and ideal for me, the school had a big assembly hall with a stage where they put on plays with proper sets, lighting and costumes.

My first port of call was the headmaster's office on the left inside the entrance: he was a mathematician named Mr Cummings and he'd fought in the war and been shot in action, so he couldn't use his left arm. In essence he was a military man, big-boned with a large head and big body, with this slightly withered arm and hand, which I'm sure made him more aggressive than he would otherwise have been. Always wearing a big black gown, he looked like a black eagle swooping down on malingerers in the school corridors.

Personally I wasn't daunted by his presence, and we soon started talking. I could tell at once I had made a good impression, as I always try to do! I passed the interview, and so was off to a flying start. I was admitted first to the 'B' stream and after my first year they put me in the 'A' stream.

I was extremely fortunate to gain a place at this grammar school. It was either this, or the more basic secondary modern, where most of those who lived locally had to go. It wasn't as if we had any other choice, or that Mum and Dad could have paid for me to go to public school.

———⊃∘∘⊂———

Apart from the puerpera, I'd passed the first eleven years of my life completely blessed, without a blemish on my happy existence, with no deaths or grief affecting my sunny disposition. By then I had been endlessly devouring films on our new television screen, which we would watch in the dark, and I grew very jealous of all those child actors I saw, for that was exactly what I wanted to do. There was one, a famous boy actor called Jeremy Spencer, who in particular inflamed me with envy.

Later, when I was fourteen, I saw Rattigan's *The Sleeping Prince* at the Phoenix Theatre, and waited to ask for Laurence Olivier and Vivien Leigh's autographs. I recognised Jeremy, who was also in the play, coming out of the stage door and

I deliberately did not ask for his autograph. But when at Cambridge as a student I became friends with him and visited his flat in Sussex Gardens, West London, I remember leaning up again his mantelpiece and reciting Hamlet's 'To be or not to be' speech, even getting tips from him on how to say the lines – quite a turnaround!

My determination to be an actor grew fiercer than ever. If there were to be shadows in the future, unavoidable mishaps and disasters, I had no idea when and where they might fall.

Strictly speaking, I couldn't be called an East Ender, but was an East Londoner: Essex Road was a popular, gregarious street, a quarter of a mile from the Underground. Quiet and comfortable in those days, Leytonstone had few or none of the more exotic or violent aspects of East London life. When I was older, I'd never let on to people that I lived in East London – never mind the East End like Hackney – but would say 'on the edge of Epping Forest': it sounded so much better that way, and was in fact true.

I would visit and play with my grammar school friend Mark Allen, whose family had a big house on the edge of the Forest, at Hollow Ponds, and we biked around or played in the skateboard area, or went boating on the lake. I'd even ride with Mark at a stables in the Forest, although this didn't last long, and brought home to me that horses and I would never become compatible. I was scared stiff, because I never knew what they would do next, and at once they picked up on my terror. I never fell off, though, and even managed to win a certificate for riding 100 yards without holding reins.

Quite a number of famous and notorious people were born in Leytonstone: Alfred Hitchcock, David Beckham, Graham Gooch, Damon Albarn, Lee Mack and Jonathan Ross – who later went to the same school, Leyton High School for Boys, as I did.

Sean Mac Stiofain, the first IRA Chief of Staff, and the society photographer David Bailey were others born in Leytonstone, but I can't exactly figure out what we all have in common, except that I had less in common with sportsmen and gunmen, and was probably most like Bailey.

But something in common always remains. In 2001 I did a photoshoot for *Vanity Fair* with David, and because he is an East London boy, and with the discovery that I too was an East London boy, we suddenly became joined at the hip and got on like a house on fire. David was great, talking about himself all the time, non-stop – what a lovely fellow he was, great career, and how he'd had a great life. I don't want to make out he was unduly conceited, because he was very nice. Like all photographers, when they're taking a photograph, however awful you look, they tell you, 'Oh how fabulous – fabulous!'

For the shoot I wore a dark suit, and he dolled me up in a kind of Noël Coward dressing gown. But even from the earliest years I was never keen on having my picture taken. I never found out if the photographs appeared.

From the start I knew I wasn't much of a looker, that I wasn't very attractive. My complexion is ruddy, my face round and cowlike. Mine isn't a face of which you think, 'Ah, he's suffered,' or 'There's something violent about him.' I don't have the mien of the suffering Dane or the harsh, angry brows of the violent Macbeth.

My face doesn't brood at all, it just looks placid and cheerful – and even reassuring. I used to ask Father Christmas to forget the toy trains and Meccano, and please give me cheekbones instead.

But he never did.

10

MY TEACHERS

'I am holding a short-story competition for this year's best boy at English,' Martial Rose announced one day in class, and in his class we all tried to think up the best idea, keen as we were to win. He looked to me to write the story to win the prize and not let him down. Striving to meet his expectation I did my best, penned my story, and submitted it in the time allocated.

Mr Rose, who taught History as well as English and who later became headmaster of Winchester College, encouraged me greatly in reading and writing, as if he believed I could have a future in the literary world. Soon I was to prove him very wrong. For while I duly won the short-story competition and received all the plaudits, I confess this wasn't at all to my credit, for I'd copied the whole of my story from a book of short stories, and was deeply ashamed.

I'm afraid this somewhat soured my relationship with Mr Rose, at least on my side, because, although he never heard or found out what I'd done, I just knew I couldn't continue in the same vein. So I rather dropped the enthusiasm and keenness to please him further and to continue being good at English. I'm not a writer and never will be.

This was far from the case with school plays, which Bobby Brown, my main History teacher, invariably directed. Here I was fated to thrive from the start. Before my voice broke I played mainly the females: Lady Macduff in *Macbeth*, which I doubled with Fleance, Ann Boleyn, several Pinero heroines, and I played Doto in Christopher Fry's *A Phoenix Too Frequent*.

These females were an astonishing and fortunate run of roles: my first encounter with the feelings of the opposite sex, although Mr Brown was diligent in making us boys understand the minds and words of all the characters we were playing. There was possibly, without my knowing it, some kind of special accord between the female side of me and these roles: a sensitivity to being vulnerable perhaps? Heaven forbid!

Often I acted with another boy, Graham Smith, who later became an artist, and we'd giggle a lot together, a habit I regret to say I carried through into my early professional life and even later. Graham was a big influence on me at grammar school. He was very camp and would shout, pull faces and play the fool, and this was in the days before scathing humour caught on in the way it has now. He came from a troubled and tragic family – his mother died when he was six. I believe – although hardly any of us at that time knew that such things happened and certainly never talked about them, as he didn't either – that he was sexually abused by an older boy in a summer house for slum kids, and this introduction by older boys and men to an active sex life continued, some of which he rather enjoyed.

Graham was quite feminine, and he liked dressing up in women's clothes. Once, when he came round to my house at Essex Road, he raided Mum's wardrobe and put on her evening dress. We went out into the garden where I took photographs of him in it. He would come to school with a purple scarf with sequins wound round his neck and perhaps over his head, and he was just asking to be bullied by the butch boys. He was the Quentin Crisp of these early days – laying himself open to be picked on – but in a way he was a toughie, too, and if the butch boys had started anything he would have fought his corner.

There were four of us – Graham, Robin Dowsett, Michael Folkard and me. Michael was thin and angular, with a sibilant voice, and later worked as a successful set designer. Robin, in future years, became devoutly religious. He was the sweetest of men. We formed a gang or gaggle; Graham became leader, mesmerising us all by being so bold and flamboyant; a wild, daring, flaming creature. We were his entourage.

It never occurred to us that being camp meant anything, and we didn't even know the word. We just spoke the same language, giggled, felt secure in one another's company. I suppose it was an early indication of being gay, without overtly recognising it. So we weren't the hearty types, the 'rugger buggers', we were just easy in mutual companionship. We never did much to flout authority – the school wasn't Grange Hill – and discipline was well maintained.

But I do remember an exception when Graham inflamed the headmaster's wrath at the assembly that was held every morning, when a boy was deputed to do the reading from the Bible. Everybody stood for assembly, we had prayers and the reading, the head would say something and give the notices. Finally another boy would put on a piece of music, a Bach or Beethoven record, or something else to inspire in us the mood for learning and study.

Graham, when his turn came to go up on the stage, did not exactly choose a rousing popular aria, or something worthy like Elgar's *Nimrod Variations*, to put the boys in the right frame of mind. He picked Ella Fitzgerald singing a very sultry and sexy song, 'I'm Beginning to See the Light':

I never cared much for moonlit skies
I never winked back at fireflies
But now that the stars are in your eyes
I'm beginning to see the light.

From the first verse this got more and more raunchy:

I never saw rainbows in my wine
But now your lips are burning mine ...

By the end there was a stunned silence. The staff were outraged, while Graham was taken away to be beaten by the head (Mr Cummings insisted, in spite of his withered arm, on punishing the boys himself).

From that moment on the head and Graham were adversaries.

        ─────◦◦◦─────

Mum and Dad were so proud of me having got into Leyton County High that every time I went to visit them where they worked in Walthamstow they would show me off to other members of the store staff. Dad looked after the crockery ware, and ran a stall outside on the street where they sold plates, crystal glass, vases, jugs, earthenware and porcelain, which influenced me so much I became an avid collector, when later I could afford them, of Staffordshire pots. I had taken over the task from Dad of standing out on the street and selling the store's crockery. This developed my hawking skills and my lungs as I learnt the street cries.

Family carried on being the pre-eminent presence in my life. I'd walk twenty minutes from school to Aunt Hilda's every day to eat lunch, wolfing down with delight my favourite cheese and potato pie. Saturday nights we had our supper upstairs with Grandpa and Grandma, which always consisted of jellied eels with mash, washed down with a lovely sauce. I hated and refused to touch the eels, which came from Manzi's pie shop round the corner. They had a great vat of these slithery eels into which they would stick a hand, pull one out and then kill it in front of you, chop and gut the thing – then cook it. I couldn't stomach the eels, but I loved the sauce they simmered them in, which tasted great with the mash.

Every Wednesday the three of us, Mum, Dad and I, went to the pictures at one of our many local cinemas, like the Ritz or King's in Leyton, or all the way to the Regal Edmonton, to see a main feature movie together with an additional feature (the B-film, which was usually in black and white and was likely to involve a bank robbery), while often the organ rose from the pit and the organist played selections during the interval while the usherettes served ice cream.

I loved all those glamorous, sultry female film stars of the Forties and early Fifties, from Barbara Stanwyck, Greer Garson, Rita Hayworth and Ava Gardner to Vivien Leigh and the young Elizabeth Taylor – a weekly diet of extraordinary women. We ate fish and chips after the pictures and would then rush back home to hear Donald Pears on the radio singing 'In a Shady Nook by a Babbling Brook' at the start of his programme. A boy or girl of my age could stand outside the cinema if they were showing an 'A' or adult film and ask a couple or single adult who arrived to buy a ticket to take him or her in with them. You paid for yourself but you pretended you were a son or daughter.

After I recovered from rheumatic fever, the two sports the doctors recommended for me to practise were cycling and swimming. Cycling was too painful, so I took up swimming. My friend Howard was the son of the superintendent of the local baths, known as Leyton Super Baths. He and I were able to go on a Sunday when the baths were closed, and we had the whole pool to ourselves.

I swam in a lot of galas. One of the disadvantages of frequent swimming was that I grew giant verrucas on my heels, which had to be injected in the middle and gouged out by Dr Byrne on our front-room sofa, an excruciating torture. Peter Head, the head boy, who was in the 1954 Olympics team, told me I had a future in swimming. He passed me to an Olympic trainer in

East Ham, and for a year I trained intensively. But ultimately I gave up from the sheer fatigue and boredom of swimming length after length with both hands or legs tied together.

Dad's second passion after his garden was his Hillman Minx, BJD 115, bought just after the war. We would make regular outings in the Hillman on a Sunday afternoon to Ongar, or somewhere in the country, where we went out to tea. Taking Grandpa and Grandma, we would drive on much longer journeys to Southend, to the smarter end of Shoeburyness, and have a picnic from the boot in the car park, then walk to the beach. It was just Dad and I who went swimming together, while Mum sat on the beach with Grandma and Grandpa.

'Dammit! I've lost my teeth!' Dad shouted one afternoon when we were down on the beach. He was in the water when his complete set of false teeth fell out.

Hearing this, I plunged in straight away to search. I kept diving and scrabbling about on the bottom of the shore, and this went on for about an hour until I discovered them. I was thrilled at my success – and you can see how much I wanted to please my dad because I shouted, 'Dad, I've got your teeth! Dad, I've got your teeth!' as I ran up the beach, waving them in triumph before all the assembled sunbathers in their deckchairs. Dad turned away sharply and didn't at all want to know: he was mortified – but I did save his teeth!

On a longer summer holiday on the Isle of Wight, Dad taught me to dance. Mum was watching while I stood on Dad's feet as he spun gracefully round the floor, carried and guided by him, able to pick up the steps and rhythm.

I became highly proficient at ballroom dancing. Later, Isla Blair and I were together in Nottingham, touring in a show about Lord Byron called *Mad, Bad and Dangerous*, and one night we went ballroom dancing. We were spinning round the floor happily for ages, quite oblivious to everything, when suddenly the dimmed lights went out and a spotlight was following just us, while a loudspeaker voice made an announcement.

Unbeknown to us there had been a dancing competition going on – and Isla and I had won. I've always loved dancing – jiving particularly – and can still clear the floor at my best!

11

INTIMATIONS OF
IMMORTALITY

St Catherine's was an evangelical church ten minutes' walk from us, rather grim in outlook. I can never quite understand how this ever happened, but when I was fourteen I boarded a chara-banc with my parents, organised by the vicar for his parishioners, to attend a Billy Graham evangelical meeting in Harringay Arena. For some reason the vicar had inveigled Mum and Dad into this. Billy Graham was hypnotic: behind him stood a gospel choir, and the combination of that voice of his and the choir had a mesmeric effect on me, all building up to the climactic moment when he drawled, 'I'm going to ask you good people to come forward and give yourselves to Jesus!'

Unwittingly I rose from my seat to follow his words. I was completely smitten. I'd fallen for it. In a dream I moved down the steps towards the centre of the arena. I could not believe what happened next. Mum and Dad, too, had risen from their seats. They were right behind me, walking down the aisle. And then all three of us were dumbly standing before the oratorical hot gospeller, heads bowed, humbly giving ourselves to Jesus.

Graham had stopped speaking. The choir behind him had stopped singing. There we were, humbly together in complete and awed silence. Then suddenly everything changed: stewards appeared out of nowhere, and we all felt somewhat different as we were directed or, like sheep, shepherded to various places below the arena to have our details taken – names, addresses and so on. At this point, for the Jacobis, a kind of shadow fell over the whole thing, and we started feeling sillier and sillier.

Later, back at home, the vicar was so mightily astonished that here was the Jacobi family, all three of us, who'd given themselves wholeheartedly to God, that he invited himself into the house, and asked us to kneel and say a prayer with him. He insisted on coming in.

So Mum, Dad and I knelt down on the carpet in the front room while the vicar said a prayer. But as soon as he turned his back we collapsed with laughter. This visit to Billy Graham put me off religion totally and for good, for we'd been conned, we'd been hypnotised and taken for a ride, and as a reaction made to feel very silly. I don't think we saw much of the vicar after that – only when he was collecting money for the church.

As a teenager I'd still attend meetings of St Catherine's concert party, which was called Sunbeams, but they wouldn't let me join. I even presented them with a programme which included a singer and a comedy sketch, but they said it was rubbish. Because I was so proficient at dancing I was much sought-after at the socials they held, much more than the macho butch boys who really fancied the girls, while I didn't at all. But I loved the companionship of girls, and most of my friends were girls. I was strongly drawn to two girls in my teens, of whom Jackie was the special one, the younger sister of a boy at school, who came from Theydon Bois.

I went out with Jackie enough for it to be assumed that we were boyfriend and girlfriend. When I asked her to the cinema I would put an arm around her, touch her breast, make all the expected moves and hope that one of us was enjoying it. But sadly that one wouldn't be me. I escorted her home, and purely physically I kissed her good night. She would cling to me and want more than a kiss. I was following the prescribed routine; meeting a girl, taking her to the pictures, dropping her home, and then I was expected to fondle and maybe more, do all that ... But for me it was different, for as soon as I knew anything I knew this was not for me. Nothing happened below the waist, so I had to back away.

The exception to this was the feet: I loved to dance, of course, and at sixteen it was exhilarating to find a girl who could follow you. Bill Haley's 'Rock Around the Clock' in the film *Blackboard Jungle* was the dance of the mid 1950s, and later in the Sixties I adored Mersey Beat. I suppose I was somewhere between a teddy boy and a rocker. In spite of my reluctance to go further than just dance, I never felt rejected by any of my girlfriends: quite the reverse, my dancing skills were much in demand, and still are, and I felt no qualms about enjoying them to the full.

By the age of sixteen I was spending my pocket money taking the Central Line to Gerard Street in the West End to have my hair cut, slicking it at the back into a DA or Duck's Arse, with the Tony Curtis quiff at the front. I was also a great Elvis fan. Although the rough element at school would call me cissy, one by one when their chums were not around each would sidle up and say, 'Where'd yer get yer hair done, mate?' Admiring on their own, they couldn't let it be seen by the others. But they weren't violent with me, just a nuisance.

Because I acted and quite often read the lesson at school assemblies and spoke the 'King's English', I was mocked to shreds by the yobs, who really had such advantages given to them, but invariably wouldn't seize the opportunities offered.

———————

But then came the biggest moment in my life so far: in black wig, with black moustaches, and now that my voice had broken, I graduated to playing Hernando de Soto, the Spanish

Conquistador, in *The Last of the Incas* by G. Wilson Knight, the forerunner to Peter Shaffer's *The Royal Hunt of the Sun*. This was a thrilling part, and it was really exciting at last to play a big male role. It was a great disguise for me to assume and I felt very happy.

Likewise I was thrilled by my visits to the Old Vic, where Michael Benthall ran from 1953 onwards his five-year plan of presenting every Shakespeare play. Richard Burton's Hamlet, with Claire Bloom as Ophelia, was for me the summit of what I aspired to be, thrilling at every twist and turn of the ascent. Harsh, ruggedly handsome, full of wild bursts of recognition, Burton was far from the romantic prince of tradition. Especially eerie and spine-chilling was his confrontation with his father's ghost: 'Angel and ministers of grace, defend us!'

I was now in my penultimate year at school. As I grew older my appearance pursued me and dogged me like a curse. When was it going to improve? I was never comfortable at that age as I had terrible acne, which deeply embarrassed me – and I still have the scars. We had a cabinet with glass doors in the front room. I could see my outline in them, but not the texture. With my carrot-red hair and loads of freckles I hated looking at myself; but facing this dark 'window' backed by books I'd comb my hair or do up my tie. To this day I can't look directly in the mirror. When I make up in the theatre I have a magnifying glass that I bring up close to my face: I do the lips and I do one eye at a time.

Mum used to wash my hair. I was very hair-conscious, for the good strong hair, my crowning glory, was a compensation for my ugly face. If it didn't fall in the right way I'd get angry. She was always calming, she never slapped me down, or said, 'I'm trying to help you.' She'd take the rough reply and she was placid, although less placid than Dad.

Placidity – that's the word that describes them perfectly. I never once heard them row, and they were together in each other's company twenty-four hours a day. It was calming.

But not on every occasion. As a teenager I found the acne worsened and it got really bad. Mum and Dad made me an appointment to see a skin man, a dermatologist whose practice was in Wimpole Street. We three set out for the West End, and while I went in they sat outside. The dermatologist shot this tube-shaped instrument with a nozzle at my forehead, then with his hands went over my face squeezing it, and finally said, 'You can go!' He didn't clean me up so I walked out of his consulting room covered in blood and pus. Seeing my state, Mum and Dad became so incensed that they walked straight in to protest. They were so angry I thought they'd kill him.

Nothing improved and everything remained awful. Everything about me was wrong. The fatty cheeks, the stubby nose, while to top it all I had no profile. Oh, I so wished to have a face like Paul Scofield! That God-given face! If I were asked who I would like to look like, if I could push a button, it would be Scofield. Handsome, rugged, pitted: a strong, sensitive face. It has got a life on it – it has lived.

And to add to this I was miserable and shy.

12

THE LADS OF LIFE

My first, entirely chaste passion was for a French penpal from the Vendée; we did an exchange when he came to stay with us in Essex Road. His name was Joël Pauvereau and from the moment I set eyes on him I was bowled over.

He was extraordinarily handsome and wore *eau de cologne* – something that to me seemed so foreign and exotic. At this time scent on a man was unknown, and the fragrance, that perfume which emanated from him, was my idea of heaven. But naturally, in spite of my crush on him, nothing happened between us, and I am sure he had no inkling of how I felt. He did not stay long and in the end became a school teacher.

With the success of this visit, Mum arranged through the school an exchange with a German boy, Fritz. The Western Allies still occupied West Germany militarily and Leyton School fixed up these Anglo-German exchanges on the basis of 'Now is the time to be friendly with the Boche,' so off I set to Frankfurt for a week to stay with Fritz and his family. But they didn't take to me at all and were very cold, very distant. For my part I hated them, and had such a rotten time that the other half of the exchange didn't happen.

As a result of the Spanish Conquistador de Soto, my acting prospects suddenly caught fire when Michael Croft, an English teacher at Alleyn's School in Dulwich, visited Leytonstone and auditioned me. For a year or two Croft, sailor, boxer and author of the semi-autobiographical novel *Spare the Rod*, had been enterprisingly directing plays with local public school boys for what he grandiosely called 'The Youth Theatre'. He was now looking for a boy to play the part of Prince Hal for his second production, that of *Henry IV Part II*.

Mainly he took his casts from Alleyn's, and some from Dulwich College. Richard Hampton, who was later head of OUDS (the Oxford University Dramatic Society), had been playing Prince Hal, but had to drop out for National Service. John Stride, another possibility at his school for Hal, was unavailable. Croft had to cast his net wider, which is how he came to our patch. As I wanted to be an actor I auditioned and got the part, a step up the ladder for me, but one which caused great unease as I surveyed those around me from a new and different vantage point.

Right from the start I was definitely not a Croft favourite. He thought I was a bit namby-pamby, for he had a footballer image of actors as 'the lads of life', into which category John Stride fitted, but I didn't.

My fellow lads of life were Ken Farrington as Poins, Paul Hill as Doll Tearsheet and David Weston as Falstaff. David was the son of parents who ran a fish shop in the Brixton Market, and he had a gutsy approach to Falstaff, with turned-up nose and a way of saying, 'I was a Cockney kid at thirteen,' as if he were confessing an addiction. All four of us were destined to be professionals, and later David acted with me when I ran the Chichester Festival Theatre, where he was my understudy as Tattle in *Love for Love*, and much later even understudy to Ian McKellen's Lear, about which he wrote a book.

The other three called me 'Strawberry bloke', for reasons unknown except perhaps the straw hair and pink complexion.

Besides the three I was with now, a lot of people started on the lowest rung of the theatrical ladder with Michael Croft, such as John Stride, Julian Glover, David Suchet, Martin Jarvis and Ian McShane.

The company had a very strong, all-male exclusiveness and ethos. This came to a head when they were going to do *A Midsummer Night's Dream*. The director of this production, Paul Hill, came to Croft because they could not find the right two boys to play Helena and Hermia. But they did have two volunteer girls who were scrubbing floors and helping in the wardrobe: the menial stuff. Their names were Helen Mirren and Diana Quick.

'With your permission I've found two girls to play Helena and Hermia,' Hill told Croft.

'Then on your head be it!' grumbled Croft, who wasn't exactly enamoured of young ladies in his company, and was the robust, bachelor type. Later Helen played Cleopatra which the Youth Theatre put on at the Old Vic, but she would decline to speak of Croft beyond saying 'that silly old fart' – I don't think she liked him much!

To rehearse Prince Hal I had to come all the way from Leytonstone to Dulwich. It was a marathon bus journey from one side of London to the other, involving six buses and twenty-seven stops. Those Sunday rehearsals in Lordship Lane didn't exactly inspire me, and I don't remember them with any fondness. Everybody was very jokey, very camp, giggling all over the place, and I was very much an outsider. The others all knew each other, had worked together before, communicated in that kind of shorthand camaraderie that long-time friends acquire. I never felt comfortable.

At first, when I saw Paul Hill cuddling up to Croft on the sofa, I very much had the feeling that Michael was a bit like a suspect scoutmaster. After read-throughs and when we moved on to rehearse properly – strangely enough, in a scout hut near Herne Hill – he could also be quite a martinet.

Yet Michael helped me greatly with my acting and made me aware of how much I had to learn, especially with my voice, which, although it had just broken, had come very easily to me so I took a lot for granted. Everything in the rehearsals seemed so professional, while activity had been much gentler at Leytonstone with Bobby Brown. I felt as if I had two left feet and was very young, extremely untalented, rather unworldly and quite out of my depth.

On the other hand I enjoyed it and learned a lot, and was glad I was doing it, although I never really felt part of the clique, the main core. And I felt confused at the rehearsals because I didn't quite know what or who the other boys were. The Alleyn's boys were such a close, well-knit lot. They all had a past with Michael, while I had no former life with him; I was a bit frightened of them all, and was made very much aware that I had taken over Richard Hampton's part.

While there was nothing ostensibly of a sexual nature going on in the all-male set-up, they would lark about and joke quite crudely, sit on one another's laps, and embrace and hug each other familiarly. Meanwhile I was feeling disorientated and unresolved in my own identity. It was strange because all, probably without exception, liked girls, yet I thought they must be homosexuals; while I, who knew I was gay, was a complete innocent, unable to join in and unhappily feeling a complete outsider. This was yet another example, I confess, of my overriding desire to be loved and accepted.

Richard's mother came in during our run to help with the hairstyling and she would curl my hair every night with hot irons into a Henry V-cum-Shirley Temple fringe. Again,

I wasn't easy with this. I'm sure she twisted my hair harder than she did Richard's out of some kind of annoyance that Richard wasn't there, probably thinking: 'Why should I be doing this for Derek?'

I only really became friendly with Barry Boys, who played Henry IV, and he was an outsider like me because he came from Dulwich College. We had that great scene together when Prince Hal tries to convince his father that he is responsible and is growing up to carry his royal responsibilities. No one can ever play that scene over and over again and not be seriously affected by it as a lesson in responsibility (and I was only seventeen).

Henry IV played four times in Toynbee Hall and won a glowing accolade in *Plays and Players*, where, in my first-ever professional notice, the critic wrote that I, like all the nobles, conveyed a real impression of aristocracy 'subject to the same weaknesses as other mortal men, yet endowed with a mettle to subdue them'. The same critic adversely pointed out that I did, in some of my emotional scenes, indulge my emotions instead of communicating them, which wasn't a bad comment to receive and work on.

'You see, what I want is not "the actor type",' Michael said. He had amazing fortune with his casts, and drew leading critics to the performances. He would have been a bigger influence on me if I had done more for him, but after I began to make a name for myself in the business in work like *I, Claudius*, I became a little surprised to see how my name rather oddly appeared in a lot of National Youth Theatre publicity, while other actors, who had done far more for the Youth Theatre, were ignored.

I had only ever acted four times for them at Toynbee Hall, and the Hamlet I did as a schoolboy was not theirs but a Leyton School production. I don't know whether that came from Michael or the journalists, but I didn't like it.

Michael and I eventually became friends and saw each other, but not that often. We were never close, for I was always the outsider with Michael. I had no idea who or what I was then. I was on the cusp of being timid, but at the same time quite other-worldly, and not at all bothered about whether I was gay or heterosexual. There were much more important things to worry about.

But I never managed to become one of Michael's 'lads of life'!

13

THE PASSPORT PRINCE

Thirty years or so into my acting career I was playing Hamlet on a tour when we visited many Middle Eastern countries, but while in Yugoslavia and before entering Egypt the company manager spotted that I had an Israeli visa stamped in my passport. There was no time to go to the consulate, so in the interval I was stuck up against the wall in the dressing room in Hamlet's mad 'antic disposition' attire, and they snapped a passport photo of me there and then, so I had a new passport issued by the British Consulate. For ten years until the passport expired, border officials had to check me against the lace collar and beard of Hamlet's 'antic disposition'.

In my final term at school, Bobby Brown – who by now was a good friend, and would often have a meal at home with the three of us – cast me for the first time as Hamlet. Bobby was tall, with receding chin – something of a chinless wonder – very clever, very kind, and with a great sense of humour. He had a terrible time with the troublemakers in my class who would riot and play him up rotten: he was not a born teacher by any means. I used to feel terrible when this happened, and I sensed there was something of the actor *manqué* about him: when he started rehearsing us he was a different person, he would relax more than when he was teaching.

He cast *Hamlet* from the school dramatic society, and we held read-throughs in the wood-panelled library, and then moved downstairs to the assembly hall. Sometimes we rehearsed out of school in my best friend Mark Allen's large house on the edge of Epping Forest – he was Laertes – and there we practised the sword fight.

Bobby was a good director: very gentle, he gave me a sense of what the words meant, who the character was and where it all came from. Mum made me wonderful costumes, and when we moved to the final rehearsals in the school hall there would be this great buzz and hive of activity: costumes and props being fashioned by parents in the auditorium, lighting and rehearsing on stage. We changed in the gym, and once Mark's brother Tim, aged fifteen, who was a very fetching blonde Ophelia, turned up blind drunk for a run-through. We had to put Ophelia under a cold shower to get her on.

After playing as usual in the school assembly hall we took the production to the Edinburgh Festival. As my Prince Hal with Croft was now being succeeded by the Prince of Denmark, I might be forgiven for thinking I was cast in the same mould – forever to play princes and royals, with the odd pope and cardinal thrown in.

As part of the Fringe we played in the hall of the Edinburgh Academy, where my performance was commended for its attack and 'sheer professionalism'. It was everything but that, and I didn't rate all that highly, but what I lacked in craftsmanship and insight I believe I made up for in terms of raw energy. I remember this *Hamlet*, which was the first of my four performances in the part, with the greatest affection and pride. It wasn't the Youth Theatre production that was generally touted, but put on by the Players of Leyton – as we called ourselves – and we experienced together, with boys playing the females, just that camaraderie I never found in my one Youth Theatre production.

Mine was a black-and-white Hamlet, very simplistic, in which I tore several passions to several tatters, but for all that it may have had something very accessible, entirely due to Bobby Brown's careful coaching, because we received a huge amount of publicity. We rather outshone the main Festival offering, *The Hidden King*, a Scottish play with Robert Edison and Robert Speiaght, at the Assembly Rooms.

Hamlet had astonishing results. Mum and Dad couldn't believe it, and were so chuffed. They ran a profile of me in the London *Observer* on the strength of which I was summoned to the Soho office of 20th Century Fox, where they told me I was too young for them. The Fox executive added that my *only* asset was my red hair, because it would photograph well.

Hamlet was a turning point, because although I had always, from a small child, wanted to be an actor, I was now really at the point where I thought: '*Yes!* I could probably make it work!' My Hamlet even caused a spat between two leading critics, Alan Dent of the *News Chronicle* and Kenneth Tynan of the *Observer*.

Tynan pontificated patronisingly, 'As Hamlet this boy would make a fine prose actor,' which Dent took to be a slur on my performance.

Dent in turn wrote, 'May I remind Mr Tynan that I once saw him [i.e. Tynan] play a dreadful Player Queen as a schoolboy?'

It was quite ridiculous. Here were these two critical giants clawing at each other's throats over me, an eighteen-year-old!

———

Twenty years later, in 1977, when I did Hamlet at the official Edinburgh Festival in the Assembly Rooms for Prospect, an American couple in the audience sent word after it ended through the stage manager: 'Can we come and see you and say hello?' This was after *I, Claudius* on television had been such a success that I was known as '*I, Claudius* Hamlet'.

'Are you here for the Festival?' I asked this very sweet couple in my dressing room.

'Yes,' they replied, 'and we're also celebrating our twentieth wedding anniversary. The reason we wanted to see you – apart from being fans – is because we were here in the year we married twenty years ago, and you were playing Hamlet, and were still a schoolboy. We were so impressed that when we had our first child we called him "Derek": and twenty years later here you are, still playing Hamlet!'

In earlier days, back in Leytonstone, Mark, who played Laertes, asked me over to celebrate with his parents, and his brother Tim who was Ophelia, and his sister. Mark had taken to wearing a large Astrakhan fur coat and trilby in the style of Bud Flanagan and his raccoon coat.

Mark's father was a chemist who ran the dispensary at Whipps Cross Hospital. They cooked octopus in its own ink, and we drank wine with it. We never had wine at home, so wine with dinner was my introduction to a more sophisticated style of living. It was strange eating this new dish swimming in black juice, and I'm afraid I almost gagged.

'Did you enjoy it?' my hosts enquired.

'Oh, yes, very much,' I replied politely, so they insisted I had seconds: I had talked myself into a second helping.

Mum and Dad were up when I got back home, waiting excitedly for news of what we had eaten for dinner.

'Octopus,' I told them.

'Octopus!'

They frowned. What kind of friends was I cultivating?

———◦◦◦———

It was entirely due to Bobby Brown that I started my theatrical career. Bobby was a fantastic influence for the good, so he was the first to stamp Hamlet on the passport (metaphorically so, in his case) that gained me entry to the wider world.

Bobby had a passion for drama and later left teaching to join the British Film Institute. We often wondered if there was a lady in his life, but we could never quite work it out. But there was never any suggestion that he was interested in boys. He followed my career later with extraordinary devotion, and he came round after the shows to give me stringent notes and say devastating things when all I wanted to hear was lavish, unstinting praise!

Our withered-arm headmaster, Mr Cummings, didn't wholly approve of acting and actors: he created fear in our eyes, not a bad thing for the maintenance of order. Now the school is a sixth-form college, stuffed with glass and hi-tech gear, overrun by security guards in luminous coats with clipboards.

'All a bit cissy' was what the headmaster thought of us then. Mum cultivated him through the PTA, to which she belonged, to look more kindly on our acting talents, so you could say she was my first agent.

I met Mr Cummings at some function years later and 'You've done all right for yourself, Jacobi!' was what he said: just like that – 'Jacobi!' But he was more than pleased to see me again, and to know me.

Grandpa and Grandma were always a benign presence in my early existence, but it was one that could not go on forever. When they were near the end of their lives they were both (though in different wards) in Whipps Cross Hospital, a walking distance away from Essex Road.

It was here that Grandpa died first. We went down the corridor to see Grandma to tell her. I was there with Mum and Dad, Uncle Henry and Auntie Hilda. We stood looking at Grandma, wondering how she would take it. I remember Grandma just saying, 'I know, I know. He came to say goodbye.'

I could feel Mum jerk a little and pull herself together as she stifled her tears. Grandma died a few weeks later.

I knew that these wonderful close family relatives my good fortune had brought me would not last forever. I wonder now how they could have lived and died in such proximity to each other. Uncle Henry, with his yen for betting heavily on horses and dogs, had been bailed out more than once by Hilda. He died from a heart attack in the front room in Essex Road, his body blocking the door when Dad found him and tried to get in. Hilda had gone some years before from cancer.

Auntie had been a very strict mother to Raymond. They waited till he was twenty-one before they told him he was adopted. Discovering this had a traumatic effect on him and he began to drink. He was twice married, and had a girl and a boy from each wife. I became godfather to the eldest, Gail, just before I reached fourteen.

Raymond died before his time. I guess life in the end just wasn't good to him. Gail became a croupier for a time working at the Trocadero, Piccadilly, and we are still in touch.

14

CLOUD-CAPPED
TOWERS

I had already picked on Cambridge as a means of entering the acting profession for good reason, and there were many there of exactly the same bent. I knew that Oxford and Cambridge were full of actors, and that it was how a lot of actors and directors embarked on successful careers. Most parents weren't keen on their children going on stage and therefore many in the acting crowd I joined as soon as I arrived there had to make the choice between pleasing themselves or their parents, while I had the luxury of both.

I'd had an idyllic childhood, and now Mum and Dad were very supportive of me in whatever I wanted to do. Of course, they still had at the back of their minds that 'Oh well, if he's brainy, it would be much better if he became a doctor or a lawyer,' because that was an accepted profession, and acting was not. It was always seen as important to have a 'second string to the bow', even by my parents, and I also wanted to continue my education as long as I could, as I loved school.

Armed with my State Scholarship I went up for two interviews at Cambridge to try for a place. My first choice was King's College, where they said, 'We'd love to have you, but you have to sit an entrance examination to confirm we have made the right decision.' My other interview was at St John's with Harry Hinsley, the Master of the College.

The Master was in appearance a rather grey man, very calm, friendly, very controlled like a schoolmaster, and quite retiring.

It was Saturday, the day of the Oxford–Cambridge boat race, and during the interview the Master said, 'Do you mind if we break for a moment and listen to the boat race?'

'No, that's fine,' I said, so we duly listened to the boat race. I was nonplussed by this unexpected turn of events. The race began and Harry grew more and more agitated and excited, while I had more or less switched off with all the prepared interview topics clanging around in my head.

'We've won!' the Master finally exclaimed. He was in such an excellent mood that he spun round and said, 'You're in!'

'But don't I have to take an exam?' I stammered.

'No, that's fine,' he said. 'Let's celebrate!' and proceeded to open a bottle of champagne.

It was almost certainly the case that, more than anything else, it was my newly acquired reputation as an actor that got me into Cambridge. The Master – whom I was later to call Harry (as he became a good friend) – clearly knew all about my recent success in the Edinburgh Festival *Hamlet*. It would not be unfair to say that as a result I arrived at Cambridge already with a certain seal of approval.

I didn't even have to do an interview or an audition, for as Alan Bennett has written, 'Being interviewed for Cambridge was like being auditioned.' Without the 'like', this actually is what my good friend Ian McKellen did a year later when he applied to St Catherine's. Asked by the tutor Tom Henn for a speech from *Henry V*, which he had just played at school, he stood on a table and recited the whole of 'Once more unto the breach, dear friends, once more.' They gave him a college exhibition.

So now I could combine my love of school and schooling with my desire to act and become an actor. However, I must add at this point that it was also my good fortune to have been blessed with a near photographic memory, which was to be invaluable not only throughout my acting career, for obvious reasons, but during my time at Cambridge, when academic studies played second fiddle to acting and I was forced to rely on last-minute 'instant revision'.

Also I had three years of paid irresponsibility ahead of me, which I was quite looking forward to. My state scholarship gave me over £100 per term, an enormous sum in my eyes. What was now coming out in me, in a more defined and understandable way – although who could ever know what was going to happen in the future? – was that I had only ever dipped my toe into life. Protected as I was, the golden boy, and now with the added protection of a scholarship, I never jumped in and wallowed. And yet when I acted, already I could feel the texture and depth to what I was doing and could dive deep down. But into real life I only ventured up to my ankles.

This is how my callow, early reasoning went: 'I can cope with the unreality of the world of the imagination because it was laid out for me what was going to happen, and what I had to do.' This was probably one of the reasons, later as a professional actor, I have never been much good at improvising – improvising is nearer to the real world when the unexpected happens, and I am not totally relaxed with that. It seems that I have always relegated my responsibilities to someone else in the real world.

Whenever I did try to improvise later I set out to try to make people laugh – the get-out, an easy way. Many actors do this: you can kid yourself you are doing it properly when you are not. A fun sketch I played later on the American TV comedy show *Frasier*, when the old ham actor, Jackson Hedley, is making his comeback, provides a good instance of this, with the audience's 'smiling faces frozen into a rictus of revenge' (by now hamming was so second nature that when the episode came out I won an Emmy for it!).

But up to that point in my life, Hamlet and the twenty other roles I played at school were the be-all and end-all of my experience: 'The readiness is all.' I was completely unattached and did my best, as Hamlet did, to avoid being asked to cope.

I needed a director, as Hamlet found one in the ghost of his father. I needed a life director. I needed, too, an ensemble, a company, because I had always been a part of a wider family – the Jacobis of Leytonstone: Mum, Dad, the aunts and uncles, my cousins and grandparents. I would have to watch out.

What would happen when I was plunged into the real world?

AGE III
SIGHING LIKE
FURNACE

15

FIRST TERM, FIRST LOVE

This was the hallowed St John's College, third on the left down King's Parade after King's, Clare's and Trinity, with its beautiful St John's Chapel, built by Margaret Beaufort, the founder, daughter of John of Gaunt, its famous choir, its Bridge of Sighs seen from the River Cam on a punt.

On arrival I felt just like a schoolboy. My parents dropped me off at my digs: in spite of my scholarship, the college had no room for me in my first year. We all cried – it was like being left on the moon. I was 54 miles from home, and to me that was a distance near to infinity. I was an only child from local Leytonstone schools where I had hardly walked more than 200 yards from home to my form room, where I had sprinted to classes with my mates, where we'd race each other along the road to the silver 1930s nude sculpture of a lady which stood in a window in a house nearby to see who could reach the naked lady's bum first. The winner had the day at his feet.

The digs the college chose for me were in a little terraced house, 32 Alpha Road, over the other side of Magdalen Bridge, where I had a bedroom and sitting room. These would be paid for by the college out of my scholarship. They discovered the dead body of a student, a girl, in the river at the bottom of Alpha Road.

'Didn't you hear about it? Took her life, she did, at the end of summer term,' said Phyl, my landlady. 'The pressure of exams must have got to her.'

This was about the first thing I heard. And weird though it was, there was to be an echo of this nearly two years later during my exams when they ran an article in *Varsity* alleging I had attempted to take an overdose, because I had taken some sleeping pills and couldn't wake up.

Phyl's news was far from reassuring, and a great chasm of responsibility stretched before me. I had never had this kind of freedom for myself before, and I had not done National Service, which many undergraduates had, and become officers or non-commissioned officers, or been involved in military action in Cyprus or Suez or Korea, and they were already young men. I wish I had known how to cope. I did not know at parties how much to drink, how many canapés – a word I had never come across before – to consume, and even to this day I have still never quite worked out the placing of knives and forks.

Mum and Dad were tearful, too, worried that I would not be able to manage. Hugs and kisses all round, and then they left me on my own. Giving them time to drive home, I was on the payphone dialling our number: I still remember it, LEY 4536, imagining Mum picking up the black Bakelite object.

Next night I would be in the booth in the porter's lodge. It really was a terrible wrench for me to leave them. I promised them I wouldn't start drinking and smoking, but what could I do when invites started dropping into my pigeonhole: 'For Drinks and Smokes'?

<hr />

That next night was my big try-out at eating in college. The hall, dominated by a great portrait of Margaret Beaufort, looked like Hogwarts in the *Harry Potter* movies. I have never much liked Dickensian institutions. I queued at the self-service counter and helped myself to soup from a tureen. Taking my full bowl I went and found a place at one of the trestle tables along a wall. I was far too nervous to strike up conversation with anyone.

I found it was the 'hearties' table, heavy with Hooray Henries. The guy opposite had finished, and the only way out was across the table, so he stood up onto it and put his foot – accidentally? – in my soup.

'Oh, frightfully sorry old chap! Oh ha ha ha!'

I only went there that once, in the first week. I felt like Oliver Twist! I fled to the Koh-i-Nor Indian restaurant and spent almost the next three years consuming curries. So as well as this I soon cottoned on to the idea that with my new land-lords, Phyl and her husband Don, who were kind, lovely and warm – and as sole lodger in their house – I would be better off than in the harsher environment of college rooms, to which my scholarship entitled me after my first year.

Gradually Phyl and Don became my protectors, my surrogate parents over the next three years. I preferred to stay where I was because I was looked after so well, and was so settled there. As they had to keep the records for the proctors, the university disciplinarians, they'd sometimes cook the books for me, saying I was in at 10.30 p.m. when in reality I'd gone up to London and was back at three.

One of the first students I met at St John's was Julian Pettifer, who was in his final year. He was extraordinarily good-looking, a *jeunesse doré* figure who might easily have stepped out of the pages of *Brideshead Revisited*.

Susceptible as I was, I was overawed. I felt so very young, so schoolboyish. I thought him the most beautiful thing in the world, and later he became a much-fêted television presenter. We had acting in common, and Julian, with whom I recorded and acted for the Marlowe Society in my first term, as a senior undergraduate kindly took me under his wing.

He lived in college, and was a leading light of a very sophisticated and amusing circle surrounding a well-known Cambridge figure, the Anglican priest Richard Bagley, who had a house in Spaniard's Row. Julian reputedly told a close friend, however, that unwillingly and against his inclination he had been seduced by an older boy at Marlborough College. He never attempted anything with me, so I was sure I was not good-looking enough to attract his attention and pursuit. I felt rather unhappy about this.

'Derek – you won't believe it, but listen to this!' Julian said enthusiastically when I was round having this first drink in his palatial rooms. I felt awkward and uncomfortable, and I behaved in a very stilted way. I was way out of my league, out of the world I knew, but so flattered that this much-admired figure was entertaining *me*.

He put on the record player to play me a priceless possession he had somehow acquired – a black-market copy of the LP of *My Fair Lady* – and we listened to Rex Harrison singing, 'Why can't a woman be more like a man?'

***

It was during my very first term, when I was rehearsing Ibsen's *Pillars of the Community*, the main ADC (Amateur Dramatic Club) production, that I met Richard Kay. Blond, blue-eyed, he was very much in the Cambridge Rupert Brooke tradition, although unlike Brooke he was not at King's but at St Catherine's.

Richard was impeccably well spoken and polite, with a quite distinctive, almost elegiac voice which gave me goose pimples. For me it was love at first sight. In particular I was attracted by his boyishness. I didn't know quite what had hit me. I think I felt rather sick and it became almost like an illness, but on the whole it was wonderful. At once our friendship gelled. We became great friends and Richard responded, but never in the way I wanted; not physically, or rather only once, and this was way down the line – much later on.

Richard, who was also destined to go into the theatre, was born in Newcastle a year before me in March. Unlike me he had been through preparatory and public school. Many of my contemporaries came from quite a similar range of public schools. In this respect I felt a bit of an outcast – an ugly duckling, so to speak. But, like me, Richard had come straight from school, so for this reason at least we felt a natural sympathy for one another.

I loved Richard from the start but sentimentally, like Viola's love for the Duke in *Twelfth Night*, I kept my love silent, like 'Patience on a monument'. We saw much of one another, went around together, and in our first vacation he invited me to spend time with him and his family at Rowlands Gill, their house just north outside Newcastle. It had a large garden and one day we went for a walk together, during which we were both forthcoming and confessed our friendship. We pledged our troth – not of love, but of 'You're my best friend.'

This friendship grew into something very steady but it was completely chaste, although at Cambridge most assumed it was much more than this. Richard, with his extraordinary good looks, his great smile and his wonderful personality, attracted a circle of gay admirers as well as of girls – and it would be dishonest of me to say that I did not desire him constantly.

Cambridge was a very tolerant society but also, compared with today, socially very mature. We seemed to live on a plateau of equanimity and good sense, although this may not have been the whole story. But undergrads could be private or gregarious as much or as little as they wished. No one was prying into the secrets of each other's sex life; no one was doing kiss-and-tell, even though we had fledgling reporters aplenty already writing for national papers. The standard was very high, the values serious.

There was no stigma about being gay, and it was never a shameful secret there, which helped me a lot to accept my sexuality without making a song and dance about it. The actor Hugh Walters, who later had everyone rolling in the aisles and weeping with laughter at his numerous comic roles, believed Cambridge was a place of spurious fame. For Hugh, 'It never crossed my mind being gay was illegal. It was just that we never talked about it.'

I've always gone with the flow, and I've never, from Cambridge onwards, been a martyr to my sexuality. However, I am also a loner and I tend to run away from conflict and decision-making. Now that I was in Cambridge I found it even more difficult to deal with the real world than with the creative side of my life in which I could make choices, which I do find exciting.

While I loved Richard, the last thing I would ever do was force myself upon him or exact demands, or provoke a conflict out of it. But somehow we suited one another, and while I tend to keep myself to myself, Richard and I interacted with one another so well, were unthreatening to one another, and preserved one another's identity. We giggled, enjoyed one another's company, went on outings, to parties, and of course primarily acted together and rehearsed each other through our lines.

We were, embarrassing as it might be to say this, like Polixenes and Leontes in *The Winter's Tale* – entire and complete innocents:

What we chang'd
Was innocence for innocence; we knew not
The doctrine of ill-doing, nor dream'd
That any did –

I attribute this wholly to Richard's equable and evenly balanced temperament. For while up until this point in my life I had generally been calm and well balanced, this was far from the case in my relationship with Richard: as time went on I became more intense, abandoning my feelings of pure friendship, and my love for him started to outweigh his feelings for me.

———◦◦◦———

Richard and I acted in just about everything together at Cambridge. The list is virtually endless, as were the number of parts I performed as part of the Cambridge student rep. I was quite happy that he had many girlfriends. I followed Richard to Paris where he played Romeo. For this he dyed his fair hair snow-white blond. We stayed four nights sharing a room in a hotel. On my own one night I managed to buy a ticket for one of the final performances of Edith Piaf at the Olympia. It was a unique experience to be able to witness that tiny, frail woman singing with almost her last gasp of breath. She was stupendous, so moving, and at the end she brought on stage her Greek boyfriend, while the audience all rushed forward to try and touch her.

In the May week production of *A Midsummer Night's Dream*, which happened on a succession of sultry hot nights, Richard and I were on stage together as Lysander and Puck. He administered love drops to my eyes but I didn't need them. The atmosphere of this production was highly charged, emotionally and sexually. But again nothing happened between us.

The only time something more with Richard happened was during the run of *Edward II* when I played King Edward, in the Marlowe Society's major summer production of 1958, a performance which did more than any other to open the way to my future career.

We opened *Edward II* at the Bancroft Gardens in Stratford, after playing the Cambridge Arts Theatre, and we had just reached my deposition scene when the heavens opened. We had to stop the performance and rush back to the tent where we changed. Here the midges in the tents were unbearable, attracted by the greasepaint, and we left as quickly as we could. Sir Barry Jackson

85

and colleagues from the Birmingham Repertory Company had been in the audience, and they promised they would come back later to see the whole show. This would become significant, although I never knew till later that they were there.

Richard and I had digs together in a cottage in Shottery. Our landlady was a marvellous old woman called Julia Hasty. She had been a great beauty in her youth, while one of her husbands had been a sculptor. Julia appears in various guises and on various buildings all over Birmingham – always stark naked. By this time she was an old lady, she had lost an eye in a hunting accident, so she had a black patch over this eye, and was known as a witch, and she was fiercely Sinn Fein. If she took a shine to you, you received this little bit of Sinn Fein ribbon to carry around. She had an inglenook fireplace in her little cottage, and a settle chair with a leprechaun on top of it. She did the full works, board and lodging, although she had only one room to let, which Richard and I shared.

'Go easy, Derek, be careful,' Richard said to me on our way back to Shottery. We were more than a little tipsy when Richard and I arrived back that night after *Edward* was rained off. We drank a few more glasses of wine. There was a great deal of groping, and then we became a bit coy: we talked about love at length, we discussed going to bed together, then we tried, but it didn't really happen. The truth was, I'm afraid, that Richard basically was just not interested. I never took it personally: it was just all too clear that he didn't find men sexually attractive.

After this incident, my feelings began to take a different path from Richard's. I became obsessive about him. I was besotted enough to spend hours under his window outside his digs in Madingley Road where he lived at quite a famous address, for his landlady was well known in Cambridge circles. I grew very jealous of the other people Richard knew, of others becoming too close to him – not of the girls, but the men friends, for instance when he went on holiday to Greece with Roddy Taylor, another of our acting fraternity. This was hard for me and I just chewed myself up inside.

One weekend when Richard and I were driving up to London (by which time I was twenty-one and had my own car), we had a terrible row on the journey over something quite trivial, and not by now the fairly predictable topic. I dropped him off where he wanted to go, but when I went back home I broke down completely and started crying.

'What on earth's the matter, dear?' Mum said, very concerned.

'I've just had a terrible row with Richard. I'm so unhappy, Mum – it's all so impossible and unfair.' I told her all about the row with Richard, and it all came flooding out of me. I told her I was homosexual, that I was in love with Richard, and that he would not have me.

She hugged me. Her reaction was fantastic – it didn't faze her one bit.

'You're in a very specialised atmosphere, dear. It's the first time you've been away from home. You've not yet grown up, and all boys go through this phase.'

She continued to reassure me soothingly in this vein. I desperately didn't want to disappoint her, but she really didn't seem to mind.

'For heaven's sake don't tell Dad, please,' I begged her, but I am sure she did.

The subject was never mentioned again, not even once, by either of them – or by me – but I had said the word, I had confessed to her, and from that moment on it was never spoken of again, and just accepted.

And as the years went by, and as I didn't marry, it was all too evident that I was gay. But now it was out there, it had been stated and was open.

'When are we going to have grandchildren?' This was said occasionally but it was spoken tongue in cheek, because they knew very well they were never going to have grandchildren, and this was just accepted, too.

And it had all started with that row with Richard. I cannot for the life of me even remember exactly what we had said to each other.

I had a group of Leytonstone friends, including a number of girls. Richard liked one of these, whom he had met through me. He fell in love with her and they became engaged. I was never jealous of this. Before I met Richard I was entirely celibate, and I remained more or less so while he was around at Cambridge and long after, when we shared a flat. As far as the world knew I wasn't gay but a romantic heterosexual, able to fuel and fulfil the dreams of single women. Our love remained, except for that one time, entirely chaste; so when at that crucial moment Richard had told me he was unhappy to continue and wanted to go in a different direction I was heartbroken, desolated, but my feelings remained. My great love for him kept on and on, and never really went away. In time he married and raised a wonderful family.

I confess I had a bit of a fling with an Italian, but it was pretty innocent stuff, as for several years I carried this light for Richard, while he was still happy to enjoy our friendship. That night in Shottery had not upset him at all, but he had decided it was not for him. And almost exactly the same thing was to happen with someone else many years later – in exactly the same way, and in exactly the same place, which was uncanny. I seemed to fall for unavailable men, the ultimate romantic torture of unrequited love, at least sexually unrequited love. So Cyrano de Bergerac was there even then in the shadows, yearning for the unattainable, beckoning to me even in those early years. Cyrano was to become one of my veils, something I was fated to do.

Later, when I joined the National Theatre, Richard, having gone abroad for a while to teach, returned to acting, and joined the company in minor roles and in the film of Olivier's *Three Sisters*. Most notably of all he was in the hilarious, all-male production of *As You Like It*, when I was Touchstone, which ran and toured for over two years. He played the rustic *ingénue* Phoebe.

'Oh God! Is this really an all-male cast?' I heard a man in the Old Vic audience call out in a loud voice. It was Richard as Phoebe who was really so extraordinary that it completely turned the audience's heads – and on stage mine. He wore a sheath-like dress of silver lamé. When he threw himself down on the ground in grief with his limbs in abandon he was so beguiling, in a voluptuously sexy way, that you could hear people in the audience, with a quick intake of breath, rustling and reaching into their programmes to find out the name.

One day, forty-eight years of age, married and with two young children, Richard drove off from his lovely new country home near Windrush in Oxfordshire – which he was in the process of doing up – to buy grouting, and minutes later he was killed in a head-on crash. The other driver, who caused the crash and was entirely responsible, was completely drunk. I was so upset I could not bear to go to the funeral.

'If Richard had followed my advice,' said Christopher Fry the playwright, who gave the address, 'the teaching profession would have been richer and the acting profession poorer.' Christopher had taught Richard many years before.

'I did my best to head him away from the theatre,' Fry continued. 'It seemed a pity that his good work as a teacher in Africa [he had taught for a while in Ghana] should give way to the uncertainties of the stage.

'But I should have known that his great qualities as a human being wouldn't be wasted, whatever he turned his hand to. They were steady and true and life-giving, as they had been I remember in his schooldays ... and his wonderful smile – the broadest

smile in the world, someone has said. The eagerness and respon-
sive friendliness were unfailing, deepening with the years, and all
this shone through his acting as well as his living. We wouldn't
be far out to suppose that this was the kind of humanity God
imagined He was creating in the first place.'

When my friend Michael Burrell, who was also with us in
all these Cambridge productions, came back and described the
service and what Christopher had said, I broke down and tears
streamed down my face.

16

THE MARLOWE SOCIETY

'My name is John Bird.'

I had been in my Alpha Road digs for only two weeks when there was an unexpected knock on the door and I went to answer it. Standing there was a small, fair-haired man, just starting to go bald, softly spoken in a very ruminative way, who introduced himself. He was, as all we first-year undergrads knew, almost instantly big-time, the Cambridge equivalent of Alfred Hitchcock.

I was quite overwhelmed, very flattered and honoured, because he asked me to play a big role in his University Actors' production of *All the King's Men* by Robert Penn Warren. So, because my reputation from *Hamlet* in Edinburgh was so high on arrival – in my view spuriously so – I was catapulted at once into a leading role.

Thus propelled, and putting on a very phoney American accent for my first modern role, into this hotbed of such discerning and mostly well-seasoned second- and third-year players, I felt dismal. I was terribly miscast. It was, 'Ooh, this boy is coming up, he's supposed to be the next best thing! Let's see what he can do. He's no good.' I was appalling. I came a cropper and for a while felt I was untouchable. If only I had had more experience and had done more acting, I started to wish.

They had read what I had done at Edinburgh, and the knives were out. I had no idea how to handle it. I remember thinking, if it is like this here, what the hell is it going to be like in the profession? To begin with, I was more than a bit frightened that I would not be able to survive. There were so many older, more mature and ruthless people around, and I was so conscious that I was a sea of emotions and instincts only too ready to dribble or rush out, to betray my *naïveté* or my innocence.

Then there were the powers that be that ran theatre at Cambridge.

'Derek Jacobi, you are late for rehearsal – *late!* You are not Paul Scofield or even Dame Sybil Thorndike! Not yet!'

This was at a rehearsal of *Cymbeline*, and the director, Dadie Rylands, peevish-looking and red-faced, bawled me out: he thought I was being grand. He screamed at me, actually screamed! It was frightening to behold. Yet by now I had played a number of leading roles.

'Dadie' (George) Rylands, lifelong fellow of King's College, otherwise had a beautiful, musical speaking voice rather similar to that of John Gielgud, who was his close friend, in its fluting, breathless, singsong high tones. He was in his mid-fifties – to me an old man. The legend was that earlier in life – and he had been at King's since 1920 – he would read Latin grace in Hall, dressed in a bright blue suit with an equally bright blue tie, with incredible panache and virtuosity. He wore a blue shirt and black tie all the time, because it was reputed he was still in mourning for Rupert Brooke.

'I'm going to drill my Marlowe players to *think* while they are speaking, think what the Elizabethan and Jacobean blank verses mean instead of ranting or throwing away the lines. You must learn how to respect the interplay of rhythm and metre of the lines.'

This is what Dadie told us, and he lined us up over the years to record the whole of Shakespeare for the British Council, stiffening the undergraduate casts with well-known professionals. Some would say that this was a discipline that after the war would transform for three decades the speaking of verse at Stratford and on the London stage. But I am not a critic or a theatre historian.

Dadie Rylands was undoubtedly the first of two great Cambridge influences on me. The other was John Barton, also a fellow and the Lay Dean of King's, who was younger than Dadie, in his late twenties. I could not ask Dadie, but I always wanted to know why Dadie never looked at the stage while directing us. One of his assistants, Waris Habbibulah, who changed his name later to Hussein as it was more appropriate for English television and Hollywood, told me why. He held the book close up to his face because he was so vain about wearing glasses, and turned his face away to catch the light from the stage to read the text and listen – thus blotting out any sight of the actors. For this he depended on the eyes of his assistant.

In *Cymbeline* Margaret Drabble, future novelist, played Imogen; Ian McKellen Posthumus. Ian was not good, being then more a character actor than a lead, while Clive Swift as Cloton was outstanding. I acted the evil Iachimo, and was much worse than Ian. I simply did it badly. Richard Kay was cast in this as Belarius, delivering so movingly the famous elegy. 'Fear no more the heat of the sun, nor the furious winter rages.'

Dadie remained frightfully annoyed with me throughout rehearsals and performances, especially when, in the most famous scene in the play, I hid in the chest in Imogen's bedroom, and emerged to examine her lying in bed and reveal her uncovered beauty. I tried every possible way to come out of that blasted chest – jumping out, crawling out lengthways, sideways and falling all over the place – never without the audience rocking with laughter. I, too, frequently 'corpsed'.

Most of all I was distraught that Dadie was so furious with me. 'Please, Dadie,' I would say, 'don't get any angrier with me than you are already!'

There was no theory about Dadie. It was entirely up and do it; no lengthy analysis of the kind directors like Trevor Nunn or Peter Brook were prone to use. No Method, no soul-searching. No fancy conceptions or contemporary theorising to make the texts burningly relevant to today, because the assumption he had was that they were that anyway.

So many names were to come out of my time at Cambridge. I formed almost at once a close and loving friendship with Richard Cottrell, later a director, but was never involved with him. In the free and easily accepting acting world of Cambridge Richard made no bones about being gay, although that was not the word in use.

His character and wit could be quite outrageous. In my second term he played Bergetto in *'Tis Pity She's a Whore*, and when he is fatally stabbed Grimaldo Bergetto says, 'Is this all mine own blood? Nay then good night with me ... Oh – I am going the wrong way sure, my belly aches so – oh, farewell, Poggio! Oh! – Oh!' Richard made such a huge, camp spectacle of his death that Dadie came round after the show and admonished him severely for overplaying.

'He's a little boy with a very bad tummy ache,' was all Dadie said.

My surprise was enormous when I was clearly Dadie and John Barton's first choice to play the name part in *Edward II*, the Marlowe Society's major summer production of 1958. The Marlowe usually had a professional or older director, and would never publish the names of its cast in the programme. We acted anonymously, which I've always felt to be a hallmark of excellence and dedication, and often needed proof that the work was being undertaken in a spirit of true love, not just for creating reputations and massaging egos. The Society made an exception to anonymity in the case of the director, who in this instance was Toby Robertson. Toby was the same age, 28, as John Barton, and had been a student at the same time.

I took to this sudden and spectacular immersion in Toby's professional direction like a duck to water. I quickly felt as if Marlowe had written this part just for me, with its amazing combination of vulnerability, doubt, passion, confusion and power – and, I have to add, specifically many and varied rhythms and musical notes. I thrived under Toby and John's tutelage, for John as *eminence grise*, as well as playing Mortimer, kept his eye on us all through *Edward*'s tour, and its brief London run at the Lyric Hammersmith, which I had to leave after the first night to play Angelo with the Leyton Players at Edinburgh.

Barton, who was marvellous as Mortimer, often tried to direct us himself, but Toby, who replaced me in London, took it on board, knowing he would have to face something like this.

I was very proud of *Edward II*, a beautifully scored and modulated production which moved swiftly as Toby injected into it a fast, relentless energy. I will never forget the way that John Bird delivered his murderer's CV as Lightborn, who kills the king –

I learn'd in Naples how to poison flowers,
To strangle with a lawn thrust thro' the throat,
To pierce the windpipe with a needle's point ...

– with his chillingly sinister face covered in oil or liquid paraffin.

Richard Marquand played Gaveston, my homosexual lover: there was something very animalistic and powerful on stage about Richard, and he and I were perfectly contrasted yet in accord. Richard became a well-known film director; he directed *The Jagged Edge* with Glenn Close and the *Star Wars* film, *Return of the Jedi*.

Tragically, he was another of that golden generation – or

'Cambridge mafia' as it was known – to die early. Driving one day on his way back from Heathrow on his return from Hollywood he suffered a severe stroke. Fortunately his daughter was beside him and able to take over the wheel. He finally collapsed in Los Angeles on 4 September 1987 from a fatal heart attack.

———

'Judy, what on earth's the matter?' I said one day during the run of *Edward* to Judy Birdwood, the wardrobe mistress for *Edward* and the Arts Theatre, when I found her sitting on a skip backstage at the Arts in floods of tears.

'Rudolph's gone, he's run away and taken the gardener with him – to somewhere in Spain!'

Judy was a very big, very pretty lady; she always had a cigarette in the corner of her mouth and would let the ash fall on her ample breasts. She was the Hon. Mrs Messel and her father was a general or viceroy. During the war she lived in the Tower of London and watched London blazing from one of the towers. She married Rudolph Messel, brother of the famous designer Oliver.

Suavely handsome like Ivor Novello, Rudolph was obviously gay. They had a picturesque stately house in Devon called Ford House, where she invited me once to stay, and two bijou townhouses in Cambridge, one in St Edward's Passage, the other in Portugal Place. She adored Richard Kay and me. We were virtually like sons to her and she made sure, as Hugh Walters joked, that 'Derek always got the best costumes; the rest got rubbish.'

She went to Spain to look for Rudolph, but never retrieved him. I think he took a lot of her money with him. She had a companion, of an equally large size, who lived and worked in the wardrobe with her whom Richard and I used to call 'She'. We didn't get on with 'She'. 'She' didn't like us either, because we were very much in the way of Judy and her.

———

I had had an amazing first year, acting all the time, and I hadn't done a stroke of academic work, but I discovered by chance that the prelims, as the first-year exams are called, were not compulsory, so I decided to go and see Harry Hinsley, the Master of St John's, to explain my plight.

'I'm afraid', I told him (this was one of my better first-year performances), 'I've not been as attentive to my work as I should have been. I'm very, very frightened about the exams.'

Harry had his back to me. He was looking out of the window. I heard him say, 'Well, you know these prelims aren't compulsory.'

Of course I knew this; that was why I was there in his study ... 'Oh really,' I said, 'is that so ...?'

The long and short of it was that he 'scratched' me – he really did make it possible for me to escape taking them. My performance of regret that I had wasted a year and my deep penitence convinced him. Of course, as I have said, he may also have felt that my acting tipped the balance in my favour.

The year ended in the May Balls – held in June – and I had never dressed up before, never worn evening dress, so I had to go. I took Freda Stratton, another close acting friend, who was such a live wire, with an attractive cackle when she laughed. The St John's Ball was so glamorous that I felt like a young man for the first time, no longer a schoolboy, with a girl on my arm, going to a dance where the champagne flowed, surrounded by all those beautiful and privileged people – such a stark contrast to anything I had experienced before.

But I was home in my bed by half past two, for I am not a late-night bird and ... well, poor old Freda, she didn't get much romance at the May Balls I escorted her to.

17

PRINCES AND PUPPETS

'Head boys direct!' John Barton proclaimed.

I have never known whether or not Barton had been head boy of Eton, but he did point to precocious powers of leadership when categorically he said this, as was his way. Already, by my second year, although in person he had never directed me, he was somehow always there in the background, coming round after the final curtain to the dressing room, making suggestions for casting – grooming us, you might say, for future careers.

While I was never head boy I was again marked out to play princes and kings. The next was Prince Hal in *Henry IV Parts I* and *II*, again for the Marlowe Society, which was rehearsed then performed in the winter of 1958–59 at the Arts Theatre. This was all very well, but I felt by now I had absurdly high expectations sitting on me. These terrified me and I had serious doubts about fulfilling them. I even thought about changing my name. If I wanted to be an actor I needed a name that was a little more theatrical, a little more eye-catching. *Mind*-blowing! Something like ... terrible, terrible names came to mind, like Ashley Clinton. This feeling stuck with me for a good while.

The two *Henry* plays were perhaps John Barton's biggest and most ambitious venture and there could not have been a greater mobilisation of the acting fraternity. In these Marlowe productions we were definitely pampered; we had coaching in verse-speaking, we had voice-training lessons fixed for us, and of course John's tuition and arrangements saw to it that the swordfights were ferocious, fantastically dangerous, and as exciting as any ever seen on stage anywhere. I did, I fear, inflict quite a number of unscheduled cuts on Simon Relph, who played Hotspur and who to this day carries the scars.

As Hal I do not believe I really advanced my game much, for I'd already played him for the Youth Theatre. The tiny part of the Ostler was played by none other than David Frost, but he had to be cajoled into turning up for rehearsals: he considered the part far too small (or so it went). But it was the Justice Shallow scenes with Silence, played respectively by Ian McKellen and Michael Burrell, which stole the show.

'Here's a brilliant Justice – but who is he?' blazed forth the *News Chronicle* headline. 'Infinitely the best performance though,' Alan Dent wrote below, 'is that of Justice Shallow who is genuinely ancient, wheezy, full of sudden changes and chortles and sadnesses ... One would like to know the name of this Shallow because it might obviously become a name to remember.'

Trevor Nunn says that when he came up to Downing College he was so overawed by these reviews of Ian's performance and his reputation that he was rather surprised to find Ian looking so ordinary, even nondescript, dressed modestly in a drab duffle coat. I, meanwhile, still dressed like my Leytonstone mates, hair sculpted at the back, very tight trousers and very dandified. I was conscious of my appearance in the way others weren't.

Barton was the first of several directors with whom I have worked who terrorised me. The reason was simple. He believed that an actor's creative juices did not flow until they were in a state of mortal terror and submission. He was, in his own mind, always right, and obsessive in getting just what he wanted. With students like me, younger than him and who would not oppose him, this gave him absolute command. These directors were far more neurotic – or, in John's case, let's say eccentric (he chewed razor blades and stood on tables to address us) – than the actors, taking their neuroses out on their casts to gain a sense of power – an emotional power.

When John, from his Olympian perch, extricated a performance from me, he made it, and I say this advisedly, a not particularly pleasant experience, and I felt I was being asked to prove myself all the time. When I went in to notes at the end of rehearsal, I would be thinking, 'Oh, please don't notice me!' and I really wanted to say, 'Please tell me something encouraging, please help me.'

Help from John in rehearsals came in the form of a sort of muted punishment, and I ended up, rather than playing the part, trying to please *him*, so that he would be pleased with me, and proud of me, and say nice things about me. But instead of encouraging me, he'd be frightening the fuck out of me. I couldn't deny John Barton had his good sides, as did the others, and that with regard to the text he worked more like an archaeologist or detective than a literary critic to dig out the best result. In addition to this his concentration was ruthless. But I'm basically a very simple soul, and he could be very hurtful.

Actors are vulnerable people – we have raw nerves. We lay ourselves on the line, we have to be emotionally open, vulnerable, though I'm not saying we should be treated with kid gloves. It's fair to say that, with Barton's energy in *Henry IV* being so huge and manifestly apparent everywhere, we all ended up – clowns, verse and prose speakers alike – to some degree or other looking and speaking like John. This is not to say it wasn't an extraordinary and brilliant production. But we *were* his puppets – puppets who at the same time were learning to be more than puppets.

Bill Gaskell, Peter Wood and above all John Dexter were all dictators. All I've said about Barton applied to Dexter in spades. They had the power of hiring and firing; from one moment to the next they could get rid of you. They flogged a performance out of you.

Girls were a particular prey. Bill Gaskell, rather than directing actors, tried to teach them how to act. These particular directors started from the standpoint that you couldn't do it, and you had to be taught *how* to do it, that you didn't have any imagination of your own, or any technique of your own, and so it became a classroom more than a rehearsal room. This is why they all liked Brecht so much. Stars were safe and hallowed, beyond the reach of their power. They would not cross their stars, so stars were untouchable. And if you had the guts to stand up to them, like John Stride, who did this with words to the effect of 'Don't you come near me, I can give as good as I get!' then you were safe too, because they then showed the other side of the coin – that they were actually very weak, they were cowards.

Years later, in a similar vein, John Dexter would say of his scathing comments to me, 'I am doing it for your benefit' – the words of the tyrant parent.

<hr>

The second-year exams, Part I of the History Tripos, imminently looming down on us, were somehow immersed, or even lost sight of, in this blaze of theatrical activity. I hadn't worked at all in my first year for Mr Pocock, my History tutor at St John's. In my second year I worked to some extent, but when the time of the first exam arrived there was one paper I was desperately worried about. It was Medieval History, during which period there were endless popes bumping one another off, and I couldn't make head or tail of it.

The night before this exam paper I couldn't sleep, so I took a sleeping pill Mum gave me. It did no good, so I left my bed and swallowed another. Over the course of the night and still not able to sleep I took three. The next morning my landlady, the gorgeous Mrs Rowlatt, could not wake me, and she knew I had to be there at the examination room for the start of the exam, so she called up Harry Hinsley, who said, 'He's got to be there, he's got to be there!'

'But we can't wake him!' she replied. 'You better come and wake him.'

Harry came over, they shook me till I was awake, and the Master of St John's put me in his car and drove me hell-for-leather to the examination hall. The exam had already started. They sat me down at my desk, while Harry went off to the adjudicators and explained why I was late. I fell asleep again, then I fell off the chair I was on, and unfortunately, I was told after, I knocked into the girl who was sitting next to me so ink spilled all over her papers.

They carried me out of the examination hall and placed me on a camp bed with a Red Cross nurse at my head, and here I stayed till the end of the exam. What they did not know was that halfway through, after about an hour, I opened one eye, then the other, and decided I would be much wiser to stay where I was and pretend to be asleep than actually get up and go back into the hall. It would be too late anyway by then. So I faked being asleep; then the exam ended and everyone filed out. I was still faking sleep.

About two weeks later there was an article in *Varsity* about attempted and successful suicides during examination time, and I was listed as an attempted suicide. Because students sitting near the adjudicators, or just one student, had heard Harry Hinsley go up to them and say that I had taken sleeping tablets and not woken up, they assumed I had swallowed an overdose. I threatened to sue *Varsity* and they printed a retraction, stating that it was an accident.

18

'HONORIFICABILITUDINITATIBUS'

In my second year at Cambridge I never stopped acting. Richard and I were together again in *Performing Rights* by Garry O'Connor in a season of undergraduate plays, perhaps appropriately in a triangular relationship. My character was Ron, a boozy Cockney saxophonist, and as such my first working-class role.

As a climax to my second year, we crammed in the musical of *Love's Labours Lost*, entitled just *Love's Labours*. It was pure thespian riot, full of humour, verbal dexterity, clever unexpected rhymes and musical parody. As Berowne I sang 'I forsooth am in love'. But the most brilliant number of all, 'Honorificabilitudinitatibus', was sung by Ian McKellen and Mike Burrell, that well-known duo from *Henry IV* – it made the audiences clamour for encores. The *Broadsheet* reviewer was less than complimentary about me, saying I 'enjoyed a prominence unmerited by my ability' (this was in the days when I still read reviews)! I appeared in only one play with Peter Cook, *The Investigator*, in which I played Thomas Jefferson, and he Karl Marx and Chopin.

Of course, I didn't know at that early age what others were thinking and feeling inside, nor for most of the time what I was thinking and feeling myself, but we all believed and were even sure that we were very happy. Ian McKellen was perhaps being rather over-modest and self-deprecating when he said of himself at Cambridge that he was 'hopeless at stepping onto the stage without any aids and just behaving in the style of myself'. He claimed that personally he felt awkward and unhappy at Cambridge, but to us he seemed far from being so: or I was too blinkered to notice. At Cambridge I did not know Ian well. I had no idea of what subsequently came to light, that he carried a torch for me, for he never showed or expressed it. Later he was to say he had fallen in love with me, and that it was a passion which was 'undeclared and unrequited'.

There was an occasion when it could have been. We were together in the summer of 1959 during the run of *Love's Labours* at the old Lyric, Hammersmith. He ended up one night (I am not quite sure how) bedding down with us. As he said, 'There was no hanky-panky, and I can't work out why I was there. I must've missed a bus or something. I can't really remember, but it was a Saturday night I know, because there was a review in the *Sunday Times*, and Harold Hobson mentioned me, and I think only me, and I read that in Derek's house, so I took the paper away with me in case he read it. I was pretty certain it was a Saturday night, and it was the last night of the run.'

Ian became part of my life in a peripheral way. We have always been close but never intimate. I admire him hugely as an actor, which first started when I saw him as Shallow. I always saw him in those early years as a character actor, not as himself but as someone else. Not confident as a face (blond and blue-eyed), he was handsome in his way, but not a great looker. But neither was I, certainly not like Michael York, who appeared in Cambridge at that time, and I suddenly realised what being handsome really meant, and the impact it had. At Cambridge Ian was not that outgoing: you could say a little introverted – very much his own man.

'Will you go out and get me a paper?' Dad said on my arrival home.

My twenty-first birthday was on 22 October 1959 and that weekend I was home for the party we were holding. I went to the shop and bought a paper. I took it in to find Dad and Mum looking at me expectantly. After a short pause Dad asked me to go back to the shop and buy some cigarettes for him. This time when I returned both were standing by the front door. They looked at me a bit oddly.

'Didn't you notice anything in the road?' Dad asked.

'No. What's there to notice? There are cars as usual.'

'Didn't you see a red Ford Popular?'

'Yes.' Sure enough I'd seen a red Ford Popular.

'And didn't you look at it?'

'No.'

'Go and look.'

I went over to it. Tied to the steering wheel was a big silver key, the twenty-first birthday symbol, and the car keys. I was overwhelmed. I burst into tears.

'However did you manage to get the money to buy that?'

'Well, we started putting aside ten shillings a week to save up for it twenty-one years ago when you were born,' explained Dad.

This must have been the longest slow-burn in history. To wait twenty-one years for the joy of seeing my reaction!

We held a glorious party given by Mum and Dad at a children's nursery in Forest Gate. Dad hired a charabanc to collect friends from Cambridge. At first the divide between my glamour friends from Cambridge and those from East London was painfully visible. My locals stood at one end of the hall, my Cambridge mates at the other: facing these two sides of my life brought together for the first time felt more than a bit hairy, but gradually everyone settled, intermingled, and then mixed famously. There was cabaret from Peter Cook, Eleanor Bron and David Frost, which was some line-up for a children's nursery in Forest Gate!

19

ENCOUNTERS WITH
A COLOSSUS

In my third year, foreshadowing Claudius in *I, Claudius*, I played my first stammerer in John Whiting's *Saint's Day*, roundly criticised by Ann Dowson in *Broadsheet*. While Jill Daltry and Ian McKellen, ran her review, 'managed to conceal the stiltedness of the writing by the conviction of their acting', I came in for the most stick.

'In the uncharacteristic part of a cringing clergyman, exaggerating Aldus's affliction of speech,' she wrote, 'until it became a comic turn ... [Jacobi] provided too many laughs of an inappropriate kind.'

That was me, all right, true to form! More afflictions of speech, already there early on, and more to follow, and even cringing or indignant gay men of the cloth.

Much more notably I played a second Hamlet at the Arts Theatre Cambridge, which we took on a tour of France and Switzerland. During this I came face-to-face with an acting legend. He was a colossus with magnificent looks, voice, stature. My very first inspiration had been of 'Rich' – Richard Burton – in those glorious seasons of his youth at the Old Vic. By chance, a member of the cast of *Hamlet* was an old friend of his from childhood. This was my dear friend David Rowe-Beddoe, playing Claudius to my second Hamlet.

Now in December 1959 once again, nearly for the last time,

the Cambridge rep assembled both for the Arts Theatre and a foreign tour. The company was the Experimental Theatre Club, which had earlier taken Richard Kay's Romeo to Paris, the producer being Michael Deakin, and the director Garry O'Connor.

After the Arts, off we went, playing *Hamlet* in the Municipal Theatre at Grenoble, the Studio Créqui in the Lyons Faculty of Letters and the Opera House in Lausanne – where you could hear the pages being flipped over as our devoted audiences followed the text of 1598. We had '*un rhythme rapide, mais avec une diction impeccable*' – what greater praise could there be than that from the *Feuille d'Avis de Lausanne*? David Rowe-Beddoe was singled out for his '*remarquable*' Claudius, while I apparently had '*une vérité saisissante*'. Every actor should be named for excellence, said the review.

Waris Hussein, who doubled the roles of Osric and the Player Queen, didn't think so, and had no illusions about his performances, saying, 'Every time I came on I could see Derek anticipating, "Oh, my God, here he is again!"' – though of course I had no such thoughts in my head.

In Switzerland, Lausanne's Opera House, where we performed, was the size of Covent Garden. Richard Burton lived in the countryside nearby and came in to watch the play, and every night he drove David back to stay with him. His house, in Selignac, was called 'Villa du Pays de Galles' (Welsh villa!) and here he lived with his then wife Sybil, whom he had recently married and whom he later divorced.

One night he asked the company back to his villa for a drink and it was here that he gave me very important advice. He complimented me on my voice, and on how well I spoke the verse, but then said, 'You have a beautiful voice, Derek, but if you don't roughen it up you will end like J.G. [John Gielgud] and risk sending the audience to sleep!' I took this advice very much to heart, although not altogether agreeing with him about J.G.

I received a letter from Rich when I was back at Cambridge, which said that if there was anything he could do for me to help me in my career he would: a letter I straight away lost. Some time later, in 1977 or thereabouts, I worked two days on a film with him called *The Medusa Touch*, and I cherish that experience of playing a scene with him. He remembered he had seen me play Hamlet nearly twenty years earlier in Switzerland.

'What are you doing next?' he asked, as we sat around on the set in our canvas chairs.

'I am playing Hamlet again for the Prospect Company at the Old Vic.'

'I'll come and see you,' he said.

He was as true as his word when it opened. In my dressing room after the performance we chatted and he said, 'Let's go out to dinner.' He waited while I changed, and as we were leaving he said, 'Do you mind if we go up on stage? I haven't stood on a stage for twenty-odd years – not for that long!'

We went up on stage. It was a very moving experience for him, and tears filled his eyes. He'd lived the life he wanted, but all that huge acting talent and power in him had never been given the chance to come out fully.

'I was a schoolboy sitting in the gods watching you play Hamlet,' I told him as I stood there with him on the Old Vic stage – it was a cathartic moment for me, too.

'You know one night when I was here playing Hamlet,' Rich went on, 'and I was starting the speech "To be or not to be", I saw Winston Churchill, who was sitting in the front row. He started saying it, mouthing it out loud with me. I didn't know whether to stop and let him go on – to finish it, or not to finish it!'

We proceeded on to dinner. He reached into his pocket as we left the theatre, pulled out a wad of fifty pound notes, peeled off I do not remember how many, and gave them to the stage-door keeper. It was such a movie-star gesture!

After eating we went to a nightclub to see and hear his step-son with Elizabeth Taylor play the saxophone (it was during the time he was married to his third wife, Susie). All he wanted to talk about was the theatre – and particularly Shakespeare. Although he no longer had British residency, and could only be in Britain a limited amount of time each year, he asked in all seriousness if I would arrange a Prospect Old Vic production for him to be in, and even suggested he'd fly me and the cast at his own expense to rehearse in Hollywood.

Rich stayed friends with Rowe-Beddoe till the end, and Villa du Pays de Galles, where we'd visited him in Switzerland, was the home in which he died, and from where his coffin was brought to the church. David arranged the music and played the organ at his funeral. In New York, David would 'cover' for Rich during his early escapades with Liz Taylor, taking Sybil out to dinner and acting as 'beard', her gentleman escort. She knew only too well what was going on, and used to lambast David for his complicity, with uncomplimentary reference to the ethnic background he shared with Rich! David and I had this bet at Cambridge as to which of us would have the first pink Cadillac. He bought his very soon after leaving, and easily beat me.

I'd found Cambridge horrifyingly competitive when I first went up. Academically I had ended up with a 2.2 – the Actor's Degree – but over three years I'd learned a lot, done so much, and was anxious to get started and skip drama school. Drama school can teach you what your good points and bad points are, what you need to forget, and what you need to bone up on, but I'm not convinced it can teach you how to act: you can either act or not.

Not only had there been a continuity of roles during my time at Cambridge, but I had played all the time before a paying public, and although most of the audiences were students, and on my side, they were far from uncritical. There was a healthy sprinkling of parents, and often professionals, visiting directors, agents, impresarios from London and elsewhere.

Cambridge expanded our minds, our emotions and our skills, and the grounding in drama at Cambridge was much broader than just the practical side of acting. Dadie and Barton have remained with me all my life. Theatre at Cambridge brought me the chance to grasp the essence of theatrical performance, and its roots in traditional classical drama.

20

THE BRUMMIE BEAST

Nancy Burman, the administrator [of Birmingham Repertory Company], took me aside before rehearsals of *She Stoops to Conquer* started and asked me to go easy on this new young find of Sir Barry's, Derek Jacobi, because he was recovering from a heartbreak brought on by an attractive young lady in the preceding Christmas show. From then on, working with him almost continuously until the spring of 1963, I never for a moment questioned his heterosexuality. I don't know whether Derek will want this episode remembered and in the light of future revelations I somewhat doubt it. Although it does go to prove yet again you don't have to be a murderer to play Macbeth.

What is described here by John Harrison wasn't exactly a heartbreak. When I read this I was rather flattered that there was never a doubt about my heterosexuality, or indeed homosexuality, because I'm glad to say neither ever really mattered to me, nor should it matter to people both with whom I worked, and especially to those watching out front. John, who wrote the above to a friend and directed me in *She Stoops* at the Birmingham Rep, isn't so far off the mark.

Here is the full story. There was an actress called Monica Evans who subsequently became famous on television in a series called *Compact*, one of the original soap operas. Monica was a very pretty girl and we got on fabulously: it was rumoured that 'Derek and Monica were rather keen on each other.' My parents heard about it and instantly had us married off to each other. I let the rumour ride. I did nothing to dissuade anybody – and apart from that we were just very good friends. Then, when she left, they all assumed I was heartbroken, and I let them assume what they wanted.

When I performed *Edward II*, Sir Barry Jackson and two colleagues had come to see it. When I wrote to them at Birmingham Rep enquiring about a job they said, 'This was the boy we saw at Stratford,' and called me in to audition for Bernard Hepton, the director of productions. As a result I joined for one play, in which I was offered a small part, and after this two others, leading to a year's contract. Young Marlow in *She Stoops to Conquer* in March 1961 was my first notable part. Mum and Dad came to see it. Afterwards Mum said, after relaying how much she liked my performance, 'There is one thing I must criticise.'

'What is it?' I asked, touchy as I could be when the 'c' word is mentioned.

'When you take the curtain call you should smile more.'

'Oh, yes ...'

'You have such a lovely smile,' she added.

That was Mum all over!

Because it was a big success we filmed it for television, broadcasting it live from the Aston Studios, and there was my photo in the *Radio Times* with an article all about me, which was not all that interesting. Filming a live theatre show was pioneer stuff, an innovation fraught with danger and difficulty. We were due to follow *What's My Line* and it overran its time, during which, while we were impatient to get going, our *She Stoops* horse became more than a bit agitated and shat all over the studio floor. The whole thing was very, very frightening because it was live.

While my parents knew what happens, one of the essential strands of the plot is that whenever young Marlow meets a lady of quality he stammers. My grandfather my grandmother, my aunts, cousins, their friends, *le tout* Leytonstone watching me on the television didn't know this. Next day my mother rings up Aunt Hilda, and asks, 'Did you enjoy the show?'

'Oh, Daisy we couldn't watch!' Hilda replied.

Mum asked why.

'Well, he was so nervous,' Hilda answered.

They thought the stammer was real, so they all switched off out of embarrassment and fear. Isn't that wonderful? I love it.

Hilda, when they came to see *Edward II* three years before, for the very first time had joined the local library. In they went and they took out a book about Edward, so it opened doors for them, it opened their lives, until the magic day would come as it did when they would go to something I wasn't in. A whole world was revealed to them to the level they never dreamed of, and they met people they never believed they would ever see.

I heard later that this stuttering performance introduced me to Laurence Olivier and Joan Plowright, who had lost the keys of their Brighton home, and booked into the Royal Crescent Hotel for the night. Joannie switched on the telly and they saw me. At least *they* knew I was acting, and my stammer wasn't something I couldn't get over.

I found a lovely flat in Edgbaston on the Cadbury Estate looked after by a starry-eyed old landlady called Winnie Banks, where I stayed for three years. She had Albert Finney as one of her lodgers before me. For the first two weeks I slept on her sofa; she had no room available, but at last Albert's old flat became free.

When I'd been there for some time I wanted to redecorate my bedroom, but she wouldn't hear of it, because 'Albert had put up that wallpaper.' And so it had to stay. I did get round to doing the kitchen, and I heard a couple of years after I had left and was at the National Theatre that the actress who'd taken over the flat wanted to repaint the kitchen, and she wasn't allowed to because 'Derek had painted the kitchen'.

I still hankered after changing my name and kept thinking up other, really dreadful names. I found my first agent when I went to Birmingham, an ebullient, enthusiastic lady called Patricia McNaughton. I mentioned to her I needed a new name because no one knew how to pronounce Jacobi: they would say 'Ja-*co*-bee' or '*Jake*-o-bee' or 'Jacoba'.

'No,' she told me, 'that's the very reason you don't want to change it. If people are talking about you, and one says "Ja-*co*-bee" and another says, "No, it's '*Jack*-o-bee,'" that means your name is being mentioned twice. That's very good for business!'

I followed her advice and didn't change it, although I've often regretted this. I have no problem about people mispronouncing it, and will not take offence, even when in an early morning show in New York when they called me 'Eric Ja-*co*-bee', and I had to be Eric Ja-*co*-bee for an hour's chat show. For some reason I can never understand, many people used to call me David, taxi drivers in particular (maybe they mistook me for David Jacobs).

On one occasion on American television, several of us had just had the most horrendous journey to publicise the beginning of the US screening of the BBC's series of all Shakespeare's plays, culminating in a snowbound Greyhound bus into New York.

There were four bunny girls being interviewed along with me, and the interviewer kicked off, 'Now Eric, you're a big classical actor, how about giving us a poem? You must know a poem!'

I thought very quickly, and, as we had just been doing a stage piece about Byron, one of his came to mind.

'Well, it's a very sad poem about the end of a love affair.'

So the interviewer said: 'Oh, that's great, Eric, that's great, Eric!'

They settled down, the four bunny girls in a circle at my feet. I launched into 'So we'll go no more a-roving ... so late into the night.'

This was at eight o'clock in the morning!

Just a month after *She Stoops*, on 3 April 1961, Sir Barry died, a colossal figure to whom so many owed so much, and with his death an era ended. He had been the father as well as fairy godmother of the Rep; although my time only overlapped with his for a short while, he had chosen me to be there, and once again this was extraordinary good fortune.

When Bernard Hepton finally left in 1962, John Harrison became Director of Productions and he kept me, the youngest player, and Arthur Pentelow, the oldest member of the company, while everyone else lost their jobs. Again, this was part of the fantastic good luck which has dogged me.

In John's regime I started with Ferdinand in *The Tempest*. I played juvenile leads in ten plays Harrison directed, mostly with a beautiful actress called Jennifer Hilary. I reckon John must hold the record for the number of plays I was in that he directed, and I'm not surprised that with his equable temper, his authority, scholarship, and his great sense of fun he was already, and was to remain, the closest, lifelong friend of Paul Scofield, my acting hero.

'Laughter', John was always saying, 'is the infallible sign of a good rehearsal.'

One evening while I was living in Winnie Banks's lovely flat, Elizabeth Spriggs came round for dinner. Liz was very glamorous in those days, with an hourglass figure, and she played Cleopatra wonderfully. That evening the wine got the better of both of us, and suddenly it entered her head that she was going to convince me that it was 'all a big mistake', growing absolutely determined that she would *prove* to me that I was 'all right', that I was straight. To do this she crushed me to her bosom, then chased me around the apartment, and in the end I literally had to open the door and *man*-handle her out – but even so, she was lovely!

I had such an enjoyable, funny time there, full of these idyllic but picaresque episodes. One Christmas show, there was another when we were performing *Beauty and the Beast*, and I was the Beast who is also the Prince. As the Prince I had to lie over the side of the couch where I sat and hide my face, then hastily put on furry claws and headpiece, and spring into view transformed into the frightening Beast.

It was Boxing Day, with a packed house mainly of kids, and I was acting my socks off to give this moment its full impact, revealing to all my horrific visage, when I heard this little boy in the stalls shouting out in a very loud voice: 'Ha, ha, ha! Surprise, surprise!' That was me, the master of illusion, firmly put in his place.

There was a smallpox scare during this pantomime and they inoculated the cast against smallpox. The following night I went down with a mild dose of smallpox, which was a one in a million chance, but I was the one it hit. I became very ill and couldn't perform the Prince or the Beast. The company manager had to go on instead of me and read my part, but he got more laughs of derision than me, because when he donned the furry claws they stuck so hard he couldn't turn the pages!

Otherwise known as God, Peter Hall had seen my work, and the Royal Shakespeare Company offered me four small parts in four different plays. I went to the powers that be in Birmingham and asked them, 'Look, will you let me go, because Stratford wants me?' They responded graciously, 'Yes, go with our blessing.' So that was it, I was leaving Birmingham and as far as I knew it was all signed and sealed, but then I received a summons from Stratford to meet Peter and his fellow directors.

Birmingham to Stratford was the kind of accepted journey if you wanted to be a classical actor, because it was so near. The doyen of classical repertory companies, it was the acknowledged breeding ground for Stratford, and many eminent thespians had done the leap. So my turn had come, for I'd been chosen to do the leading roles at Birmingham, and I was almost automatically being asked to go to Stratford by the new triumvirate of directors.

When I arrived, they put a copy of *The Tempest* in my hand and said, 'Would you like to read Ariel?' I was suddenly caught on the hop, because this wasn't at all what I expected and I should have said no, but I was cowed by their presence. They gave me just ten minutes to look the speech over, and then, when I went on stage, not only with Peter Brook, Peter Hall and Michel Saint-Denis out in front, but also Clifford Williams and John Barton, I felt it was like walking out onto Mount Olympus. I was terrified, and did the reading like a sick choir boy.

Peter Brook came down to the lights of the Memorial Theatre and said the equivalent of 'Don't call us, we'll call you.' A few days later I received a crushing letter from Peter Hall saying, 'We don't really think you'll fit in.'

I was utterly devastated. Auditioning for the RSC was my first big disappointment. I hadn't experienced anything like this in my whole life, and I became very depressed.

Birmingham has many canals and for a while I wandered around gazing at the water, thinking a quick brick round my neck would finish it. People say about the brickbats life throws at you that they should become learning experiences, but, out of work for the very first time, I wasn't remotely in the mood to learn from this experience.

I went back to the directors at the Rep and asked, 'Could I have my job back? Stratford doesn't want me.'

'Of course you can,' they said. 'Sorry it didn't work out.'

This extraordinary kindness turned out to be a great stroke of luck. It was the Rep's fiftieth anniversary year. Sir Barry Jackson had founded the Birmingham Repertory Company just before the First World War: born into a rich family he put up the cash to build the small and intimate theatre in Station Street as a home, 'to serve', as he said, 'an art, instead of making that art serve a commercial purpose'.

To celebrate the anniversary they put on three Shakespeare plays they had never previously done: *Troilus and Cressida, Titus Andronicus* and *Henry VIII*. They gave me three leading roles: Troilus, Aaron the Moor, and Henry. During the run of *Troilus*, Peter Hall came to see it. I reckoned it was Peter who had initially offered me four parts at Stratford, but then thought he'd better call me in to show me to the others. At the interval he met Harrison, who was directing me. Peter, in shocked amazement, told him, 'Derek wasn't at all like this at the audition!' This says something many of us would agree with about auditions, namely that they are unreliable, and rarely show or truly reflect an actor's abilities.

I had twelve weeks with three spanking roles in these three productions, which celebrated the Golden Jubilee year. Blacked-up as the villainous, bloodthirsty Moor, Aaron, I had plenty of anger and frustration over failing the Stratford audition to work off in Ronald Eyre's production, while as the tortured, quivering lover Troilus I could portray my whole world of love and trust falling apart before me when betrayed by Jennifer as Cressida. But it was the third of these parts that became the most significant, when I could rant and rampage as the bloated, padded tyrant.

We weren't told *he* was there, but one Wednesday matinée Sir Laurence was out front. I was sharing the dressing room with Cardinal Wolsey, and he always stayed in costume between shows, while I always used to go out. I could take off my make-up very quickly and go to the Kardomah Café for tea and egg on toast.

When Sir Laurence came backstage I was in my outdoor clothes and had shed the wigs, the facial hair and the padding, and was ready to leave. I instantly turned to water and jelly. Sir Laurence marched in, looked at me and said brusquely, 'Hello, well done!' and then went over to Arthur Pentelow and enthused over Arthur's Wolsey. Eventually he said, 'Thank you both very much,' and left.

I breathed again, but really I was a bit miffed, a bit upset because he hadn't said anything more.

Less than a minute later there was a knock, a head peeped round the door, and it was Sir Laurence again. The peremptory bark of Richard of Gloucester was there.

'*You* played Henry?' He must have met someone outside and said, 'Who was that?'

'Yes, sir.'

'Oh well, my great apologies,' he said. 'I didn't recognise you. Well done!'

He locked eyes with me and left.

This was our first meeting. In the next few days I got a letter offering me the role of Brother Martin in *St Joan* at Chichester. That was beyond my dreams, because I imagined he had really hated it, but the fact was that he hadn't recognised me, and for a man who had spent a lot of his career putting on false noses and disguising himself as someone else, I thought, really, I can chalk this one up!

Albert Finney came to see *Henry VIII*. Afterwards Winnie Banks invited him and the cast back to the house. All of us sat round while this energetic young actor just talked and talked about theatre and his life. It was so inspiring, for he had all the coherence of successful talent. He had it all made, and he was mesmeric.

After three years the time came to leave the Birmingham I loved. I had my red Ford Escort, and they had paid me £11 a week, which nowadays will hardly buy a prawn cocktail. Out of this I settled my rent, ate out mostly in restaurants, and still saved £2 a week.

In particular I loved the intimate theatre and its surrounds; loved, too, the paint shop next door where they made the marvellous sets, but which later was depressingly turned into a porn cinema. On stage, wherever you were, the audience could see you: to me, with its sharply raked auditorium, it felt as if I were acting in a huge theatre like the Palladium.

And there was Auntie D, who played the piano during the interval, and Georgie who ran the tea stand: altogether such a happy time in which, on average, I was in a new production every four weeks.

But it was time to move on and I was about to fulfil the dream every young actor had, that of becoming a fledgling in Laurence Olivier's company at Chichester, prior to opening as the new National Theatre at the Old Vic. Yet I was soon to be submitted to what I can safely say, at the hands of my first director there, was the worst and most shaming humiliation I've ever suffered.

So much did it hurt me that I still remember it every day.

AGE IV
SEEKING
THE BUBBLE
REPUTATION

21

A SHAMEFUL EPISODE

As the new boy on probation, I joined Sir Laurence's company playing Ladvenu, or Brother Martin, the young but ascetically fine-drawn Dominican monk who puts the case for mercy and compassion towards the Maid of Orleans.

The first rehearsal of *St Joan* was in a rehearsal room in Chelsea called Pettit House. Sir Laurence came in with Joan Plowright, cast in the title role, and we all dutifully lined up.

He proceeded down the line like a king, shaking hands with each of us and saying a word or two, with Joan at his side. Joan was wearing dark glasses and a little hat, a kind of cloche hat, covered in mother-of-pearl beads. Every time she moved they glittered and clinked. When we started to rehearse she hardly ever took off that bloody hat!

As Sir Laurence came down the line, as he came nearer to me, the shirt was sticking to my back, and then he shook my hand, and he *absolutely* locked eyes with me again, as he had in the Birmingham dressing room. He was talking to me, eye-balling me, and it was, 'Who is going to drop the eyes first?'

Of course it was me, it would be. This was a game for real he used to play – who was going to break eye contact first? He had piercing eyes. Then he went away, and I didn't see him for a while, because he wasn't directing *St Joan*. John Dexter was.

Well, it came to the dress rehearsal, and all the bigwigs were out there in the darkened auditorium. I was the new boy, no doubt about this fact, and as John had directed all the monks at the trial to surround the apron and be seated with their faces to the audience, only I had my back to it. I had to stand up, turn around – which was like giving me an entrance – and say my first line, 'Is there any great harm in the girl? Is it not merely her simplicity?' which I duly launched into the darkened auditorium.

'*What does Daisy Jacobi think she's got on her face? She's supposed to be a fucking monk!*' screeched Dexter at me from out front. The selection of 'Daisy' at random, not knowing it was Mum's name, was an added insult.

I had on the usual make-up, five and nine, and I think I was ascetically fine-drawn enough, but I guess Dexter did not. So I was sent shaking with fear and completely humiliated back to the dressing room, while Miss Plowright, Max Adrian, Sir Laurence, all patiently waited in the auditorium while I washed my face and re-applied my make-up to come back on. But that was only the beginning.

———

When we transferred to the Old Vic, just after we opened there, during the Epilogue, twenty-five years after the trial, I had been given by John this important entrance behind Robert Stephens, who played the Dauphin. Now crowned as King Charles the Victorious, he is lying in bed when Brother Martin enters carrying the huge cross from Rouen he bore when Joan perished in the fire.

As, after delivering my denunciation of Joan's end in the dreadful and final wrong of the lying sentence and pitiless fire, I backed away with my final proud words, 'Henceforth my path will not lie through palaces, nor my conversation be with kings,' I must have let the top of the cross become hooked up onto the curtains around the royal four-poster.

The result was that I was walking backwards with the bed coming with me, and it is total disaster as I slither all over the place and fight to free the cross, extricate myself and leave the stage. Fortunately the lights came down just as the wind blew out the candles.

Charles says, 'That was a funny chap. How did he get in?'

I and the cross, with help from stage hands, had at last succeeded in disentangling ourselves. Fortunately Bob didn't play his line for the obvious laugh.

This was the night Mum and Dad came to see the play. As I walked through the stage door to go and meet them I met Dexter, who said to me, 'You fucking university amateurs! The sooner you go back to Birmingham Rep the better!'

I straight away became hysterical and burst into tears. I knew I had done wrong, but it was just too awful with my parents waiting for me outside.

John then said, 'Come here, Derek, come here.'

I followed him into an empty dressing room, where he gave me a handkerchief and coaxingly said, 'Stop crying.'

I eventually stopped and calmed down, but I was still shaking.

'I give you a hard time because I think you are a good actor. You must believe me, Derek, I do it for your own sake.'

This wasn't what I wanted to hear, but he had shown me his soft underbelly for a brief moment or two. He then opened the dressing-room door – outside people were milling around – and reverted to being hard, saying loudly, 'You'd better be fucking better tomorrow night!'

I suppose this was when I felt he had let me in, and we became some kind of friends. From then on I laughed at his dirty jokes, and this, too, was a way into feeling a degree of companionship. He thought in extreme, crude terms almost without exception: when he was casting Salieri in *Amadeus* for that hit production he wrote to Peter Shaffer:

If we are prepared to think of JG [John Gielgud] and Paul S [Scofield] as Salieri, then why dismiss Jacobi and McKellen? None of these four is exactly expert in the expression of passion for 'tit and slit', but whereas the older pair suffer either from problems of memory and energy (and saintliness) the other two can produce energy, venom, and astonishing vocal variety and are adaptable enough to be unflustered by the constant changes of text.

'Anyway,' he added to Peter, 'this should stop you whingeing around like an old Jewish authoress suffering from hepatitis.'

Charming, no? Laughing at his filthy humour was an easy way for me to cope with him. While John was a stickler for perfection, it was hard to feel much sympathy for him sometimes at a human level.

When he died, all too prematurely in 1989, I did not go to the funeral, but my close friend Brenda Bruce did, and she remarked that the congregation, consisting of all the theatrical great and good, had attended not out of love but to make sure he was burnt to a cinder.

Perhaps there was bit of affection in the contempt, but I doubt it.

Joan Plowright was marvellous as St Joan. One remarkable aspect of her great performance was that at the moment when she cried, and when I was kneeling in front of her, her tears used to hit me in the face: they popped out of her eyes and wet me. I was so moved I used to shudder.

At Chichester I met Michael Redgrave for the first time, as I understudied Sir Michael in *Uncle Vanya*; his health was deteriorating, not as yet badly, but he had begun to suffer from the shakes, and fits of amnesia, due to the onset of Parkinson's disease. Everyone mistakenly put this down to alcoholism.

A SHAMEFUL EPISODE

One Saturday morning, when we were on tour at the New Theatre, Cardiff, the stage manager rang and told me Michael had 'flu, and I had to go on in his stead for the matinée. Tony Hopkins understudied Sir Laurence, and once a week Sir used to take a rehearsal of the understudies. Our brief was to reproduce exactly in meticulous detail what our principals did. With Michael this was virtually impossible because he was totally, seemingly spontaneous, and while I could follow his moves, what he did was so close and personal to him I couldn't make it work for me.

I rushed to the theatre, rapidly went through all the moves with the stage crew, put on the make-up, the wig and the costume, and sat quivering with fear in the dressing room. Olivier and Dame Sybil Thorndike dashed round to wish me luck, but fifteen minutes before the curtain was due to go up the door to the dressing room swung open, and there was Redgrave, pale and clutching at the wall to steady himself.

'While I have breath in my body you're not doing the part for me!' he uttered in a quavering voice and sank into the make-up chair; then he changed, prepared himself, and went on, as usual superbly. I was not the slightest bit resentful – rather the opposite, by which I mean relieved, for at that age I would have looked ridiculous and made a fool of myself.

One day at Chichester I had a terrible toothache. I went to the dentist's where they put me out with gas to extract it, but they didn't give me enough gas, so when I came round the tooth was half in and half out, and they were pulling and pulling without success. I reacted badly and kicked over the gas cylinder, with the outcome that I ended up in St Richard's Hospital under another anaesthetic, where they took out two of my wisdom teeth.

I had to stay on the ward for several days, and during this time Dame Sybil and her husband Lewis Casson, theatre royals although quite ancient by now, on their habitual constitutional walk around the park, visited me, the junior novice player. Dame Sybil brought along a book, and they sat down on my bed to give an impromptu poetry reading to all these ailing gentlemen in the ward. It was so thoughtful and kind, so touching and lovely.

Back on stage for the next performance of *St Joan*, I suddenly found my mouth full of bits of bone, of shards, and I suppose bits of chipped jaw. I had to move swiftly upstage with my back to the audience, spit out all the shards and bits into my hand, then carry on as if nothing had happened.

During the last days of that Chichester season the entire company was summoned by Sir Laurence and Co. to be told whether they were going to be kept on in London or not. Over we went, biting our nails, at five-minute intervals, to the offices, which were just a little away from the theatre. All day there was this continuous stream of actors passing in and out to learn their fate. It was such a hideous way of carrying on, because I could see from the face of the actor or actress coming out before me what his or her destiny held. About five didn't get in, but the rest of us did.

22

'I THOUGHT HAMLET LOOKED A BIT DOWN AT THE WEDDING'

I now had my foot in the new National Theatre Company, which opened at the Old Vic on 22 October 1963, the exact date of my twenty-fifth birthday.

Imagine my luck, for in the first production, that of *Hamlet* with Peter O'Toole in the title role, I was understudying Jeremy Brett, who was cast as Laertes, when he suddenly left the cast for Hollywood. Jeremy would become marvellous and famous in the future as Sherlock Holmes, but people hardly remember that he was a very fine classical actor. Warner Brothers offered him a contract to play Freddy Eynsford-Hill in the Hollywood version of *My Fair Lady*, so here was I, a greenhorn, in the relatively major role of Laertes, playing alongside Peter O'Toole in the title role, with Redgrave as Claudius.

Rehearsals of *Hamlet* were bumpy and unpredictable and somehow a good rapport between 'Sir' and Peter failed to get off the ground. Peter wanted a shortened version of two and a half hours, while Olivier insisted on the uncut version which takes nearly double that. Then, too, Peter wanted to wear a beard. Olivier made him be clean-shaven with dyed blond hair. Of course, Peter worshipped the very ground Olivier trod on, like everyone else in the company, and as he put it, 'I'm hooked on Larry Olivier: he's sat on the top of Everest and waved down at the Sherpas.' But it hardly stopped him being defiant.

131

I fell into a bad scrape with Sir over my sword fight with Peter at the end. We were practising, and Peter didn't care for the movements that had been arranged by the fight director, as he wanted it to have more swash and buckle. So he said to me: 'Let's go up to the rehearsal rooms and work out our own fight.'

We did. There was a lot of me slashing at his feet and he would jump, and then I would slash at his head and he would duck. He would jump on tables, and turn them over, and imaginary furniture would fly in all directions – very Errol Flynn. We rehearsed it pretty savagely for several days. One day the inevitable happened. I cut at his head and he jumped instead of ducking, and the sword went right across his cheek. It hit with the flat of the sword, fortunately, not the edge, so it didn't cut him, it just produced a weal, just this terrible red mark.

I was far more scared than he was. He took me up to his dressing room and gave me a brandy.

Next day Sir Laurence called me into his office.

'I hear you had an accident yesterday,' Sir said.

'Yes,' I replied, and explained what had happened.

'Well, it really doesn't matter whose fault it was, or how it happened, but it happened. You do realise he's a film star, and you do realise he's only doing twenty-eight performances of *Hamlet*, and then he's going off to make a film of *Lord Jim*, so if you cut him they can't photograph him. His agent has been on the phone and there is now an insurance on him for £60,000!'

So rehearsals were fraught for reasons other than star and director not seeing eye to eye. Michael Gambon, who was holding a spear in this production, recalls that O'Toole turned up in evening dress after having been out drinking all night. There was a lot riding on Olivier's inaugural production, and his choice of O'Toole, at the height of his fame as Lawrence of Arabia, was a high-risk strategy, especially with no pre-London opening.

When we did open it was even worse, for the critics to a man hated it. They hated Peter and they hated the production.

They had put in a new revolving stage at the Old Vic, new seating, new sound systems; as the set was too heavy for the revolve on two occasions, maybe three, the revolve broke down. The first time this happened Sir came on and told the audience there would have to be a pause in the proceedings while they winched Elsinore Castle into place. As he entered with a walking stick this was, for most of the audience, probably worth the price of admission. But the second time it happened we had all begun to make our entrances. At the start the battlements were facing the audience, and there was the Ghost of Hamlet's father positioned high up on the tower; then the whole stage would revolve so we were now inside the castle, while the battlements, turned inside out, were at the back.

We were proceeding onto stage when suddenly the whole structure shuddered to a halt. We knew from now on it would be winched by hands below stage and a number of us, or rather everyone, in full view of the audience, decided to grab a bit of the set and start pushing hard to give a hand to the winching and the stage staff down below.

So there was me, and Frank Finlay and Redgrave, Rosemary Harris and so on, all dutifully pushing it round ... But there were these three court ladies as well, who each grabbed a piece of the set. Everyone was trying madly to stay in character, and pretend this was quite usual in Elsinore. As they were passing the front of the stage – it couldn't have been timed better – the court lady in the middle, desperately trying to keep in character, turned to the court lady beside her, and in a voice that ricocheted round the auditorium she said, 'I thought Hamlet looked a bit down at the wedding!'

This rebounded through the building, and of course it killed the rest of the evening. You couldn't really blame her, she was right in the part, saying what the court lady might have said. But what a wonderful moment!

The more or less universal bad notices had a terrible effect on Peter, who had been very good up to then, and been on the wagon, but he reverted straight back on the booze. Laertes is offstage much of the play, and I'd be sitting in the dressing room in a state of tension during the four hours, often discussing acting at length with Rosie Harris, who talked of her acting mentor, the American Eva La Gallienne, for my duel with Hamlet didn't happen until the end. I would always be wondering what disaster might happen that night.

I come on to do battle. Peter, being seriously out of condition, having done as much as he could with no movement in any direction, is by now absolutely cross-eyed. He looks at me across the stage, and as on every night he gives me a big wink – then starts fighting for his life. And I have to fight back for *my life*.

The trouble was that it always ended up with Peter getting hurt and not me. I cut his finger, then his shoulder … I didn't mean to but this was because I was a bit more nifty, and I was not drunk, while Peter had slowed himself down with the drink. His fury with the role continued after the appalling notices, although he remained a great crowd pleaser (and one matinée had even gone on wearing glasses, he'd been mugging up his lines beforehand, and this was met with a snigger from the house). So he would begin to slash at the audience in his rage. He'd go downstage to the front, slash madly at the front row, as if there was a line of critics sitting there. We received letters about this.

Notorious as it had become in the eyes of the general public, the whole run was a complete sell-out with tickets changing hands in the Waterloo Road for as much as £60 each. Larry went around saying it was the worst production of anything he had ever seen, and when Bob Stephens asked why, he replied, 'Because I don't have a Hamlet.'

Peter's blame of Sir was equally outspoken. He claimed he wasn't sure Larry should be running the National Theatre, and that he had little to contribute as a director. Larry's business was 'acting', he said. 'He belongs in the stable as head stallion. In *Hamlet* I wandered amazed among scenic flyover and trumpets: I didn't know where I was ...'

I heard all this as it were indirectly, for the blame game rather passed me by.

———⊰•⊱———

Sir Michael, whose memory by now was not too good, was the absolute master of gobbledegook Shakespeare. He would dry in the long plotting scene which I, as Laertes, had with him, but he did not stop, he went on completely off text, careering along madly in Redgravespeak. It had brilliant rhythm, plausibility, power, conviction. In fact it had everything Shakespeare requires, except that it didn't make sense.

I was in my element. 'Sir' gave three-year contracts to only a very select few, including Finney, Stephens and John Stride, and I was the only unknown to get one. Being installed at the National was endless fun. We laughed all the time. Olivier homage was at its height among the young bloods who had just joined, and we'd hang around waiting for Sir to leave and notice us, for all had to pretend he was our friend. We would walk the long way round just to say hello.

That first night of *Hamlet*, on my twenty-fifth birthday, was for me especially a magical night. At the opening-night party on stage and in the stalls I was boring the arse off everyone, telling them it was my birthday. Shirley Bassey went up on stage and sang 'Happy Birthday' – to shut me up – so I would always know when the National was fifty years old. It was my baptism by fire as well as my birthday.

23

SIR

Sir Laurence had a look of anonymity about him which would have been very useful for a spy. I once travelled with him to Bradford in a crowded compartment, and nobody knew the world-famous actor was sitting in the corner. They always said he looked like Harry Worth playing a bank clerk. He had the classiest kind of fame because he was recognised as the greatest actor in the world, and probably the most famous. Yet you could meet him in the street and not know you were talking to Laurence Olivier. This is what I would call class. He had many hats, many faces, as a performer, but also as a person.

One day I was at the house in Brighton where he lived with Joan, and this is what she told us. When she had been given only an hour or so of warning, Princess Margaret came to visit her, and it wasn't long – perhaps a year or two – after Larry's and her first child, Richard, had been born.

As the conversation wasn't fluent – you could say a bit sticky – Joan thought it might be a good idea to bring up the topic of children, because Margaret had recently given birth to Viscount Linley, and so she started talking about the children.

Margaret suddenly stopped her, and put to her a direct question. 'Do you remember the first words that Richard said?'

Joan thought a little while and answered, 'Ooh ...' She was struggling hard to remember. 'I think the first words Richard said were just one word: "Car" because – well, he used to see Larry go off to work – yes, I feel pretty sure it was "Car".'

And she went on, 'So, can you remember Viscount Linley's first words?' Margaret paused for what seemed an eternity, then answered: 'Chandelier!'

The image of this little baby, in his cot or chaise, looking up and saying 'Chandelier!' It defies all sense!

A group started to form at the National, made up of Charlie Kay, Ronald Pickup, Jeremy Brett, when he came back into the company later, and myself. We were known as 'The Daughters'. This was a rather silly camp joke, if you like, but very much of the era. This league or cabal, as you might call it, of 'Daughters' was created by an actor no longer with us called Ken Parry.

Ken adored Tom Courtenay and made him the original 'Daughter', while Ken was 'Mother'. He was a friend of Charlie Kay, and you didn't have to be gay or even male, so Louise Purnell was a 'Daughter', and so was Maggie Smith. There wasn't only a ridiculous campness about belonging to this sorority, but also an eccentricity, a sensitivity, a lovability, which is hard to describe. Anyway, it was a little in-joke of the 'elect', and of course rather childish or childlike.

The all-male production of *As You Like It*, which ran successfully for years from 1968, was calculated to throw the whole notion of 'Daughters' into confusion. Sir Laurence (I went on calling him 'Sir' and still do) was deeply against the whole idea of doing *As You Like It* in this way. It somehow stuck in his throat and made him feel very uncomfortable. It was John Dexter's idea, endorsed by Kenneth Tynan, but 'Sir' had summoned Dexter, and in a ten-minute interview sacked him from this production. 'Merely confirming what I already knew,' commented John tartly, 'I was trainee material,' whereupon Clifford Williams had taken over.

The point was that the men who were playing women played it absolutely straight in their own voices. 'Sir' was especially sceptical of this approach when he had reluctantly acquiesced, and wondered why the girls didn't pad out their breasts and slap on nail varnish. He sent us a *very* encouraging telegraph on the first night from Canada, where he was performing in *A Flea in Her Ear.* 'Don't worry if this is a flop!'

Among the straight male performances Robert Stephens was Jacques, and I played Touchstone. We had the heavy fellas playing the girls, not boys, as they would have been in Shakespeare's time, and this was the main part of the humour. Ron Pickup played Rosalind, Charlie Kay played Celia. Both were made up 'straight' as women. Ralph Koltai, the designer, dressed them in ski boots, and they wore big plastic earrings.

We said to them, 'You look marvellous!' when they were terrible and they knew it. So they went away and designed their own costumes, Charlie appearing in a mini-skirt, Ron in a trouser suit – and both now did look wonderful.

───────

I approached Touchstone with trepidation, but when you have Tony Hopkins playing the love interest opposite you as Audrey, with Brünnhilde plaits, you've got it made. I kept in mind something Dame Edith Evans once said, when someone asked her to explain the basis of her comic technique, and she answered, 'Well, I say everything as if it were dirty.'

It is that kind of innuendo which was going to work with Touchstone, and when I was playing with the likes of Tony dressed up as Audrey, the uncouth country wench, a lot of the lines couldn't help becoming *very* innuendo. They were funny because they became dirty – in other words they became sex funny. But the laughs fell mainly on Tony as the butt, and he was the only one who was really unhappy, desperately so, apart from Sir. He just didn't want to do it. In spite of this he was so funny, and very sexy in a bovine kind of way. This made my job as Touchstone so much easier.

We took this production from the Old Vic to Stockholm, Copenhagen, Belgrade and Venice, and even when the audiences didn't understand the verbal humour they laughed themselves silly.

To show support for us, Sir had flown out to Stockholm where we were playing. We were having a jolly after the show in the bar, and it was here we tried to make Sir a 'Daughter'. We explained to him what it meant. But no, heavens no, he wouldn't have any of it, and he suddenly got terribly macho – he did not at all want to be a 'Daughter', and he thought we were all screaming poofs!

Another little revelation to me of this mixed-up department in Larry's psyche popped up in Franco Zeffirelli's *Much Ado About Nothing*. I played the villainous Don John to begin with, in a very thick Spanish accent, and with a liberal supply of facial tics. The production was a curious hodge-podge, set in nineteenth-century Sicily, with brass bands and exaggerated *opera buffa* trappings and some reworking of the text by Robert Graves.

Graves had been called in to tinker with this on Kenneth Tynan's initiative. Tynan painted a grim picture of the National's financial plight to convince Graves to accept a risible £250 to rewrite Shakespeare, then Graves saw his 300 corrections trashed.

Everyone was very miserable, and as Bob Stephens (who was Benedick) said, our costumes made us look like Sicilian toy soldiers. Bob was forced to strut around like a temperamental Italian; not at all the true Benedick, who is defensively fending off the truth of his feelings for Beatrice. As for Maggie Smith as Beatrice, she was 'excused being Italian because of her colouring' – in other words left well alone, a wise tactic with Maggie.

As with O'Toole's *Hamlet*, the public fell for the swagger and confectionary, so people queued for hours to get in and exchanged tickets at extravagant prices.

Albert Finney as Don Pedro was unequivocally marvellous and as part of his performance and throughout the run he smoked cigars – provided free by W.D. & H.O. Wills. At the end of the play there were two banquettes on stage, on either side, and Don Pedro would be left on his tod, puffing thoughtfully on his cigar. Albert would blow a smoke ring and the smoke went curling slowly round, expanding beautifully into the auditorium. He was such a master and it was a lovely moment.

Some time during the run, which went on for years, the cast changed and Ronnie Pickup took over Don John from me. I took over from Albert the part of Don Pedro. There was a great drawback here because I couldn't blow smoke rings, and also by now they had to buy the cigars for me – no Albert's name on the programme! – so I sat there at the end on the banquette in a single spotlight wondering what the hell I should do. Then I had a sudden brainwave. I noticed the spotlight on me and decided to 'blow it out', telling the electricians 'Blackout!'

At the end of the dress rehearsal when I tried this out, Sir Laurence rushed forward to hug me.

'Baby, darling, baby boy, great – and I so wondered what you were going to do! That was marvellous! But I've got a better idea, darling, baby boy – I think you should jump up onto the banquette, pull off your wig, and shout "*Je suis un homme!*"'

I was nonplussed and stepped back a pace or two. It was just a joke, a very involved joke, at which I laughed dutifully, but what he meant was that I hadn't got Albert's balls, and that compared to Albert Finney I could have been in drag. This is what he was saying. Maybe it was a bit cruel.

Again it was this sexual complication he had, this hang-up. He adored his boys – us I mean – but he was always wary. He must have known by now that I was gay. He must have known Charlie and Jeremy were too, and it was something that irked him. So he was not, or could not have been, happy with that side of himself. It was very exaggerated of course, much later, when rumours about some gay affairs came out after his death, but some of it I remember feeling must have been true, and served to feed his insecurity.

He didn't quite know where the borderlines lay in that area, and was over-sensitive as a result. But there was no doubting he was the most courageous actor of all of us. Who can ever forget the awesome moment in the film of *Hamlet* when he threw himself off the landing at Elsinore, the heroic way he led from the front as director and actor in his film of *Henry V*, to the extent that he had his face smashed up when a camera crashed into him? Or that even more extraordinary death scene in *Coriolanus* at Stratford when he was stabbed in the belly and fell, hanging upside down from a promontory caught by the heels by Albert Finney and his fellow Roman?

I took over Tattle from him in *Love for Love* when he went into hospital for cancer. He was due to go in on a Tuesday, and I was called in the preceding Thursday. I was in the other half of the company, so I was asked to play Tattle, as he wasn't keen on his understudy. I did not know the part, so I learned the lines over the weekend, then I was taken through the moves. Sir Laurence played it on Monday and I was out in the audience with a pair of field glasses trained on him. I rehearsed it on the Tuesday morning and was then prepped up for Tuesday night.

When they announced Sir Laurence wouldn't be playing that evening you could hear the groan of the audience all the way to Waterloo Station. I was standing in the wings in gold costume, the full Restoration dandy rig-up, because Tattle is always waiting to go on and make them laugh.

During my first scene, my goodness they were cold – they were so disappointed they turned into a solid brick wall.

But as the evening went on the pendulum began to swing in my favour.

'Well,' they were saying to one another, 'the kid's doing well, at least he knows the lines,' and by the curtain call it had swung so that, 'Oh, good on the kid, the kid's done well, great, great!' and they were applauding rapturously.

For me the real pay-off came later with an American couple who had arrived late and been placed by the box office manager Pat Layton at the back of the dress circle.

Pat said to them, 'I'll come and pick you up in the interval, and take you to your seats.' He collected them and said, 'Are you enjoying the show?'

'Yes,' they replied, 'the old man's doing great!' They didn't realise they weren't seeing Sir Laurence.

Larry, aged sixty-two, as Tattle performed a number of hair-raising physical manoeuvres which I couldn't even begin to replicate. He came out of a window way up in the flies, rapidly pulling on his clothes, to escape discovery from an amorous escapade with Miss Prue, at the same time speaking the lines rapidly so you could hear every word.

Along this ten-foot-high narrow wall, wearing high-heeled shoes, he would teeter, jump off onto a wicker chair with a roof to it, which would then sway from side to side. This was a wonderful bit of business, and during it he would have his stockings rolled down, and try to pull up his stockings – first one, then the other – and they both had false calves in them, so when he pulled up the second it was back to front and it fell out. Gales of laughter greeted this. Nearly forty years younger, I could do all this except for the walk along the wall in high heels.

———

Sir Laurence's physical courage and prowess were amazing. In the most famous role of these later years, he played Othello, which was filmed, and I enjoyed the perfect role for me, that of

Michael Cassio. As always Sir Laurence's preparation for his role was extraordinary and meticulous, and we had a ten-week rehearsal period, much longer than usual.

When the cast first assembled to read the play we were utterly transfixed at the performance he gave, especially as he was clad from head to foot in black leather. During rehearsals and performance, John Dexter, who directed, was sacked and reinstated, and Sir was extremely uncomfortable with his Desdemona, Maggie Smith.

Dexter's casting of Maggie was probably a bit wilful, and John wrote defiantly in his diary:

Casting Maggie as Desdemona. Nobody wants her. I do. A strong-willed, mature woman who's been around and knows what she wants. She wants that big black man. Isn't everyone tired of pretty blonde ingénue Desdemonas?

He probably had the notion that this would sting Sir Laurence into action and put him on his mettle, which indeed she did, but it built up personal tension between them. I remember how Olivier would shrink from any physical contact with her as if he thought he was literally and metaphorically untouchable, so much so that one day she burst out, 'I've come all the way from Venice to see you, you've won the war, and what do you want me to do, back away in fuckin' 'orror?'

Apparently he said to Bob Stephens: 'Please tell her to stay away from me on stage, I don't mind if she looks like a cunt, but I'm buggered if I'm going to look like one.'

Maggie could be very disdainful; this was very true, even to Sir, if you didn't keep up with her. One night during that Cyprus scene after the battle he says, 'Honey, you shall be well desired in Cyprus,' but on this line he dried totally, saying something like 'You will be well looked after in Paris.'

Hearing this, Maggie buried her face in his neck and howled with laughter, but it must have been awful for him. She could be stupendous, and on stage she thought and acted with the speed of light, and in the scenes I played with her she always set the pace and rhythm. I gained so much from her. But her unconventionality irked Sir Laurence, and he made no secret that he didn't like the way she sounded. One night she went round to his dressing room, knocked on the door and, opening it, said in a very loud voice, 'How now, Brown Cow!' and then left. When Billie Whitelaw took over from Maggie it is not surprising he felt much more comfortable.

Every night Sir Laurence as Othello used to come on stage holding a red rose. The rumour was that they were supplied by Vivien Leigh, but by now he was married to Joan, so this could hardly have been true. His dresser Christopher used to sell the roses off nightly at the stage door. He gave me one, which I pressed in a book to keep, but promptly lost.

Before the production opened, when we were in Cardiff, Dexter really overreached himself in front of the cast, and tore into Sir Laurence, saying he played the Moor like a Jamaican bus conductor, and was equally scathing about the company. Sir Laurence was furious, summoned John to his dressing room and told him he was never, but *never*, to speak to him and his company like that again. John retaliated by telling him it was not his company, but the National Theatre Company, whereupon Sir Laurence sacked him on the spot – for the second time.

The performance did, to be fair to Dexter, put others in mind of London Transport: Michael Gambon thought of Sir Laurence's Othello as a black bus conductor, too:

'No standing on the top deck! Sir was experimenting all the time, and once even put padding up his nose.'

Everyone persuaded Sir Laurence to take John back. This was a rare occasion for John, because he usually left stars alone, but that day he had gone for the star's jugular.

It took Olivier three or four hours to black up each night and it was an ordeal to wash off the make-up afterwards; Bob Stephens and John Dexter were in Larry's dressing room after one performance when suddenly, in front of the mirror, looking at himself, Sir Laurence uttered the words, 'What a tragedy that such a very great actor should have such a very small cock.'

I'm not altogether sure if this is what exactly happened or was said, for the version I heard direct from his dresser Christopher was not quite the same. As Bob told it, it made a good story, but it was Christopher who helped him in the shower after each performance, and Chris told me it was to him that he made this observation.

Neither Bob, Finney, or anyone else – except of course Scofield – could ever challenge Sir in his undisputed position as leader of the acting profession. I never wanted, or indeed was capable, of doing this, but some years on I did take up the taxing, indeed punishing performance of repeating his famous double act of Oedipus in *Oedipus Rex* and Mr Puff in Sheridan's *The Critic*, at Birmingham Rep.

I didn't realise I had broken two ribs until the middle of the night after one performance. It was not until I stopped acting and my adrenaline died down that I then realised I could have bled to death. These roles earned me a congratulatory telegram from Sir.

He wrote just two words: 'Cheeky bugger!'

24

CLAY FEET AND
OTHER PARTS

It was during one of those performances of *Othello* that I saw for the very first time Sir's feet of clay, and realised he was just another actor. It happened one night when Frank Finlay and I were waiting in the wings to come on stage, and Olivier was screaming with grief, 'The handkerchief, the handkerchief, the handkerchief!' before coming off.

That night he won a great round of applause. Now for this scene he was in bare feet, and he had several pairs of slippers dotted around in the wings to slip on after his exit for the next scene. As he did this he would lean on Frank or on me, as we were waiting to come on, and put a hand on our shoulders to steady himself.

As he came off to thunderous applause, he leant on my shoulder, and he was pulling on his slippers when he said out loud – but to himself – 'What the fuck can I do for my next exit?' It was the actor saying, 'I have peaked too soon.' Depressing in one way, but a good lesson for instilling self-restraint. Even so, it was a significant moment in my never-ending learning curve.

———◇◇◇———

Sir's attack was prodigious, the emotional energy stupendous; he rolled as he walked, in costumes with padded shoulders, like

146

a god. He was godlike, but there was always a light-heartedness around in all of these years in the company he led, so the 'Daughters' laughed much of the time.

Dexter commented, somewhat morosely, or perhaps it was with envy, that Brett, Pickup and I were 'usually in a state of convulsed hysterics, compared to which my strained nerves on a cold spring morning were as nothing!' Later during the run of *Othello* we gave a special performance on a Sunday just for members of the profession, when practically every member of the audience worked in the theatre in some capacity or other. They didn't just stand up at the end to give him an ovation, they stood *on* the seats. It was such a display of affection and admiration. It made him ideal to lead the profession – and lead he did.

Sir seemed to consider there was an important closeness between himself as Othello and Bob Stephens as the Inca God in *The Royal Hunt of the Sun*. He told Bob to be careful of his voice, asking him rather discreetly and shyly whether it was possible for him to make love to Maggie after giving a performance in this role. Bob answered that he found there was no problem, but Sir Laurence said he couldn't rise to anything much in that department after playing Othello, so Bob pointed out that the comparison was false: Othello was so much more demanding a role!

The funniest moment for me on stage throughout my theatrical career came in *The Royal Hunt of the Sun*, when I played the first Indian the audience sees. I walked out onto the mountain range set, shining with a hairstyle somewhat like Cilla Black's in the 1960s: a black Cilla, covered in that terrible make-up called Texas Earth. My character attempts to rape one of Atahuallpa's daughters, and as a result suffers short shrift, dying at the end of the second act.

We then come to the immortal moment! It was in the scene when all the Indians have to prostrate themselves flat on their faces, and all in feathers. So here was Ted Hardwicke and Ted Petherbridge, me, and the rest of the Indian crowd, including by this time Michael York, and we were all lying flat on the stage, naked but covered with feathers, and we were creating a stunning visual effect.

Then somebody explosively farted!

When you get a large group of actors, all nearly naked and in feathers, and somebody farts, the effect can only too easily be imagined. At once the whole stage was a-quiver, positively palpitating with all these feathers shaking. It was awful, truly awful – and wonderful. We couldn't stop laughing.

As the run extended, some of the Indians grew bored. During the picturesque scene where the Spaniards, my character leading them, were climbing to the peak of the Andes (all beautifully choreographed), and were ranged up high at the back of the stage, the Indians, on their first entrance, entered down below from the side, backs to the audience, about six of them spaced across the front.

They opened their feathered cloaks to reveal to us upstage, as salutation to the visitors, that they were all stark naked – and one of the Indians had fixed an oil lamp to his cock: the lantern was simply hanging down from it. The entire line above at the back folded up helpless with laughter, myself included, and behaved more like giggling schoolgirls than conquering *conquistadores*.

As my character suffers an early death in the play, I remember one of the perks was that I was allowed to 'shower off' with Fairy Liquid the nightly coating of 'bole' or Texas Earth, and leave the show early without staying for the curtain call. There were so many Indians to wash down, and few showers in the theatre.

There was a time when I almost took to the bottle out of boredom. This was when I played the unrewarding part of Mr Worthy in *The Recruiting Officer*. It was all very well for Sir

ady for my first close-up,
ed three

Taking Mum and Dad for a walk

ad as proud shop-owner

Mum before her hair turned
white

The gang, from left to right: Michael Folkard, me, Robin Dowsett

Richard Kay, the mischievous Puck; Garry O'Connor as Oberon

Coming of age in style – I'm just above the cake (below)

Members of the Cambridge 'Mafia': Ian McKellen and me (above)

y 'cheeky bugger!' roles: Oedipus (left) and Mr Puff in *The Critic* (right)

Three 'Daughters' in the all-male *As You Like It*: Ronald Pickup, left, as Rosalind; Charlie Kay as Celia; me as Touchstone

entors of my NT days: Olivier and aggie Smith in *Othello*

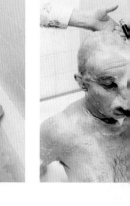

Claudius with snorkel: the 'Emperor Fool's' make-up removal and bath time

My American debut in *The Suicide*, with John Heffernan

A pensive Alan Turing

Claudius: 'I'm thinking of writing a book about my family'

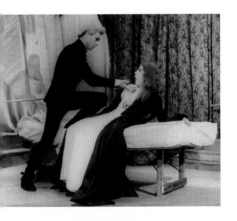

A hoop of Hamlets: (top left) the Edinburgh closet scene with boy Gertrude; (top right) rehearsing the Cambridge Hamlet with Garry O'Connor directing; (centre left) Old Vic 1977; (centre right) Old Vic 1979, which played at Elsinore (bottom left); (bottom right) BBC Television 1980

In the master's footsteps: a stern
John Gielgud as John of Gaunt;
me as Richard II

Prospero: 'I'll drown my book'

For love of Sinéad: Cyrano and Roxanne

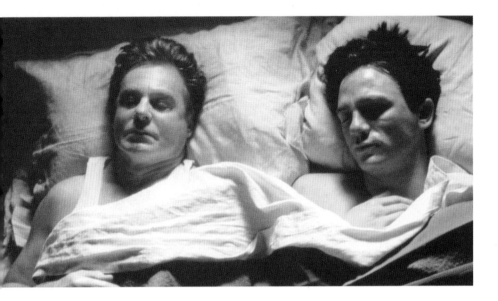

bed with 007: *Love Is the Devil*

Hollywood 'co-stars':
Kenneth Branagh and
Emma Thompson

Doing my own stunts
in *Dead Again*

My far better half
– Richard (right)

Masters of all we
survey! (far right)

Beloved
Bella
Sinéad

On Lear's journey to forgiveness
and understanding (above)

To end where I began: Mum
and Dad (left)

Laurence, Colin Blakely, Maggie Smith and Bob Stephens – they had wonderfully funny parts. But Sarah Miles and I had to play these two impossibly wet juves who come on, chattering together nothing but plot-plot-plot, and nobody was the slightest bit interested.

We would go off, and then in would swan Maggie and Sir Laurence, and they would get the laughs again, and it was all wonderful – for them. Sarah couldn't bear it and walked out, and Mary Miller, who'd been her understudy, came in instead. Before the show one night I was meeting a friend at the pub next to the stage door, and I did something I had never done before: I drank a large whisky. Not for any other particular reason than that my friend offered me one, but I thought, 'Why not? It's only *The Recruiting Officer* tonight!'

The whisky went straight to my head, anaesthesia took over, and the effect was that I actually enjoyed the performance. I got two laughs, and I was *so* relaxed. Before the next performance I thought, 'I'm going to try that again.' I went to the pub, bought a large whisky. Again, it was great. I even raised a few more laughs. It was then it suddenly hit me: 'What the hell are you doing, Derek? You're relying on this to get on the stage, and you could easily end up a piss-artist – like so many of us have.'

So for me that was it – *finito*.

25

GIVING AWAY
MICHAEL YORK

To begin with Michael was a walk-on and my understudy in Coward's *Hay Fever* and Shaffer's *Black Comedy*. We had met at Cambridge, when Michael had come over from Oxford in an OUDS production. Like me he had been to grammar school and acted for Michael Croft. He joined the National Theatre Company just over a year after me, in early 1964, at the time when Albert had joined, and also Ian McKellen, who stayed only a short while.

Michael and I acted together in John Arden's *Armstrong's Last Goodnight*, written in Arden's abrasive and often incomprehensible Scottish. I had twenty-one lines in the first scene, which I felt utterly ill-quipped to deliver until mentored by Frank Wylie, a real Scottish actor in the company, who pointed out that it was very simple: every time I had an 'i' in a word I had to pronounce it as 'u'. So my line, 'Ah you've won the King but you didna win the kingdom,' should be said as, 'Ah you've won the Kung but you dudna wun the kungdom!' It worked a treat, and still does every time I play a Scotsman (which is very rarely).

Ian was in this and he remembers that 'We were covered in hair, in this scene of such complexity speaking this Lowlands dialect – Derek, David Ryall, Ted Petherbridge and I. It made us all laugh behind our beards. And then Derek, having played his scene, went off to watch the tennis!'

Ian didn't stay long at the National: there were 'an awful lot of us *jeunes premiers*', too many for him. 'I got out because I could see there was no future. What with Derek, Jeremy Brett, Ted Petherbridge, John Stride, Ron Pickup, Tony Hopkins, you just had to wait your turn to get the parts.'

⸺◦⊷◦⸺

Noël Coward's *Hay Fever*, starring as it did Dame Edith Evans and Maggie Smith, was one of the biggest hits of these golden years and stayed in the repertoire for a very long time. I was landed with the young juve Simon, my counterpart again being Sarah Miles. Living with her lover, the impresario William Donaldson, Sarah was at the time carrying on a clandestine affair with Sir, which only Noël knew about, and he strongly disapproved. She tried to get Noël to change some of her inadequate and underwritten part, that of Sorel, which offended The Master, and brought down on her fierce retribution from Sir, who didn't want to put Noël out of humour.

One night after a row with The Master, Sarah gagged on a fish bone, and she left the cast. Noël delivered the parting shot on the effect of the chop bone on her throat: 'We all heard *it* at the read-through!' Noël was directing, or rather non-directing: in fact Noël did no directing, but mesmerised us by his presence into giving good performances. So Sarah repeated her trick of early departure and again abandoned me.

Edith Evans was Judith Bliss. 'The Dame' – God rest her soul – engendered little love in the cast. The battle lines were at once drawn between the legendary Dame, sadly now a bit past her prime and shaky on her lines, and Maggie at the very first dress rehearsal. For Act II Maggie wore a ravishing black cocktail number with an exotic, fish-tail fan behind. When The Dame plonked her elbow down on the sofa where Maggie was seated, there issued forth a great tearing sound and off came the fish-tail fan.

'Oh, that looks so much better!' said Dame Edith.

When Maggie came on next it was with a large cigarette holder and she made a gesture of shedding a longer fish tail with the holder, twisted round and raised the holder in triumph. As well as being wary of Maggie, The Dame was wary of us young-sters, giving us notes, summonses to her dressing room, and tellings off. She did not like us getting laughs, declaring regally, 'I'm like a well-bred racehorse and when I'm not expecting it (she meant a laugh she did not get) – I rear! I rear!'

As a first-night present Noël gave her a box with a box inside, with another box inside this, and another and another until it got down to a tiny box. Inside this were just two lumps of sugar.

She kept slipping up on one line in particular: 'On a clear day you can see as far as Marlowe,' saying instead, 'On a clear day you can see Marlowe.'

Noël pulled her up sharp. 'If you can see Marlowe, you can probably see Beaumont and Fletcher as well, but it's not the line I wrote!'

To be fair to her, we had all been told before rehearsal to learn our lines and the message never reached her, so from the start she felt at a disadvantage.

Before we opened at the Old Vic we had a week at the Opera House in Manchester. Given The Dame's variable humour, Noël had had the forethought to ask Maggie to under-study her. Just before we opened, Dame Edith refused to go on, claiming she suffered from 'a dropped stomach', and no saliva. Hearing this, Noël had gone to her room in the hotel, apparently shaken her like a rat, and told her she was a disgrace to the acting profession. A doctor had then been summoned to visit her, in spite of her allegiance (like Harold Hobson) to Christian Science, and had endeavoured to convince her to take a bromide.

'Bromide?' exclaimed Noël. 'What she needs is a firecracker up her arse,' and he sat down at the grand piano in his suite and bashed out 'All Things Bright and Beautiful'. I wasn't there, but did think by now they were ganging up on her.

When The Dame heard Maggie had been asked by Noël to take over her role of Judith Bliss, and had played a midnight dress rehearsal when The Dame failed to appear, sending her up so mischievously that Olivier and Noël were lying around on the floor in fits of laughter, she miraculously recovered. With help taking her through the lines from her old friend Gwen Ffrangcon-Davies, also a Christian Scientist, she opened on the Monday.

When at last it came to the first night at the Old Vic, Noël gave a party in the dress circle bar. Mum and Dad came with Aunt Hilda and Henry, the only time all four were together to see something of mine. Judy Garland was there, and Rudolph Nureyev, and they were thrilled to meet them. I introduced Noël first to Mum, then to Dad. I was about to say, 'This is Aunt Hilda,' but stopped short because I saw The Master looking at her. No one said anything. Then he spoke:

'You look like a Hilda to me.'

She practically fainted with joy. He had guessed her name.

At the Vic, The Dame and Maggie occupied adjoining dressing rooms. One matinée day during the run, between shows I could hear Maggie playing rather more loudly than necessary her favourite 'Baby Love' by The Supremes, so The Dame couldn't have a nap and would be too tired to cause trouble in the evening performance. I even overheard The Dame berating Maggie backstage:

'I understand you are covering [i.e. understudying] the role of Judith Bliss,' she said, as if she did not already know. 'I should like to tell you, here and now, that I shall not be off!'

To this Maggie answered in a flash, 'Well, I sincerely hope not, because the cossies won't fit!'

Yet The Dame was, after all, amazing, instinctive, commanding, and Maggie was to some extent standing up to her for everyone else.

Once we opened *Hay Fever* Noël invited each member with a speaking part individually out for a night on the town. My turn came and we spent a lovely evening together. We went to the theatre, then back to the Savoy where he was living, for dinner, then up to his suite for a nightcap. He reminded me how years before he had seen me play Edward II in the Marlowe production, and how much he had enjoyed it. The gossip was riveting, and it grew late (it was half past one), and next day I was rehearsing.

Still green as grass, I rose to leave.

'Derek,' said The Master, 'might I ask a very personal question?'

All atremble lest the lovely evening was about to be spoiled by a Spriggs-like lunge, I stood my ground.

'Are you circumcised?'

'No, no, no,' I stuttered in answer. 'Why do you ask?'

'What a pity. What a great pity!' Noël answered mournfully. 'You're a very fine actor, Derek, but you'll never be a great actor until you're circumcised.'

'But why?' I asked frowning. By now, not at all knowing but fearing where this was leading, I was edging towards the door.

'Freedom, dear boy,' Noël explained airily, mystifyingly. 'Freedom!'

And that was it. But freedom from what? I had a bet with myself he had said this before, but I was out of the door and away.

Next day I considered further what he might have meant. The Master must know something I didn't, and maybe I should check myself into the London Clinic immediately. I did so want to be a great actor! And I was still far away from achieving this. I told this story to everyone in the canteen who would listen. The majority verdict was that at my age it would be too painful. I decided to carry on risking it as I was.

Michael York 'covered' for me as Simon in *Hay Fever* but never once went on to experience among other delights the pleasure of Maggie, a picture of enamelled nauseated horror, stroking my horribly sticky hair, and finding her fingers covered in grease.

While the 'as luck would have it' principle applied to me, to Michael it was 'as looks would have it'. These stunningly handsome looks provided him with a springboard into his career, the glamour that demands attention and reward. Films are about looking at people, and Michael was soon to become a successful star.

Here again it seemed as a worshipper of beauty I was falling for a very attractive but straight man, so it was, as far as a sexual relationship went, unrequited, but a deep and close friendship. We greatly enjoyed being together, which was rather frustrating on my side as I wanted more, which was not forthcoming. It was virtually a prequel to the Sally Bowles–Brian Roberts relationship in *Cabaret* which Michael was later to film with Liza Minnelli!

When he was my understudy in *Black Comedy* we shared a cottage outside Chichester, and then shared a flat together in Neville's Place, Earls Court, for a while. In the break between seasons after *Black Comedy*, Michael and I decided to drive to Italy in my soft-top Triumph Herald with the top off, and on the way back we passed through Switzerland.

'Let's call on Noël Coward,' I suggested. Noël had said if ever I was passing through Switzerland to visit him at Les Avants, his home there, and he would be delighted to see me. We duly found where The Master lived, and knocked on his door. A butler answered.

'It's Derek Jacobi,' I said. 'Sir Noël told me, "If ever you are in Switzerland, do call on me."' The butler left us to confer with The Master, came back a little later and gave the reply: 'Delighted to see you.'

In we went and at once Noël came over and embraced me. 'Derek, darling, how lovely to see you! How lovely to –'

He turned to Michael and did a triple-take.

That was it! I was immediately ushered into the sitting room with a drink, and Michael was taken off on a tour of the house. I was the wallflower!

History now repeated itself in a strange fashion, for Michael and I ended up sharing digs in the same cottage in Shottery near Stratford belonging to Julia Hasty, where I had stayed eight years before with Richard Kay.

Getting very drunk one night, we jumped over the gate and pissed in Anne Hathaway's garden. I'd like to have imagined it could have happened but it never did. Wasn't this a further echo of my previous experience with Richard at Shottery? At some moment in the farcical proceedings, Michael was so drunk he projectile vomited across the room. That really put an end to any passion which may have started.

On the holiday in Italy we had been sharing beds but nothing ever clicked there, which again had been frustrating, but it was better than nothing, because I was madly in love with him.

Michael soon after met Patricia McCallum, a photographer, some years older than him, and they married in 1967. I was best man at the wedding and so I might claim that I gave him away. By the 1970s and 80s, after *Accident* and *Cabaret*, he had become very famous, but he started to live the trappings of fame and not the work, to my regret. One instance was when he was cast as Benedick in *Much Ado* opposite Penelope Keith for the BBC television series of Shakespeare's plays, and would miss rehearsals because he was dining with Prince Rainier and Grace Kelly, or the Aga Khan. What they filmed was so poor they pulled it, then remade it with Robert Lindsay.

I was outraged as well as saddened by a dinner I attended with Pat and Michael at their house in Eaton Terrace, where I met Angela Lansbury for the first time. They now had the butler, maid and cook. We finished our first course. Pat would ring a little bell, a flunkey would come in. It was all so piss-elegant. Pat was outwardly sweet but she tended to shoo away his girlfriends and his close friends – though he was still so handsome that I'm not surprised if she had felt possessive.

However, I wonder if that had an adverse effect on his acting potential.

26

LEADING IN THE DARK

I was embarking on my first lead at the National in the dark – or pitch black – of Peter Shaffer's *Black Comedy*. The idea is that dark is light and light dark, and all the comedy stems from this brilliant reversal. In the first five minutes the stage is in complete darkness and the actors are acting naturally as if it is not. The lights come on, and Brindsley Miller, my character, says, 'Blast, a fuse!' and we all start acting as if we are blundering around in the dark. The physical gags are endless.

Cast as the lead, I was very cautious about my role because I had two star players up against me, Maggie Smith and Albert Finney. I was in complete awe of both. Albert took the initiative and asked me out to dinner.

'Now look, I'm Albert Finney,' he said. 'I've got more experience than you. You've got the bigger part, so don't you worry about Maggie and me, we can look after ourselves. This is your play and *your* big part. Get on with it!'

I was still, to be honest, a bit shaky with Dexter directing. This would be a huge demand on every comic device.

Finney played Brindsley's neighbour, the limp-wristed antique dealer Gorringe, from whose flat I have surreptitiously removed the antique furniture in order to impress my fiancée Carol (played by Louise Purnell in a delicious squeaky voice). Maggie was my ex-mistress Clea, who turns up to queer my furniture

158

machinations and compromise my wooing. In the dark–light reversal I slink about the apartment, shifting the furniture so as not to let anyone else see, and stagger from crisis to crisis.

I could feel the audience on the first night, in the first five minutes of complete darkness, batting on our side for a minute or so, but then their patience began to wear a bit thin: 'We're not going to sit here much longer without something happening.'

Then the lights came on and Brindsley said his first line and as the trick registered they went absolutely bananas. It was such a thrilling, unique moment. During that first night a stern-looking man who sat in front of Peter suddenly fell out of his seat into the aisle and started calling out in a voice hoarse from laughing, 'Oh stop! Please stop it!'

'This is what you mean by a blind date!' Maggie as Clea imperiously pronounces as she arrives without warning and finds me with my new girlfriend.

In these conditions something unexpected always happened. In the play I hide Gorringe's Buddha statue under his raincoat, Gorringe enters in a fury, carrying his lighted candle, sees his raincoat, grabs it, and pulls the statue onto the floor which then breaks, but one night the business went arse over tit. Albert came on, seized the raincoat, pulled it off the table, the Buddha hit the floor but it didn't smash as expected. Albert went 'Ah!' blew out the candle and stood on the Buddha, all with the speed of light, a fantastic moment of inspiration.

———

After the first night of *Black Comedy* in Chichester we held a little celebration in The Crossed Keys. When this was over Sir Laurence and I climbed in a car and were driven overnight to Shepperton, where we were filming *Othello*. Next morning Sir was sitting in his canvas chair surrounded by the daily newspapers, for he had been reading the reviews when I joined him. I was about to pick one up.

'Don't read them!' he warned.

I dropped it, for he could only mean the reviews were bad. I knew we had scored a fantastic hit so I frowned and was unhappy. If the critics shat on it, this was most unfair. Whether he was being naughty, as he could be with me, I will never know, but from that time on I stopped reading reviews, and have never read them since.

'That curtain call you do at the end of *Black Comedy* is terrible,' Sir went on. 'You rushed on, you nodded at the audience, and you rushed off. You mustn't do that, it's rude, it doesn't do you any favours. You've got to learn how to take the call as you can gain a lot by doing a wonderful curtain call.'

'Oh yes, I'll try,' I said, but my instinct stayed, and even today I still hate it when I take a solo call, and cannot wait for the company to come on. Then I feel better.

But Sir was right. I have even seen a curtain call rescue a show, which happened at the first night of *Applause* in London with Lauren Bacall. While the applause at the end was passable, the show wasn't enough to make you stand on your seat. But then, in the space of a second, Bacall changed dresses three times as the curtain lowered and raised, and each time the applause went up and up. She had someone behind the curtain ready to slip her into her new outfit. Finally everyone left thinking they'd had a wonderful night.

This may not necessarily have anything to do with great writing, acting or directing – but of course it has everything to do with show business!

―――――≎≎≎―――――

When the film of *Othello* was finished, Mum and Dad came to the première. Mum was outspoken at the reception after, when she told Sir what she thought of her son's performance as Michael Cassio.

'Only one criticism,' she blithely informed him. 'That was a bugger of a wig you gave 'im!'

Quite right, too. I looked like Jane Wyman! This toe-curling episode slightly redressed the balance sheet with Sir.

One night, acting in *Black Comedy* when I slid down the stairs, I twisted my knee. Michael York was my understudy. Dexter insisted that Michael went on instead of me, although he hadn't covered the part since Chichester. He only knew half the lines, and felt he was being led, 'after rehearsing the moves, down to the stage like a convict to an execution'. During the opening minutes he felt in the dark in every possible way, and somehow Louise did not deliver the first or right cue. He froze and panic engulfed him. Finally he brought out the first line, 'Well, what do you think of the room?' and it had kept its effect of instant laughter.

Michael was being over-modest when he wrote in his autobiography, 'The measure of my success was that I was forbidden to go on for the evening performance, and a feverish Derek was dragged from his bed to amuse his monarch!'

'Dragged from my bed' I certainly was not! I had sat in the wings through the matinée to steer Michael through. I was upset over being off, for I knew the Queen was due to attend the evening performance and I was determined not to miss the opportunity to play before her. I pulled myself together and struggled through.

'My sister nearly died of laughter,' Princess Margaret told me years later when I had dinner with her.

The consequences of that shock performance never left Michael. He had nightmares of being on an empty stage not knowing what to say or do. I understood completely how he felt. Later it would happen to me – big time.

27

THE IDIOT

After my first lead I had a bigger and much more difficult one. After seven years and twenty-five roles at the National, and without ever once coming into contact with the commercial theatre, I was to be given my big chance. I was once more a prince, although in this case he was epileptic.

The role, that of Prince Myshkin in Simon Gray's adaptation of Dostoevsky's *The Idiot*, looked perfect on paper. Dostoevsky's character is a man for all seasons, which was convenient when you realise the book was first published in serial form. On stage it was going to be impossible to reveal every facet of his character, for he changes so often and is so many different things to so many different people. Simon's idea was to pick out one through-line and be consistent to this, so he seized on the character's goodness and gentleness, specifically in relation to his disease.

The challenge became how to show for three hours, when I am on stage virtually the whole time, this man who often appears to be saintly without becoming an insufferable prig. I had to convey an inner life of innocence that is not on overt display, but is brought out by the reactions of the other characters. I had to get onto a different place, and not just be relentlessly good.

To find the details of epileptic behaviour I watched films which the BMA and the British Epileptics Association supplied me; I read papers on the subject, and I learned that such fits sometimes do not have any visible manifestation, but from a movement or a sound may lead to a state of total immobility. Myshkin's fits are ecstatic, and he even knows when they are about to happen. Dostoevsky is specific about them starting with a cry, but I never found anyone like this in all I saw and studied.

One doctor suggested the kind of scream Myshkin made would be like that of a peacock, so I went off to Holland Park and tried to provoke the peacocks into uttering their cries for me, but they were not very obliging. One main problem was that Simon kept changing the script every day in rehearsals. He would arrive with fistfuls of new stuff to learn overnight. I think he suffered from a variation on the theme of writer's block: if you looked at the scripts they were full of dot-dot-dots.

Anthony Quayle, who was doing eight performances of *Sleuth* a week, rehearsed and directed *The Idiot*. We performed a run-through in front of Sir Laurence, who straight away cut several scenes, which meant several actors losing their entire roles. We had a set designed by a famous figure called Josef Svoboda, who wanted to show off his skill and win prizes; while it looked quite impressive, it was hell to work on. This added to the general sense of incompetent direction.

We had only two public dress rehearsals before the first night, and while I am never at my best on first nights it went surprisingly well. The reviews were good (so I was told), but as a whole I'm not sure ultimately it worked in Simon's adaptation. Needless to say I loved playing Myshkin; I loved his character, his innocence and his goodness.

Tony Hopkins had been cast as Rogozhin, but he left during rehearsals so they upped his understudy, Tom Baker, the future fourth Doctor Who. Diane Cilento, an actress of celebrated beauty and talent, played Anastassya. At the time she was married to Sean Connery and sometimes couldn't come to rehearsals because of his 'golf tournaments' – a euphemism, I believe.

During Wimbledon we were rehearsing round at her house one weekend and after about half an hour Diane said, 'Let's call a halt. It's the men's finals. Come on, we have to watch.'

We sat down to watch the Men's Finals. It was Ken Rosewall versus John Newcombe, another Australian, who finally beat him. During the match the door opened behind us. A man came in and sat down. I turned and did the most enormous double take as Diane introduced Lew Hoad.

Imagine watching these two champions, Rosewall and Newcombe, with Lew Hoad sitting right beside you!

After *The Idiot*'s first night Olivier threw a reception in his flat in Victoria. At one point I said to him, 'Can I ring my parents to tell them how it's gone?' and he said, 'Yes, of course, there's a phone through there in the back room.'

I went into the bedroom and rang Dad and Mum; I had just finished the call and was leaving the room when the door opened, and Sir Laurence came in. He wasn't drunk, but I'd say he was a little bit tipsy. He said how marvellously well the evening had gone. And then he hugged me to him.

'You're my third son,' he said, 'you're my third son.'

That was a great moment for me. Of course I melted, I completely melted, and I adored him for it.

Larry was so generous to the younger members of the National Theatre Company. He had lived through some very bad years. He had not long before turned sixty when he began rehearsing *Three Sisters*, in which I was cast as Baron Tuzenbach, and in which Joan played Masha, while he was playing *The Dance of Death*, waking three or four times a night wet with pain and worry.

'Prostate pain,' he wrote in his diary. Doctors at St Thomas's diagnosed prostate cancer, which he chose to have treated with radiation instead of having an operation. Not far from his flat in Victoria, his former wife Vivien Leigh, in her flat in Eaton Square, was dying of tuberculosis.

He went on rehearsing. He did a tremendous amount of homework. He had a little stage in his study, and he would come back next day with his idea of where he wanted all of the actors to be. He would bark at us in his famous manner: 'Walk to the door! Come back!'

You plucked up your courage: 'Please, Sir, can I try something?'

'Yes, you carry on.'

But you always ended up doing exactly what he wanted, even if you had the chance to flap around and do your own thing first. I had a natural deference towards him. Even after eight years of friendship I could never call him Larry to his face. Behind his back, of course, to my friends it was always 'Larry said that ...'

Just a fortnight before *Three Sisters* opened, he promenaded his two young children on the beach in Brighton, then found at 2 a.m. that night he could not breathe. He was driven with Joan by his chauffeur to London and behaved as if he were dying, shaking hands next morning with stage staff and taking his leave before they brought him into hospital where he was treated for pneumonia. While he was there he persuaded nurses to let him watch a heart operation.

From his St Thomas's room Sir Laurence had a direct line to the stage manager in the prompt corner, so she could tell him how *Three Sisters* was progressing on the opening night. After a triumphant performance we went along to his room and brought champagne with us.

Together with courage went extraordinary largesse. He'd invite us down to Brighton for the weekend, asking us in pairs. I went with Louise Purnell. We were dined and wined, plied with nightcaps, and next morning he came into each of our bedrooms with a tray. Just think: this was 'Sir Laurence' in his dressing gown, the most famous actor in the world, bringing me up my breakfast on a tray!

———

In the summer break after *The Idiot* Diane invited me to the Connerys' Marbella villa. I stayed there with their son Jason and Graham Hill's boy Daimen. Sean was not there because he was away on a golf course somewhere – presumably playing golf. Diane and he divorced not much later and she married Antony Shaffer, Peter's brother, who wrote *Sleuth*.

I saw my first bullfight with the famous toreador El Cordobés. He had been up drinking all the night before in Torremolinos. He had a hangover, and was not at all on form. At the end the crowd gave him the bird, booing and whistling him. At the exit he turned, strode back into the centre of the ring, stood there, threw out his chest, raised up his fist and started turning and stamping his feet in rhythm.

By the time he had made the next full circle they were screaming with delight: it was a real two fingers to them, and they erupted in adoration. I didn't approve of bullfighting and I could just about watch the Cordilleros, but not the kills.

One evening we were invited along the coast to what should have been an exclusive celebrity party. The hostess had once had Sammy Davis Junior and orchestra perform for her. The food was lovely, while to follow there was a cabaret. As a curtain-raiser a man wheeled on a trolley on which sat a tape recorder. He switched on and we listened. I couldn't work it out, but Diane sussed it at once.

'Come on, we're getting out of here!' she explained, and I couldn't believe my ears: it was the Moors Murders Tapes, presented as entertainment. How sick could you get!

———

After *The Idiot* the time had arrived to leave the National and go out into the big wide world. I made an appointment and went along to see Sir.

'I would like a leave of absence.' This was the way I put it. He said yes immediately and I was out of the room.

Well, I thought, he didn't exactly put up much of a fight, did he? I had talked myself out of a job with a single sentence. We did discuss a little about 'leave of absence' with the idea I would come back. But at the end of that year he himself was out and Peter Hall was in, so that was me up the spout. I wondered if I hadn't made a big mistake. It was a leap in the dark: eleven years I'd been in work without a single break, and when they gave me my National Insurance book it was filled up like a collection of Green Shield stamps.

Along came a film job straight away, absolutely out of the blue. I owed this entirely to Fred Zimmermann who, unlike most film directors, was a fervent theatregoer. He had seen practically everything at the National so he had seen a lot of us juniors growing up and must have heard I was leaving.

Zimmermann was making *The Day of the Jackal* with Edward Fox as the star. He offered me the role of the French detective, Inspector Caron, which was my initiation into big-time movies. I was flown to a hotel in Provence which was to be used as one of the sets. I arrived for my first pure camera work on location.

On my first night I knew nobody. I found my room and took myself down to the restaurant, ate some supper on my own, and went back up to my room. I couldn't sleep and I had a terrible night for I was in agony with what I thought was food poisoning. I rose at 6.30 next morning, went to the make-up room for the first day's filming, but I was green, I was so ill that they put me straight back to bed.

Within minutes Zimmermann, with his producer, were up in my bedroom. They called in a doctor and he diagnosed appendicitis.

167

'Wait a minute,' I said, explaining I had eaten some fish the previous night and that was why I was bad.

'It will be all arranged. There will be a helicopter to take you to Cannes. The surgeon will be ready waiting to operate. They'll whip it out, and all will be fine.'

'Please, please, please,' I objected, 'give it time, I'll be better soon, I'll be better!'

They wouldn't listen. At this point, fortunately, the wife of the producer came in and she took my side. 'Give him a couple of hours,' she said to them, 'and if he's not better in two hours, take him away and cut him open.'

Two hours later I wasn't exactly at my best, but I was recovering. Then, by the afternoon, I had improved enough for them to use me on the set. The location was only a hundred yards away from the front gates of the hotel. As I left the hotel to walk only that little distance away, a big limousine drove up alongside me, and the driver stopped, lowered his window, and said, 'Mr Jacobi, this is your car.'

'No, it's all right, I'm fine, I'm OK ... I can walk,' I protested.

The driver insisted. 'In the car! Mr Zimmermann's orders.'

I gave in. Seconds later we were there.

This was my introduction to the film world, and I understood at once that you do as you are told. If there's anything wrong with you then, 'We've got the surgeon ready, the knife is in his hand!'

AGE V
AND THEN
THE JUSTICE

28

THE INTANGIBLE 'IT'

In the late 1960s I lived mostly on my own without any steady relationship, and this went on for a further ten years, nearly up to the age of forty. I shared flats with others, first with Richard Kay and Michael Burrell, opposite the Seymour Swimming Baths by Bryanston Square W1, and had been in that flat for a few years when Richard and Mike had moved out, Richard in order to marry.

Then I rented a flat on my own in Sussex Gardens. Mum and Dad with dusters and cleaners would arrive where I lived, and go over the flat with a toothcomb, take away my washing and fill up the fridge, while Dad would clean my car. Mum would never come and just sit down and have a good chat, but would spring clean the entire place from top to bottom. I would go home at weekends to Leytonstone after the show, and they would have coffee and banana sandwiches ready for me. I would drive back Sunday evening to my flat.

During these nomadic times when I was living in Sussex Gardens I made a very dear, new friend. I had always had a great love of ballet, and to begin with I became acquainted with, and then close to, Iris Law, Frederick Ashton's secretary, whom I had met through Wayne Sleep. Again I suppose she was one of my mother substitutes or surrogates; I used to sit with her and her friend Gwyneth in the staff house box at Covent Garden overlooking the stage, and then be taken back stage afterwards to meet the dancers. Once we went round and Rudolf Nureyev and Margot Fonteyn had just finished dancing, so Iris said, 'Come and meet them.'

We stood to the side while the audience screamed and applauded like mad; Rudolf and Margot would go out and bow, then come back and be pumped with drinks, take a glass of champagne, have a little chat with us, and go out again while cheering went on and flowers were thrown. This lasted for twenty minutes.

Nureyev, with his defection from Russia, had a glamour which eluded other dancers. Everything was so dramatic in his life, and with his talent, and looking as he did, he pushed everyone else aside. I saw Rudolf in action, and he had incredible charm, and my, wasn't he sexy when he put it over – man, woman, or dog! I had a brief fling with someone in Greece who had been one of his lovers. He told me, 'I learned all I knew about sex from Rudolf!'

When interviewed during the 1970s, I would claim that I had no personal life and for the most part this was true. Always in the background I had Mum and Dad to whom I was as ever deeply and constantly attached, and I had my passion for acting. Every day, all day, I aspired to become a great actor, but it always seemed beyond my reach.

My parents still went on their holidays, but without me now. I had been trying to persuade them to go abroad for years, but they would only go if I went with them. I was hardly relishing the idea: as much as I loved them both I expected to have an incredibly boring time. I dutifully took them away to Mallorca in the summer of 1967.

One day, when sunbathing, I had this absurd notion. I found two big copper penny coins and put them over my eyes and lay back in the sun. When I removed them an hour or so later they had become quite hot and I couldn't see anything. I panicked. Everything was black. I had gone blind. That's vanity for you! Dad prevailed on me to stay calm and some time later my sight came back.

Lying on the water's edge one day I thought I must be hallucinating when I saw Maggie Smith paddling in the shallows.

During the National Theatre years I had been quite close to Maggie. We shared little trysts together. I used to go at the weekends and stay in the house in Kensington where she lived with her playwright husband Beverley Cross: I would be sleeping up in the loft, and we had this covered-over living space where we listened to music together. We used to dance, and one very appropriate number was 'Up On the Roof'. She had a different room, but it was a sort of chaste flirtation. If I had been straight we would have gone to bed together, but she knew she was safe with me, and when Bob Stephens came along she fell in love with him.

I carried on gazing at this phantom Maggie in the water and then I stood up and looked again, and it really was Maggie.

'Maggie, what on earth are you doing here?'

'I came in that,' she said. She pointed out to sea where there was a cruise launch bobbing up and down at anchor.

She was staying with Robert Graves, and she invited me to join her at the weekend and meet Graves, whose Claudius I was to play ten years later. Mum and Dad didn't mind my short absence, so I was picked up and whisked off for a wonderful weekend. Ava Gardner was there, and so was Jeffrey Hunter, the actor who played Jesus in the 1960 film *King of Kings* – the first time we were shown Jesus's face on screen.

Graves was about seventy-five, a giant of a man, full of energy. His house was on the top of a cliff and he went swimming daily, hurtling himself into the water, and hurtling himself back up the rocks to his house.

I bought a house in Chelsham Road, Stockwell, but it soon became rather like a hotel. When I first bought the house, to help me with the mortgage I had two lodgers from the ballet company. I do not and cannot cook, and I relied on the house guests, who later on were often temporary lodgers from Australia, to do the cooking and washing up. Thankfully I had a constantly revolving coterie of male and female acting friends and I spent many a jolly evening with them and their friends. I was by no means a recluse, and that was the rent the lodgers paid. There was an actor, a trainee accountant, a former secretary to the Australian premier Harold Holt, who had drowned in 1967: all were delightful and eccentric companions.

I am very good at hoovering, emptying ashtrays and plumping up cushions. I like order and pattern. I used to say at the time that this was one reason I would be difficult to live with on a permanent basis. So heavily was I still under Mum and Dad's domestic influence that I had the net curtains and heavy drapes of home to cocoon me: Mum said Stockwell needed net curtains.

I still smoked very heavily – two packs a day or, to be more truthful, nearly three packs a day, and I was getting quite breathless. Fags were my prop, I would light up when answering the phone and I drank to lubricate my throat for the next ciggy. As for fitness, my preferred exercise was *thinking* about using my rowing machine.

Michael York wrote in his autobiography that although I shared the usual actor's insecurities (this was only too true) I was 'obviously' marked out for greatness. If this was the case, which I rather doubt, and never would feel it even if it were, so far so good. But when would it come? I could not wait for it to happen!

'As well as chain-smoking, a self-deprecation about his looks also made him go out of his way to avoid being photographed. Even later, when film acting inevitably embraced him, he would refuse to watch his performances at the rushes.'

This was true of all my performances on film and television, and still is. Maggie Smith and Sir insisted when we filmed *Othello* that I see the rushes of my scenes as Cassio. They would march me into the viewing room and plonk me down between them so I couldn't escape. I shut my eyes, although I had to listen.

I wrote to Michael on the subject of films (he was filming now with Franco Zeffirelli): 'What you've told me is very interesting. I think it is quite significant that Franco is not rehearsing you, but directing you on the spot, so preventing you from letting your theatre technique blur your photographic image. In other words *his* is the technique, *yours* the expression. As the medium is so individual, what the actor requires above all is the intangible "it", which, and I'm sure many others tell you, you've got.'

Movies are a director's toy, but movies make you rich. TV makes you known, but theatre is what it's really all about. At this juncture in my life I could see, increasingly, the way everything was going, namely that I could no longer make a name for myself solely in the theatre.

But did I actually have that intangible 'it'?

29

FROM KAISER TO EMPEROR

After filming *The Day of the Jackal* in 1971, I did a BBC classic serial called *Man of Straw*, which was a six-part adaptation of Heinrich Mann's famous novel. It satirised the obedient, authoritarian Kaiser-worship before the First World War. The protagonist, Dietrich Hessling, was my first big television lead. I was on screen for virtually all of the six episodes in a role which by turns was comic, bullying, ranting, vulnerable, and altogether a rather frightening embodiment of all that was most evil in German society. *Man of Straw* reminded us what happened before Hitler came to power, and how Germany was culturally disposed towards Nazism under the Kaiser.

The director was Herbert Wise. Herbert had been born in Vienna. He was sent out of Austria just before the war, when he was placed on a *Kindertransport* train, and settled in England, where as soon as he could he joined the war effort at the age of 16 by working in a factory, and then a lead refinery; he was always much older in looks than his years, and from the start he wanted to be a film director.

When the war was over he attended New Era Academy, a drama school started mainly for ex-servicemen. This led to his first acting in rep at Shrewsbury in Rattigan's *Flare Path*, in the part of the Polish flying officer who is given up for dead when failing to return from a bombing raid, and then, after being ditched in the English Channel, survives and miraculously turns up. Herbert managed to convince the management that his real passion was for directing. After directing every other show in weekly rep for 18 months at Hull he worked at Dundee, and here he came to the notice of the BBC, who in 1956 brought him to London.

Before they interviewed me for Dietrich, Herbie and the producer Martin Lissmore had already cast someone, but this other actor was uncertain he wanted to play this rather despicable worm. The image wasn't right. They were dithering. Out of the blue, Patricia McNaughton phoned and asked them if there was any work for me. I went along to see them, and they decided I would be just right (despicable? A worm?) and so I was cast as this quite awful main character. The other actor was correct: the image was not a happy one.

Here I was, decked out with white collar and huge handlebar moustaches, seducing and groping the local *fraüleins*, and ridiculously ranting and raving that everyone who did not love the Kaiser and extol the virtues of the Fatherland was scum. We rehearsed and filmed everything on set in the BBC studios in North Acton – at that time the Hollywood of West London.

The atmosphere was amazing. There were three rehearsal rooms and numerous studios. Everyone who was anyone in television would be in the canteen. Christopher Biggins was cast as my jolly Hun drinking companion. One Sunday rehearsal, before they shot the big scene where the brotherhood is drinking, they brought on real booze for the twenty actors sitting around toasting each other.

Everyone got paralytic, so when subsequently they trained the cameras on us we knew what it was like and could replicate stone cold the heavy drinking session. Long scenes were filmed in one take, so this one turned out particularly authentic. Christopher, whom when drunk I meet in the *Herrens* loo (in the serial, I hasten to add!), had to take off his real glasses, and put on prop glasses, but he forgot them and had to brave it out in his Specsavers.

My part was a great gift for comic invention, and for all the varieties of lust, power, manipulation and vulnerability anyone could muster. Dietrich is always making a fool of himself, and then always recovering his petty Teutonic pride and self-regard, so as well as being despicable and rebarbative, I could laugh and smile, look innocent and play the clown. Herbie, having acted and worked so long in rep, as well as knowing from first hand Teutonic barbarism, was fantastic at supporting me and bringing out the many shades of character. Nobody could have been better and more brilliant in initiating me at such depth into the world of film and television, as well as dealing with this particular subject.

In 1975, Martin Lissmore, the producer of *Man of Straw*, asked Herbie if he would be interested in directing *I, Claudius*, which the BBC hoped to film. Jack Pullman had been asked to write the whole adaptation; however, the American company, ironically called London Films, the old Alexander Korda stable, had a legal claim on the Robert Graves book, so that project was cancelled.

Nothing was heard until a year later when Martin phoned Herbie and told him that *I, Claudius* was definitely on, and meanwhile Pullman, who had been contracted at the earlier time, had written ten of the thirteen scripts, all of these by a curious coincidence in the house he owned at the time, which I bought in 1983 and where I now live.

London Films had to approve the casting. Originally they wanted two people, one to play the young Claudius and one to play the old one. Charlton Heston was approached for the older one, and so was, at the other end of the scale, Ronnie Barker, a great comic stammerer. Both said no. They decided to try and find an actor to tackle both: Alec Guinness was another idea, whom they thought could do the ageing, but they couldn't get him.

The BBC went through the whole casting directory before they thought about me. I became quite paranoid when I heard about this later.

'What about Derek? He aged from seventeen to fifty in *Man of Straw*. Let's ask him,' suggested Herbie and Martin.

The moguls of television and film drama move in mysterious ways. The men at London Films said, 'Derek who?' I was never the star they sought.

To sell me to the Americans they paraded me out to dinner at a restaurant in Shepherds Bush and I turned on the charm. They were impressed enough to say, 'OK, we'll go along with that.'

But before rehearsals started Herbie saw another actor on stage and said, 'That's my Claudius,' and was going to change me for him.

The show in question was *The Norman Conquests*, the actor Michael Gambon, I found out later, but Herbie says the gossip wasn't true that I was nearly taken off it, just malicious. It stayed with me for years until I had sorted it out with Herbie.

We had three months to prepare. When we congregated we rushed to our Livy and Suetonius for historical exactitude, but Herbie warned, 'Don't do that, we're not doing Roman history, we're doing Graves's novels. Do no more than look into them if you want to find out what's happening.'

The BBC showed me the documentary about the unfinished Joseph von Sternberg's film of *I, Claudius* with Charles Laughton, a fascinating piece with extracts of scenes and fragments that were actually shot, a very Hollywood version with a hundred vestal virgins! They wanted me to see it to exorcise the ghost of the great man, and to make sure I did something entirely different.

It was difficult for us to work out how to play these first-century figures. The first four episodes mainly concerned Livia and her ambition as an imperial mother to propel her son,

Tiberius, played by George Baker, onto the Emperor's throne, using a variety of advancement techniques, none of which involve studying for civil service exams. It was very slow burn as far as I was concerned, for I mostly topped and tailed each episode and I was gagging for Claudius to come into his own.

We were very much at sea with the first episode, as there was so much information and so many complex character back-stories to convey. A case in point was Caligula, played by John Hurt: he was supposed to be Livia's great-grandson, while Siân Phillips was only three years older than John.

But this was historical drama, not documentary. At first in rehearsals we just didn't gel with the personages and we feared it would be a disaster, until Carol Weissmann, Herbie's assistant, pointed out, 'It's a *Jewish* soap.'

At last we began to hit the right note, but it was still difficult for the audience to cotton on to all the names, and it was even more difficult when they ran the first two episodes together. For both actors and audience the hardest thing was getting to know that imperial family, as so many different members came into view, and some didn't last very long because Livia bumped them off. As soon as you grasped who someone was, you would find by the next episode that he or she had been murdered.

I was the stammering, twitching, limping, over-the-top imperial chronicler who constantly avoids death, and who in the end, as luck would have it (Claudius calls his luck 'fool's luck'), becomes Emperor. Playing Claudius as an old man I wore an uncomfortable prosthetic mask and, throughout, a false nose, so the luck came at a price.

First they made a cast of my face, covering my whole head in plaster of Paris, with two straws stuck up my nose to breathe through, a notebook and pen in my hand to record my agony for forty minutes until it set. It was claustrophobic, just like being buried alive. From the cast they made a mask of innumerable rubber strips placed next to one another and then glued on, then blended.

I had to arrive at the studio at 4 a.m. for this, and it took six hours to put on. To take it off was very difficult, too. They had to use spirit remover and acetate, and it broke blood vessels, so once I got the rubber off I would be bleeding. We found the best way was for me to soak in a hot bath filled with Badedas and put my head under using a snorkel. Then if I was lucky I could lift off the face in one piece.

It brought back the visit to the Harley Street specialist years before, while Mum and Dad waited outside, and the 'Oh, I've got to cover it up!' feeling. But, because they had to soak me first in a bath, this was worse.

Claudius was a *stammerer*, not a stutterer, as I had to make clear so many times. I was very lucky in that Richard Cottrell, one of my great chums at Cambridge, had a stammer that exactly fitted the bill, and so I copied him. It had been extraordinary that Richard, who played many roles, never stammered on stage. The assistant set designer, who was always around, also had a pronounced stammer; I listened to him, pinned him to the wall, and cried, 'Talk to me, talk to me!' Much later one old lady, when she saw me stammer as Turing in *Breaking the Code*, remembered me as Claudius, and commented that it was 'lovely to see Derek has a part which accommodates his disability'!

The twitch was more hazardous – the twitch was a good third of the performance. In one early scene Claudius visits the oracular Sybil to discover what the future might hold; how to address the Sybil was the question, and the answer we decided was to raise my arms in supplication, bow my head, and twitch! Doing this I severely cricked my neck and had to wear one of those white-collar supports which I took off when the camera rolled. But I couldn't disguise the pain in my eyes.

Graves came to the filming and he loved it so much that when it was time for him to leave he insisted, 'No, I'm staying here.'

By now he was mentally on the decline and had Alzheimer's, but he looked amazing because of that great mane of white hair and his proud, craggy face. When he came out to lunch with us he was taciturn and just sat there. Then he suddenly came out with, 'I've always had a great deal of trouble with Scots!'

'Why?' I asked.

'It's probably my age. You do know I'm 125?'

Beryl, his wife, butted in: 'Don't be stupid. You said you were only 100 this morning.' She defused it.

Graves's only comment on the acting was on George Baker, who was very tall. 'You're the right height for Tiberius,' he said.

It was spooky: the make-up was applied for the old Claudius, the latex wrinkles and jowls, then the wig – and I found Graves was staring back at me from the mirror, especially before the grey hair was trimmed. His Claudius was a version of himself, I am sure, so my Claudius tried to be more than a bit like Robert Graves. At the same time he was the best ever of my veils. Some people held that there was a curse on Claudius, but when this question of a curse was put to Graves he was insistent that there was absolutely none. A previous dramatisation by John Mortimer, with David Warner, had been jinxed, 'because Claudius did not want it,' Graves declared at the time.

The diabolical Livia was not only an austere character and decidedly on the cold side, but also it was appallingly difficult for Siân to make her seem human. 'They say a snake bit her once and died,' says Tiberius – and this describes Livia. To justify to herself how evil Livia actually was, Siân understandably wanted to psychologise it, to find a reason. Herbie in the end had to tell her she was inexplicably evil, a Cruella de Vil, and it was her nature to manipulate everyone. It did the trick and she was brilliant.

Brian Blessed as the Emperor Augustus could sometimes be a bit mutinous, but then Brian is always gloriously mutinous. When the others, excluding me, were dispatched to a viewing room to see what we had shot so far, time after time they came back to the rehearsal room looking doubtful and saying to each other,

'Oh dear, this looks really strange. I really wonder if this is going to do right.' Peter O'Toole, Siân's husband, popped in to see one early showing, and told us the critics were going to hate it but that the public would love it, which, with critics hating it and the public falling over backwards to see it, would have been right after his own heart! Thankfully, though, the critics loved it, too.

The main criticism Herbie had to give me was that I mustn't let my own personality colour what I was doing, and that I tended if I relaxed to become lazy and play from myself, rather than reach out and get the character. This was good advice. Apart from my neck I slipped a disc in the base of my spine. It was painful, but all part of the character. Two months later I went and did it yet again. One of the legacies Claudius left me was a permanently weak neck, and when I become over-tired or over het-up I get neck-ache.

Herbie's approach was to see the whole story as if looking through the keyhole, and he used the camera as an actor participating in the drama, so he made the action come to the camera, rather than have the camera commenting on the action. Directing for television is immensely complicated, with so many different functions and crafts involved, but as a director he never lost a vision of the whole work, and always had an innate eye for a good shot. Like all good directors he saw himself primarily as a facilitator, having to make decisions quickly on his feet.

All 615 minutes were recorded in the studio without a single outside shot. The result was that, buoyed up by Tim Harvey's universally hailed sets, we actors went for it in an electrifying, theatrical way. Although this was television, it was a stage performance by a closely knit and integrated company, who relished and enjoyed to the hilt Jack Pullman's bracing and mordant scripts.

If it had been made now it would all have to be filmed rather than recorded, on locations where the light was Mediterranean, or thought to be, and the games and the other great set pieces could be realistically staged with hundreds of extras, all at the expense of dialogue and character: in other words at the expense of intelligence and quality. The legato structure, which even Herbie admits to having been nervous about at the deliberation of the first episodes, would be right out. So, too, would any actor like me, who was nowhere near starry enough to be entrusted with such a gigantic role.

Yet I was given this wonderful part, and, scoring a number of firsts, it became a classic from the start. Herbie was probably the first director who demanded that he do it all himself, and we had the same studio camera crew throughout a long serial. Much of the craft was executed on the wing. Barbara Kronig designed the costumes – 'Just keep me in touch,' was all Herbie said to her; and on the production side everyone was pushing the boundaries. Pam Meager's make-up used prosthetics in a completely revolutionary way. The six hours for my age-old face set a record. Everyone was under severe financial constraint and never moaned.

'The costume designers and I each gave back £1,000 of our budget at the end because we were under such pressure,' Pam said. 'The Romans weren't the only ones who got away with murder.' At this time there were BBC department heads who were not just deviously jockeying for power and a bigger slice of the budget, but who led and bolstered the craft services.

None of us ever imagined *I, Claudius* would become such a cult phenomenon. Roman history? Thirteen parts? Patrick Stewart, who gave an amazing performance as the evil fixer Sejanus, told me later how *Claudius* is on cable regularly in the United States, where it has a huge cult following, so that even today he is more easily identified as Sejanus than as *Star Trek*'s Captain Picard.

30

'HAMLET, PLAYED BY DEREK
"I, CLAUDIUS" JACOBI'

Claudius opened many doors. Every actor in the course of his career longs for one part that becomes his. Some actors have more than one in the course of their career, some actors don't get any of those kinds of parts. For me, Claudius was that part. When asked when the supposed jinx would operate as it had in the past, Robert Graves said, 'I've always been very good to Claudius and he's always been very good to me, and he knows I need money.' I can echo this. Within two years I was on Broadway.

Even so, *Claudius* did take its toll. At our cast party at the end of shooting one of the extras had a heart attack on the dance floor and died. Two years after we finished, our brilliant producer Martin, aged only twenty-eight, was tragically killed in a car crash. A year after this Jack Pullman fell off the bed upstairs with a heart attack and died in this very house where I am describing this.

By now Herbie was ringing up, saying, 'It's you or me next, Derek ...' It didn't happen, but for a time it did seem the jinx was working. Later on I hosted a.programme for PBS in America when they were intent on finding out and celebrating the most popular English series with their viewers. They held a poll, and because they were pretty sure *Claudius* would easily win they asked me to be in New York to announce the result. But we only came second! *Upstairs, Downstairs* won the poll.

Once again a portrayal of the English class system triumphed. Roll on *Downton Abbey*!

When in 1996 the BBC threw a party to celebrate the twentieth anniversary of the first transmission of *I, Claudius*, billed as 'an orgy of reminiscence', they showed us a digest of the show made with clips, which we all found not only amusing but absolutely amazing, to see how it stood up after all these years. *I, Claudius* made me into a property, especially in America where rows even erupted between well-known personalities if one of them was going to miss the next episode. When it first came out in Sweden it emptied streets. I had been a classical actor and worked hard for sixteen years before *Claudius*. And now I was known to a vast audience who had never heard of me. I used to get letters asking if I'd ever acted before.

Peter Hall had not, however, asked me to join and play in his new regime at the National Theatre, and possibly at least partly because of this – and because the Cambridge bond of fraternal rivalry still held very strong – Toby Robertson, with whom I had done several productions for his Prospect Company at the Old Vic, had posed the question even before *Claudius* was filmed. 'Would you like to play Hamlet?'

By 1977 we felt it was time for me to take up the suggestion. At first I felt great trepidation. Of course I was thrilled and excited at the idea, for while I had played Hamlet twice already this had been once as a schoolboy and once as a student. Everyone who aspires to be a classical actor has Hamlet somewhere inside. It has become a sort of examination, a hoop to jump through. You can do all sorts of classical parts, but this one is the test. People say, 'Yes, but what was his Hamlet like?' The character is such that he can be played more than once by the same actor, because there is no end to him. You keep changing all the time, too, and you find a different rhythm for each change and development. So I was to embark on Hamlet again, and I was on the threshold of forty, perhaps the best age for the most rounded portrayal.

Tim West, a tough, gruff heavyweight with excellent sponta-
neity and range of effects, was cast as Claudius, and Barbara
Jefford as Gertrude. There could not have been a better balanced
trio of principals. For me the problem was going to be one of
pacing and energy. Hamlet was now to be played, as the posters
billed it, by 'Derek "*I, Claudius*" Jacobi.

———◦◦◦———

Hamlet is on stage for nearly three hours, and has 1,100 lines to
deliver. Unless you learn to pace it correctly, it is the most
knackering show ever, as I had witnessed only too painfully
before at the National playing Laertes to O'Toole's Hamlet. I
had to find out how much energy I needed to use in each particular scene, so that I did not exhaust myself too soon. Health
is terribly important, too. I had to be very fit. I grew my own
hair long, and a beard and moustache. The part is so active that
using a wig would become impossibly sweaty and hot.

I was terribly worried about my return to the stage, even
after so short a time. All through rehearsals I had an unspecified
throat infection which baffled the doctors. Although Toby had
been up at Cambridge he had no overall directorial mission to
fulfil, nor was he an intellectual wanting to impose any reading
or specific interpretation on the part and play. He was not out
to create a style, or prove that Shakespeare was our political
contemporary. He looked more to Shakespeare's universal and
timeless appeal. As such, he was perhaps much more in the
Dadie Rylands tradition of letting Shakespeare speak for himself, in fact – if I dare say it – content to let the director take a
back seat and leave it up to the actors and the play.

For Toby, the rehearsal and run-throughs reached a certain
point, and he confessed, 'I feel it belongs to the actors now.
There are things which will never be quite as I want or would
like them. But you have to work with your actors and especially with your Hamlet. This Hamlet is perhaps a more

187

rational man than I saw originally, but Derek has defined his own interpretation.'

Almost at the same moment, and this was now the day of the opening performance in Oxford, I was saying exactly the same thing: 'In the end you can only say that's how *I* play Hamlet – although Toby brought more aggression into my performance than might otherwise have been there.'

Even an hour before the curtain went up that fateful evening we were still practising the big fight, and had been doing this daily for a month. The fight lasted over two minutes and in all there were seventy-two moves, with cup-hilt rapier and dagger – 'one each for lunge and answering parry' had been written down in the ballet-like notation with the tiny drawings and the name of each position written beneath.

Apart from my fight, I had been in my dressing room two hours before curtain-up, since 5.30 p.m. I hadn't slept for two nights and that afternoon there had been a shatteringly loud drill digging up the tarmac outside the Randolph Hotel. I spent the sleepless nights with the show going round and round in my head – entrances, exits, cuts. I had stopped being able to eat. Both Toby and I showed the strain in the form of imaginary ailments and mysterious pains. My body was saying it didn't want to do it. I was living on Dextrasol and I was desperately tired.

How am I going to get through it? a voice was crying inside. But at the same time there was another, more hopeful voice saying, *There must be some way of doing it without flogging myself to death, and I've got to find it.* And yet, if I didn't go flat out, I wouldn't be giving 100 per cent of my energy. My throat was still hurting from the infection, so I had glasses of water set out for me at strategic places in the wings.

'Five minutes please,' came the sepulchral voice of the dressing-room loudspeaker, and behind it now I could hear the subdued roar of the many-headed beast waiting for us out there in the dark!

Particularly at this moment everyone feels so naked and vulnerable, so superstition runs deep. We spread charms out on our dressing-room tables. Tim had a collection of glass animals set up in front of him; Barbara had a special stone, a red chestnut colour. On my table I had marshalled my make-up pots and sticks and liners like toy soldiers on a parade ground, with telegrams and good-luck cards stuck behind in impeccable order. I always set up a ritual for that first performance which I stick to. If on my first journey to the stage I hold onto a handrail I repeat this for all performances; if I trip on the steps going down, then I have to trip each time I go on. These and similar rituals I've kept to throughout my career.

'Beginners please.' Then the distant auditorium voice. 'Ladies and gentlemen, will you kindly take your seats. The curtain will rise in one minute ...'

'Standby, please,' Marje the stage manager quietly utters in her supercool voice into the prompt corner microphone, about to take down the house lights. And then I have to get out there on stage and somehow find the energy, at least that I know.

Then Doctor Theatre takes over.

I have found that the first night is the most uptight, nervous and unrepresentative performance that I'll ever give. When I've worked more into the play with audiences I'll know more about it. The critics never see those performances. It's so unfair – as judgements are often made prematurely based on first-night performances. Even without reading them I can get to know what the critics have said very quickly, I get the drift, I read it in people's faces. I can judge by the tone of their voice, if they don't tell me themselves, that the critics are good, or the critics are bad. Even friends will ring up and say, 'Oh, marvellous, congratulations on the reviews. Whatever you do, don't read *The Times*!'

It was so evident that Toby's production and all the cast had become very well regarded, and we went on to give hundreds of performances. But it is the actor who knows when it is or isn't working, or when it needs work on a particular area. Good actors – no, not 'good', that's a bad word: *proper* actors, the *real* actors, know whether it's working or not. Critics, on the other hand, most often attend a very special and highly charged performance which, however, is not necessarily indicative of the true strengths of a theatrical production.

———

I was now playing *Hamlet* for the third time and I thought I'd better try and give up smoking, so I went to see a hypnotist who promised that for three sessions at £25 a go he could cure me. At the first session he made me lie down on a couch. I closed my eyes and as he began his soothing words of persuasion I pretended I was going into a trance, although I wasn't.

'You do not smoke, you must not smoke!' he repeated sonorously in a mantra for about half an hour, then he said, 'Wake up,' so I duly opened my eyes, not having at all been in a trance.

That evening I went along to a Greet and Meet party at the Old Vic for the new show, and while everyone smoked I made an effort and didn't light up. The next session the hypnotist did exactly the same as at the first session, except it was speeded up, and a second time I didn't go into a trance, but pretended until he told me to wake up.

During the third session he came over to where I lay and sat next to me, pressing nerves in my shoulders and down the back of my neck and going through the whole rigmarole again while once more I faked being in a trance and complied with his instructions. However, I decided to come clean and at this session I said, 'I have to confess, I fooled you, because I've never been asleep.'

'Look into my eyes,' he said, and paused for five seconds while I did this. 'Have you heard the phrase double bluff? I knew exactly what you were thinking all along, and all the time you thought you were awake and fooling me I was controlling you, and you were in a trance. The bottom line is, have you stopped smoking?'

Well, I had stopped smoking straight away, so I did believe he was controlling me. Since then I have not smoked. His sessions had no after-effects, and I suffered no withdrawal symptoms.

31

ENTER RICHARD II

At the start of the last week of the *Hamlet* run at the Old Vic someone sent round to the stage door two dozen red roses and no card of explanation, just a 'Thank you for your performance'. We were about to set off on the Prospect tour and the first port of call was Amman in Jordan.

After the show in those days I would always go for a drink at the local pub next door on the Waterloo Road, and here I 'clocked' this young man, who was perhaps a student, little older than a boy. I would see him there, and I must have seen him at least a couple of times. We reached the last night of *Hamlet*, the Saturday night, and this time I saw him standing up at the bar, looking over towards me. Then eventually a group of us had formed in the corner, and the young man came and joined it.

He introduced himself. He was perhaps aged twenty-one or twenty-two, I would have said, no more than that, and his name was Richard – Richard Clifford, a name straight out of the *dramatis personae* of a Shakespeare history play.

'Are you connected with the theatre?' I asked him.

'I've just finished drama school, and I'm working at the bar – front of house,' he said, 'so I've seen your performance many times ...' He then asked, 'Did you like the flowers?'

'What flowers?' I said.

'Didn't you get some flowers I sent?'

'Oh God, yes ... on Monday I got these fantastic roses. And I thought it was my birthday! – it's not far off. So it was you who sent them!'

It was indeed Richard who had sent them. So now this ended up with me driving him back to his flat in Olympia, where I went in for a cup of coffee. We chatted, and then it was getting late so I said: 'Look, I must leave you. Tomorrow morning I fly off to Amman. There's a taxi coming at eight o'clock to pick me up, and bring me to the airport.'

We exchanged numbers and addresses, and that was about it. I said goodbye, and that I would be in touch when I returned from the Prospect tour. And so I went home.

In Stockwell I had a lodger, a former actor; he was in the process of taking holy orders, and he had the front bedroom on the first floor. Next morning I rose at 6.30 and prepared myself for the journey; I had all my luggage packed in the inner sitting room ready to load into the taxi, and be off; but then a big surprise. Richard had been there since six, and was sitting there waiting for me. He had brought along a bottle of champagne and a red rose.

I was quite put out and asked, 'How on earth did you get in?'

'Your lodger opened the door as he heard me coming up the steps just when he was going out.'

I felt pretty fussed. 'Look, my taxi will be here in fifteen minutes. I don't drink champagne, so it'll be wasted on me, but thank you for coming.'

And that was that. If I had missed the flight to Amman, after our last performance at the Old Vic, the penalty would have been dismissal, for there was not another flight for four days.

I left, and Richard went on to a friend in Fulham where he continued drinking, and had a few lines of cocaine. Well, I had to face it, I had already heard he was a Hooray Henry who threw bread rolls at people, while his friends had double-barrelled names – they were almost royal; quite the opposite of me.

———

Two more plays had been added to the Prospect repertoire from March to July as we began a strenuous foreign tour, feeling the effects of cholera and typhoid injections. In Amman I gave in instantly to the first temptation, and had an affair with some-one who was sent to interview me, an astoundingly good-looking young man who came on so strong I could hardly resist. By now, in my thirty-ninth year, I was just beginning to think, 'Well, after all these quiet years forty must be the age. It's all happening!'

Traditionally actors are 'players away' when on tour (not that I had anyone at home from whom I could 'play away'). On the previous Prospect tour, when we were out in Australia, I had a tortured, abortive scene with a stage manager, with whom I had fallen madly in love. I was playing Chekhov's Ivanov, which Toby considered to be one of my very best parts, and Bucking-ham in *Richard III*, with Richard Briers compelling and superbly sinister in the title role.

Dickie Briers and I became boon companions, and shared digs everywhere we went. I was deeply in love with this Aussie SM, who was leading me a merry dance, while Dickie was in the throes of a great passion: he'd left his wife for an actress. His love life, like mine, wasn't going well, so after the show we found a restaurant, had a meal and told each other our heart-breaks while sinking deep into our cups, until we became very maudlin. I would do the maudlin drunk, but Dickie would get a bit out of hand. While I would just get silly, he became just a tad aggressive – in language, not at all towards me – but he was a good and wonderful friend, both then and after.

I had slipped unawares into this affair with the Aussie boy, which for once was far from platonic, but then I discovered there was someone else in the company with whom he was also carrying on an affair, and this was so incestuous it became ridiculous. There had been no one else in my life, and he was all there was on offer.

But now in Amman there was Richard, this gorgeous interviewer with whom I was having a rapturous fling, and lo and behold one night it turned to farce. He had borrowed his father's car — it was parked outside the hotel — and I was in bed with him when his father came into the hotel hunting for his son. Susanne Bertish, another girl from the company, was sleeping on the same corridor.

'Christ, it's my father!' Richard exclaimed when his father found my room and banged on the door. He ran into the bathroom just as I opened the door to his father. He stayed there while I said to his father, 'I believe he's along the corridor!' pointing towards Susanne's room.

She rose to the occasion, came to the door and covered beautifully, hinting Richard was with her — and no more needed to be said. So, for the father who tactfully withdrew, hetero observance and decorum were preserved. It was Feydeau with a gay twist!

───

Amman, Dubrovnik, Cairo, Istanbul may all sound wildly romantic, but the reality was make-up running and sweat pouring from under costumes weighing 20 pounds or more in heat reaching 90 degrees even at night; then, if this was not enough, there was gastro-enteritis. The British Council representative gave us tips on how to behave prudently, and suggested we remove Marks & Spencer labels from both male and female underwear before entering an Arab country.

In Amman we played before two kings, King Hussein of Jordan and his guest King Constantine of Greece in the Palace of Culture, a basketball stadium seating 6,000. There were so many bodyguards waving sub-machine guns clogging up the wings that we had to push them aside in order to make an entrance.

At Ljubljana Airport, owing to industrial action, our skips with wigs, swords and armour failed to arrive, so the battle scenes and duels were fought unwigged and unarmed. We had another problem doing *Hamlet* at Lovrejenic Castle. Where should we put John Turner as the Ghost when he appears on the Elsinore battlements? With extraordinary temerity John opted to stand on the very top of the keep, on the wall itself, unprotected, 70 feet above our heads. Picked out by a single light, he was a truly unearthly Ghost, and looked as if he were standing in the sky.

In Dubrovnik we played *Antony and Cleopatra* against the exotic backdrop of the Ducal or Doge's Palace. This was at the end of one thoroughfare, where the café next door mercifully agreed to close for the performance, but hundreds of house martins roosting on the palace pillars suddenly saw the stage become floodlit, so their body clocks indicated it was dawn. They started up screeching and twittering, and never stopped, deafening our voices so nobody could hear a word.

In Split we played in Diocletian's Palace. Every actor exiting stage left had to thread his way down steps through a narrow public alleyway into a side street, a maze, to come back on stage right. Andrew Sear, wearing a bulky robe and carrying his sword, found a very fat Yugoslav blocking his route, and he had to shout 'Back off!' But the man would not budge, claiming he had the right of way. Andrew drew his sword, and the man turned and fled screaming.

As for Cairo, when I now had the Hamlet photo on my passport, we played only a hundred yards from the Sphinx. Nearby, a nightclub gushed forth endless Arab music, while from under the stage columns of half-inch ants were on the march, crawling into and invading our cloaks and costumes. There was no room for subtlety and all I could hope for was audibility and knowing where to get on and off. Muezzins punctuated the performance at the Rumelar Hissar Castle in Istanbul, providing a strange multicultural infusion into Elsinore. When I spoke Hamlet's final line, 'The rest is silence,' it was met by the hooting of ferries and barges on the Bosporus below.

Back at the Old Vic to play more performances of *Hamlet*, they were rehearsing *The Gingerbread Man*, in which Richard Clifford was acting as well as working as an assistant stage manager. So we met up again, and from then on the romance flowered. It was extraordinary when I think he was only twenty-two, but I felt taken over because it was what he wanted, and he was going to make it happen. It was the first time in my life someone was taking the lead with me.

I had thought about him while I was away on tour, but never 'Let's share, let's be together.' It was not on my horizon to find someone to settle down with. It was never what I was after. I never thought there was going to be a Mr Right, and I am going to be with him for the rest of my life. I did not know any long-term gay couples: of course, I knew of Dirk Bogarde and his partner, and Terrence Rattigan's long-term lover, but I had reached the age when I thought, 'It just ain't going to happen to me. There is maybe going to be a series of close relationships, but not one that rules out all others.'

Being older than Richard didn't mean I felt responsible: quite the reverse, for it was I who was being asked to commit. It was so unusual for me; for once in my life I was the one who was being chased, an unexpected luxury. I was the older man pursued by a twenty-two-year-old. This was not long before my fortieth birthday and I cannot pretend I was not set in my ways, for I had ended up thinking only of myself, dealing with myself and my domestic life, and up till this moment I had never shared, never been close to anyone, never committed.

Richard was born in Assam, India, where his father was a tea-planter; at the age of six and a half they sent him back to Seafield prep school; later his parents returned to England, where he boarded at Canford public school in Dorset. At this time his mother, having met another man, left his father and moved back to India to Darjeeling. He went on to study acting at the Webber-Douglas School in Kensington.

Our backgrounds were very different: I, a day-boy, a grammar-school boy, very cosseted and loved by my parents; he, a boarder who had to make decisions for himself, or had the decisions made for him by his parents – not always in harmony either with him or each other. In his teens his parents divorced, which had a shattering effect on him, so while he had mastered the art of what was expected of him, by fourteen or fifteen he failed all his exams, and then went so much off the rails he grew rebellious; because of an incident involving cannabis he was expelled from Canford in his final, second A-level year.

The headmaster relented and allowed him to return to study and take his exams, because he was considered to be – or excused for being – from an 'unstable background', and therefore should be given another chance. Richard felt that had he not wanted to become an actor, he would have drifted into the world of drugs, although with his phobia of needles he believes he never could have become a heroin addict.

In December of that year, 1977, with the actor-turned-priest who had been my lodger leaving the Stockwell house, Richard moved in with me, and we lived together from then on. I was increasingly well known from I, Claudius, especially abroad. One bizarre result was when a Dutch magazine phoned my agent and offered me £250 for an interview. The interviewer, an attractive young woman and her girlfriend, spent a whole day in London with me, and during this, having met Richard, made hints about my personal life.

Later the Dutch pair had dinner with Richard, my agent and me. Just before the end, in a throwaway manner, the journalist

stitched me up, asking, 'Oh, by the way, are you a homosexual?' Looking pointedly at the pair of them I skirted round
it in my answer. When the article appeared it carried a huge
banner headline with a picture: 'I asked I, Claudius "Are you
a homosexual?"' I couldn't complain as I'd taken their money,
but it was uncomfortable.

Richard joined the Prospect Company, playing Fortinbras in
a further revival of *Hamlet*, and as we went abroad on tour there
would be accommodation problems, because we would not
cohabit in the hotels. For a young man at the beginning of his
career starting up with the star of the show, one could imagine
the combination would be pretty lethal. I would be allocated
a suite, while Richard was staying in a room down the end of
the corridor or on a camp bed.

It was not easy, this discrepancy in status, and neither of us
dealt very well with it. I couldn't help but think that I was the
star of the show. It was difficult, and made more difficult by my
not realising what I was doing to him, my insensitivity to what
he was going through. In Sydney one morning Toby Robertson
came up to me very fussed and upset, and asked, 'What on
earth's the matter with Richard? He's trashed his room.' So he
had – he had done the full rock star bit, because he was so pissed
off at the way he was being offered a put-up camp bed in the
corner of this beautiful suite.

32

A MARRIAGE PROPOSAL

Prospect was peripatetic, with no home of its own, except for the intermittent and much-contested Old Vic, which is possibly one reason why Toby Robertson has been so undervalued for the huge contribution he made to the theatre during these years.

The whole Danish royal family attended the opening night of *Hamlet* in Kronbörg Castle, a building of springing spires, of gables and steeply pitched roofs of weathered copper. Toby decided to put back the famous speech 'How all occasions do inform against me'. I had only had three hours to relearn it. The wind howled, and the rain poured down so mightily I had to shout all the way through: possibly appropriate for the weather, but hardly for the ruminative 'To be or not to be'. Then it rained more heavily.

The audience had been issued with Cellophane covers to put on when the rain started, and the signal to abandon the performance would be given when the Danish royal family put on their hats. First the audience, making an incredible noise, put on their Cellophane covers which made them look like rows of boiler chickens, then the royal family put their hats on and we stopped. They said they would come back again another night, so, as in *Edward II* at Cambridge, history repeated itself. They kept to their word, while the Queen Mother came several times, and passed through the dressing rooms to arrive at her seat: she became a sort of mascot for us.

My Danish knighthood, first class, Order of the Dannebrog, was awarded during a celebration in Tivoli Gardens, Copenhagen, for Queen Margrethe II's fiftieth birthday held by the two crown princes. It came as a complete surprise, for a number of favoured artists had been invited to perform. They insisted that I recite 'To be or not to be', and I had to do it as a 'turn', which I found embarrassing. The Queen visited me in the dressing rooms afterwards and asked me, face to face, just like that, if I would like a Danish knighthood, and if so she would confer this on me. I was utterly shocked, although I knew the production of *Hamlet* had been a hit with the royal family. I formally received the honour later through the Danish Embassy in London.

The final week of this tour, when we were now at the Dassos Theatre in Thessalonica, we began playing but again the rain so bucketed down we had to stop, and then had to cancel the rest of the performance for wardrobe to keep the costumes dry for Bradford the following week. I sat down with some of the cast to eat dinner at a restaurant nearby, as the disappointed audience trooped by on their way out: this was not the spectacle they had come to see.

More trials came in Russia on another Prospect tour when we were hauled over the coals by the British ambassador because the company was misbehaving. At this time the Panovs, a pair of famous ballet dancers who were well-known dissidents, were in the news, but still living in Leningrad, where we were playing, although they later defected to the West. Someone in the company had made contact with them, and they invited us to their apartment for an after-show party. The Soviet authorities refused to allow transport to take us, so we had to walk there in crocodile, followed at a walking pace by KGB agents.

We arrived at the Panovs' flat, carrying the drink we had brought while they were providing the food; we had been there a few minutes when the KGB knocked on the door. They took

Valerie, the husband, into the kitchen, grilled and verbally threatened him for about an hour, after which he came back and joined the party, looking a bit white about the gills. He wouldn't talk about it.

<hr />

After this party we started to be punished as a company. The coach to take us to the theatre would be late. There would be no programmes on sale at the theatre. After the performance, when we got back to the hotel, we found the kitchen closed and there was no food. Suddenly, when I went up to my room to wash, the soap had gone: it was that petty.

The old-fashioned lift stopped at every floor, except the thirteenth, where it would never stop. So we naturally rebellious actors pressed the button or asked for floor thirteen, knowing it wouldn't stop, but curious about what went on there. One night Ben Cross, one of the actors, was a bit drunk, and instead of using the lift he walked up the flights of stairs and when he got to level thirteen, in the state he was in, he had to have a look around.

At about two o'clock a phone call woke Toby: the heavily accented caller said, 'We would like you to come and collect your cast member!' On the thirteenth floor 'they' (whoever 'they' were) had seized Ben and had beaten him black and blue: he had a broken lip and a black eye. Next day the British Ambassador called us in: Toby, me as leading actor, and the Leningrad head of the British Council, under whose auspices we were there, and he gave us a roasting.

'You know you mustn't behave like this. You're in a goldfish bowl. Everything you do, everything you say, is noted. And don't think that everyone here wants you to be here. You have to behave yourself as a company, and it is no good coming into a reception saying, "If I want to say fuck I'm going to say fuck! Fuck the Soviet Union!"' Some of the younger members of the company were doing just that. From then on we had to mind our Ps and Qs, but even so our ultimate slight or punishment came the day we left Leningrad.

There was a bus waiting outside the hotel to take us to the airport. The Panovs came to the hotel to say goodbye, but they were not allowed in, not even to stand at the foot of the steps in front of the hotel. There was a little park opposite: the Panovs were told to wait at the other end of this park, that was the nearest they could approach. So we, the company, descended the steps, again in crocodile, walked through the park to the other side, met the Panovs, said goodbye, came back along the path, and boarded the bus.

When we arrived at the airport to fly to Cologne there was no plane. They made us wait six hours. Later we were told our bus driver, who had patiently attended while we said goodbye to the Panovs, copped it: although it was nothing to do with him he was punished, for his job was to keep us on schedule. As our punishment the plane had been deliberately delayed.

We had two interpreters with us on every journey or outing, two lovely girls who were clearly fully paid-up CP members. Marina was the name of one – a committed Party girl – and when at long last we were about to board the plane she came over to say goodbye. I shook hands with her and said, 'Thank you so much.'

'Don't say anything!' she replied and palmed me a little amber necklace, which she didn't want anyone to see she was giving me. When at last we arrived in Cologne and left the plane it was extraordinary, for we felt like kissing the ground in gratitude like Pope John Paul: we were reaching civilisation again! It was a weird experience.

In my pigeonhole in the hotel very early on during the Elsinore run of *Hamlet*, I found a letter from Timothy West. It just stated,

'There's a lady I have met called Cynthia Wood. She is a fan, she was an *I, Claudius* fan, and she's coming to see you and would like to say hello. When she gets in touch – and she's an American Lady – you'll know who she is.'

After one performance this American Lady did make herself known to me. Cynthia was blonde, quite attractive, and in her fifties. She was very clever and, as I found later, talented in many ways, from breeding horses to learning Egyptian hieroglyphics, being a qualified vet and a world champion equestrian. We chatted, and at one moment I said, just making polite conversation as one does, 'How long are you due to stay here?'

'I've only flown in for a couple of days to see you in the play,' she replied off-handedly, 'and also to put a suggestion to you.'

'When do you go back?' I asked.

'I think the pilot's bringing over the plane the day after tomorrow ...'

Only then did it click that she had flown in a private jet, *her own* private jet, so the lady was obviously loaded. I must have frowned, or could hardly keep a straight face.

She went on, not registering my reaction: 'I have a proposal to put to you ...'

'Err ... yes ... well ...?'

'A *theatrical* proposal,' she added quickly so that I would not misinterpret her. 'I live in Santa Barbara, in California, and I am in touch with a group of people, all Los Angeles based. Three of them are ex-Disney producers, and they have formed a company, and they want to be involved in the theatre, not movies, and the theatre means obviously New York. We have read reviews of this fantastic production in Providence, Rhode Island, of a Russian comedy called *The Suicide*, by Nicolai Erdmann. Our idea is to buy that production, bring it to New York and present you, the British star of *I, Claudius*, as the lead.'

This is what it was all about: a big leap for me from the dingy, rain-sodden roar of the Waterloo Road to the lights and glitz of New York. The play, a satirical farce originally banned by the Soviets in 1932 after being read by Stalin, had been smuggled out of Russia and directed in Providence by Jonas Jurassas, once the director of the Lithuanian National Theatre, an anti-communist dissident who now lived in New York with his wife.

To cut to the chase, I read the script and agreed. I learned the role of Semyon the peasant, symbol of the oppressed individual, whom the regime tries to absorb, integrate, and make work for false dogmas. We rehearsed in Hoboken where they had built the entire set and we opened on Broadway. It was a marvellous, heavily Eastern European production with New York actors and myself: the set was pure Meyerhold, a whole scenic extravagance with 120 doors all in different styles. There was a banquet scene where the table was 30 feet long and set on a fulcrum, like a seesaw: some of us were on it when it went up; others when it came down.

In the last scene, when I am supposed to have committed suicide, I am lying in a coffin 20 feet above the stage and I am lowered down in it. Then, from behind, and by three gypsies, it is swung out over the audience for me to deliver my last soliloquy over the heads of the spectators. When we opened, all the blue-rinse ladies in the stalls were frightened when I suddenly sat up in the coffin, swung my legs over the side of it, and was propelled out over their heads. They ducked to take cover. It was terrifying for me, too, especially when I had to climb up to the 'flies', the overhead gallery, and into the coffin. In spite of the title, which put some people off, both the comic aspect and the passionate anti-Soviet content worked. It had great reviews, full houses, and it did well. Even John Dexter came to a performance and wrote in his diary that I had made a big hit in New York.

I brought Mum and Dad out on Concorde. Cynthia gave them her plane to go private-jetting down to Washington, where she laid on a stretch limo which toured them round the sights: they thought they were on the moon. Richard made his first trip to New York, too. He stayed with me in the twenty-second-floor apartment lent by Cynthia on West 57th Street off Madison Avenue in an area of gourmet restaurants and world banks. Cynthia had another apartment nearby. Then Richard returned to England where he was touring with Prospect in *Trelawney of the Wells* and *The Merchant of Venice*.

———✦———

I found Cynthia very attractive, a sparkling as well as commanding personality. In one way I loved her, the qualification of which sounds rather mean, but this is why I went along with her. She was lesbian, and along with her mother had inherited a considerable fortune from her mother's second husband, who before he died had owned and run one of the largest privately owned oilfields in California. Her mother had been the oil tycoon's secretary; she married Mr Wood, but Cynthia was not the offspring of that marriage, because she had already been born, but she took the mother's new name. When Mr Wood died they both inherited this fortune which ran into many millions, so Cynthia had something like nine million dollars of oil revenue to spend every year. But while being seriously rich, she was also great fun.

During breaks in the run we would fly out to Santa Barbara where she lived on a hill she had inherited from her stepfather, with six houses she owned spread over it. Whenever I stayed in Santa Barbara I had a whole music studio to myself. The studio had two Bechstein grand pianos, which she had bought because Karl Boehm, the famous Austrian symphonic conductor, was a great friend, and often stayed there (she owned an original Mozart score, given to her by Boehm).

When I walked into her main residence there were Pissarros and Picassos hanging casually, not ostentatiously, on the walls. She owned, too, a substantial ranch with luxurious stud and breeding stables, in Montecito, which after her death was eventually bought by John Cleese (he sold it in 2006 for many millions of dollars). Here she bred horses, naming one of them 'Super Dane' after me as Hamlet. She rode often, she was a trained vet and she was a world champion with her Saddlebreed horses. She had to spend so many million dollars a year, and what she also adored doing was giving money to the opera, to the Metropolitan Opera House and the San Francisco Opera.

During one visit she took me to the Louisville Horse Show, where Super Dane won one event, so they asked me to walk out into the centre of the huge arena carrying a blanket of yellow roses, while the loudspeakers boomed out 'Ladies and gentlemen, *I, Claudius!*' I then had to throw the roses over this steaming horse.

But I soon found out that she was a little schizophrenic: she had two sides to her. She could be very loving, very friendly, but then she could turn and become really vicious, really nasty. One day when we were down at her stables she objected to something I said, and she let fly at me. She became terrifying, really frightening: but that was part of her too! Next minute she could switch on the sophisticated charm.

Back in New York, one day during the run, she said cheerfully, 'Let's go out to lunch.' We went to the Tavern on the Green in Central Park, and that was when she came out with it, straight out of the blue:

'I think we should marry.'

She delivered this thunderbolt just like that, without any warning.

I must have looked blank and said nothing. She then tried seriously to persuade me, saying, 'Look how well we get on.' The sexuality was not mentioned. 'It would just make sense if we did, and you can still go on seeing Richard.'

She certainly had thought it through and taken Richard into account. This was a conversation I didn't want to have, so I 'tactfully declined', which meant I said 'No' as politely as I could. Was I to be the trophy Hamlet? Never.

But even so I was cowardly in the way I turned her away, because on my side I wanted us to stay friends. I quickly thought afterwards that it was all over, for having said no I felt relieved that this embarrassment was out of the way, and we could just carry on as friends like before.

33

TERRIBLE NEWS

All he said was, 'Hello, son.' It was Dad, and I knew at once from the way he said it on the telephone during the run of *The Suicide* that my mother had died. No actor could ever reproduce his tone.

I knew something catastrophic had happened: and I knew it was Mum.

She died of a brain haemorrhage while she was cooking both of them Sunday lunch. It was fairly quick for her, but terrible for him. She had always had problems with her ears, and with her head, but this was a normal Sunday, she was just preparing the lunch; he as usual was out in the garden; and then at three o'clock in the afternoon, after it happened, he was sitting there numb with grief, holding in his hand her rings and her watch.

I do not know how he survived it, or at the time how he would survive it. Anyway he did, for twenty years afterwards he survived it.

―――※※※―――

Richard, when he had been on tour in Norwich, had been informed first in England by Dad. He had phoned Cynthia, and then tried me without succeeding. Richard made sure the producers were waiting by the door when I was told by my father.

They knew before I knew, and they were sensational in their generosity. They booked me on Concorde that day, it was a Sunday, and I flew back to London next day.

When the cast came into work on Tuesday for the evening performance they were told, 'Show's off, show's gone!' The death of my mum, which had happened all too unexpectedly, closed down my appearance on Broadway in *The Suicide*. In spite of them all losing their jobs, nearly everyone in that cast wrote Dad a letter of condolence, which was a very kind gesture.

Back in London with Dad, I was utterly shell-shocked by Mum's death. I was so full of inconsolable grief that I couldn't work. We were both trying to be the strong one for each other. We were together, paralysed, not knowing what to say, what to do, utterly lost, feeding each other's grief, possibly feeding off it too, and after a time I felt we had to put some distance between us. But how could I leave Dad on his own? He and Mum had been joined at the hip, worked together, been in one another's company 24/7.

By now it was coming up to Christmas, so Cynthia, who had been constantly on the phone, suggested, 'Why don't you come out to California for a while?' It seemed a good idea, but what about Dad?

'You go, son. I can look after myself. Don't you worry about me. You have to get on with your life.'

He insisted I go, so I did. Richard was still on tour during December and somehow I wanted to be on my own.

The extraordinary thing was that after Mum's funeral Dad and I never talked about Mum again. I couldn't do this without breaking down; over the years Richard told me I should mention her more, bring her into the house, although she was no longer there, but make her part of our lives, but I never could. My grief was too great. Even now it is hard to talk about this.

Richard and I had been together for three years, but he had been away on tour, and this had not yet ended. Cynthia and I, while we were doing the play in New York, and in spite of her proposal, had become very close. I looked forward greatly to this visit, while she had high hopes of what might come out of it. Dale, her PA (and later business partner), was with her all the time, and while once I believe the two of them had been in more than a work relationship, she now generally 'looked after' Cynthia.

I made the trip out to California and during this we flew to stay in New York. One of Cynthia's great chums in Santa Barbara was Judith Anderson, a very famous and formidable Australian actress. She was Dame Judith Anderson, and she had played Mrs Danvers in the Olivier film of *Rebecca*. One night Cynthia and I were going out to dinner, and I had been sent round to pick up Judith, who was to accompany us. We had a drink together in her hotel bar, and she said out straight, 'I think you should marry Cynthia. She's got all the money; you're a very good actor, Derek, you'll have no worries ever again. You'll just work, you'll just act: you'll get on, you're great companions, and at dinner this evening she knows I'm talking to you. If you could just give her a look, to suggest, you know, it's going to be all right to ...'

Oh my God, this was just terrible! I was flabbergasted! I had to give Cynthia a look to suggest it was going to be all right between us? I knew what that meant!

I did not look at Cynthia all night. We left after dinner in the car to go back to the galleria on West 57th Street. In the car it was very, very difficult, because nothing was said. I felt acutely embarrassed once again.

Only much later did I realise she had planned every detail all along. I realised in my naivety I had been set up from the start, and Judith, as go-between, was only the final stage. I had been warned this was going to happen and taken no notice. I realised this powerful, wealthy lady was still making a play for me, and would accept Richard as part of the baggage or deal.

And even so it seemed Cynthia was not going to give up. I had come back to England to rejoin Richard. Cynthia was visiting, for she came to London occasionally. We met again, and she invited Richard and me for a summer holiday – for five weeks. Her plan was that we would meet in New York, fly to Florida for the Fourth of July, and then to different places across America: Orlando, Disney World, then New Orleans, then the Grand Canyon, Yosemite, where the famous hotels had to be booked well in advance. Richard wanted to visit Mexico, and this would be fitted in, too. The script now was that we were all going to get on and be happy. Richard was accepted, there would be no more talk of marriage, and it was all going to be lovely, indeed fabulous. Foolishly we agreed and fell in with her plan.

We flew from London to New York. We did Orlando and Disney World – it was 4 July – and we then flew to New Orleans, after which it started to go wrong. Suddenly Cynthia wasn't happy, and she started being vile to Richard. In front of others she called him 'Derek's bum boy', and then I heard language come out of that woman's mouth no navvy would speak.

I should have said, 'Come on, we're off!' but I allowed it to happen. I will always castigate myself because I did not stand up for Richard nearly enough, and I have to admit I played it terribly badly. He had such a rough time but he never retaliated. If Richard had left me I wouldn't have blamed him for a second. But he couldn't drive, and anyway we were right in the middle of nowhere.

Overnight Cynthia changed the plans. We flew back to Los Angeles. She booked Richard and me into the Royal Suite in the Beverley Wilshire Hotel: two floors of it. She took another suite for herself, while Dale had a third. Then she disappeared, completely disappeared, leaving us totally in the lurch. We didn't know what had happened to her or where she had gone. Next – this was now about two days after we had arrived in Los Angeles – Judy Shepherd, who was Louis B. Mayer's granddaughter, asked me to a party in Malibu to introduce me to people in Hollywood and help me circulate. I was informed Cynthia was going to be there, and this was to be the reconciliation; but although she was there and we went along, it never happened.

By now we had made plans to come back home, and this desperately awkward lunch signalled the end of our closeness. Here I met Natalie Wood and Robert Wagner, the idyllic Hollywood couple before Natalie mysteriously fell off her yacht and drowned. I sat on a balcony and chatted with Rock Hudson. It was such a heady world. I was quite smitten, but also disorientated.

Cynthia flew us back to New York, and that is where she left us. Richard and I boarded a plane back to London and saw little of her again. She and her producers put money later into the New York run of my *Much Ado* and *Cyrano* performances, and on my birthday in 1982 she threw a party for me on the Hudson River, the Circle Line, a generous treat. But when Richard another time attempted to take us out, the four of us with Dale, and insisted he foot the bill, she swore at him and refused to let him pay. She had no reason to hate him, and again she couldn't bear it because he didn't retaliate. She could have had a great friendship with the two of us, but perhaps control was more important.

She insisted over one weekend that I sit and watch all thirteen episodes of *I, Claudius*, which I had never seen. She also did this to Richard when he was out with me at Santa Barbara – he hadn't seen them either. She and I went out to dinner and left him, which I should never have agreed to. Richard soon switched to one of the 800 other channels!

She had thought Richard was just a passing phase, but she was wrong. The last time I saw her was when I played in *Breaking the Code* on Broadway, and she came to the first night, and attended the dinner at Sardis afterwards. It was a very hot night and she arrived wearing a cashmere turtle neck with long sleeves; I could see she felt very cold inside. When she saw me arrive with Richard she sat with her back to me and we didn't speak. Some six years later I heard that she had fallen very ill, with two brain tumours.

I was in San Francisco and Dale, with whom I remained great friends, was in touch: 'I think she would like to talk to you.' I called her and we spoke, but that was all: she died several weeks later.

Her mother had remarried some years before, to a Belgian whom no one liked very much. When her mother died the Belgian inherited the mother's fortune, and when Cynthia died in the late 1980s the Belgian inherited her fortune too. He ended up with the lot.

I reflected that if I had married her I would certainly be worth knowing today – but I would have had ten years of absolute hell.

34

SO WE'LL GO
NO MORE A-ROVING

The first time I met Brenda Bruce had been in the early 1970s. There were five of us taking *The Hollow Crown* on a world tour: Michael Redgrave, Paul Hardwicke, Brenda, myself and our musician Adrian. I knew of Brenda Bruce of course, and of her fame. She, like me, had done her time at Birmingham Rep, twenty years before me, and her extraordinary resilience and well-seasoned skill were now legendary.

I went to meet her where she was staying in a friend's house near Lambeth Bridge, bringing a big bunch of red roses. She came to the door, and she was very much in her Laura Ashley period, with dresses down to the floor, hair in a pigtail. I presented the flowers, and immediately we established a rapport. I discovered later that her main reason for coming on tour was that Sam, her fourteen-year-old adopted son, had just died from asthma, so she was coming out with us to get over it. She had no children of her own: she had four adopted children, twin girls Jennet and Casey, and Annabel and Sam. She semi-adopted a black boy, too. I believe she fostered him.

Brenda came originally from Shipton. Her first husband was Roy Rich, who created Southern Television; her second was Clement McCallin, a leading actor at Stratford and father of Tania, the set designer who married Michael Blakemore. She was a much greater actress than people thought; although she worked much at the Royal Court she was originally a West End leading lady, and she'd tell stories of how Binkie Beaumont summoned her to his office, telling her she must dress more like Margaret Leighton, the doyenne of fashionable actresses.

But Bren was into trousers: she looked like a boy with her short cropped hair, and at that time in the West End elegance was *de rigueur*. Actresses like Maggie Leighton would arrive at the theatre in a hat and gloves, and would leave equally attired. When Bren was fêted for a string of West End successes, there was a huge photo of her on the side of London buses with the caption 'Is this the plainest face in the West End?'

On a cold rainy January day we flew to Miami with *The Hollow Crown*. We worked our way across America, across the Pacific, across Australia, New Zealand, a bit of Eastern Europe, Greece, Israel, and we had a great time, met a lot of fantastic people.

There was one very odd performance in Fort Lauderdale at the Poncianna Theatre. It was the gala first night, for the ladies came dressed up to the nines, and there were photographs next day in the papers, and on the front of magazines. There was a big commotion when one woman in the stalls turned on and used a handheld hairdryer. Then, about halfway through the second half of the show, the audience started to leave in droves; the seats were banged up, and we had no idea what was going on – they made no secret they were leaving. We reached the end and immediately asked, 'What was up, what happened?'

This was the first night, they told us, and the ladies had to get their jewels back to their safe deposit boxes by 9.30. So these heavily bejewelled women, who were not there to see the show at all, were traipsing out to take their jewels back. They were there to be seen, not to see us: we were incidental, jesters at the court.

Redgrave wasn't well on this tour, and we did our best to look after him and love him up. We took him out to a gay tea dance in Florida at Fort Lauderdale which he loved. We had drinks and they played Gloria Gaynor's 'I Will Survive'. Everyone danced, including Michael, who circled the floor with Bren very gently.

In Honolulu we brought him with us to a gay bar after the performance, and here he got a little tipsy, and really let his hair down, had a ball, and the four of us then went for a stroll across Waikiki Beach. But next morning he reverted to Sir Michael.

The Hollow Crown wove a spell and lasted so well we were still doing it in the Nineties. We went out later with Diana Rigg, which was great fun, and then with Janet Suzman. But it was with Brenda that I loved it most.

Brenda was not beautiful, but she had a wonderfully characterful face, with huge blue eyes and snub nose, and a warm, appealing, husky voice; she was extraordinarily versatile, because she could do the classics, and also the kitchen-sink stuff. Her energy was prodigious: she was at one time playing leading roles at the RSC at Stratford and running a pub, for she was a landlady in a pub just outside Stratford and looked after the lunches and dinners.

She had so much tragedy in her life, losing in a short space Sam, her second husband Clem, her father, then her mother. As the years passed by, Richard became much closer to her than she was to me. He adored her and she adored him, and he did for her what a child would do when she died, but it was not like that to begin with. Initially there was great jealousy between Richard and Brenda, for she was very jealous of Richard being with me, while we were fraternal brother and sister. This passed. We spoke practically every day and she really became part of our family.

Unfortunately the Prospect Company came to an end in something like acrimony – in public poses and unruly emotions. We were in Beijing or Peking with *Hamlet* after many successful tours, when Toby and the Chairman of Prospect were sacked, while it was announced from London that Tim West was taking over.

By this time Prospect had painstakingly earned that semi-global pedigree suitable for the first-ever British theatre company to appear in the People's Republic of China. After a rapturous welcome in Japan, where we had been fêted by the traditional Kabuki actors, we flew west into a very different atmosphere of outward conformity and protocol, yet unpredictably noisy audiences.

When we opened in Shanghai I carried my own private sense of occasion, for it was my 200th performance as Hamlet. Looking through a hole in the curtain I saw an audience of identically dressed, identically shorn men and women, all with white transistor wires for the translation issuing out of their ears. Rather rudely I thought of Alcatraz, confirmed by the disquieting barrage of sound, giggling, eating, very loud hawking and spitting which went on throughout. There were five Chinese actors at the back of the stalls in a booth translating simultaneously, and we received a barrage of feedback from this, too.

There was one line, and I don't quite know why, which always got a big laugh: it was when Hamlet kills Polonius and says over his dead body, 'Thou find'st to be too busy is some danger.' Whether there was some political comment implied, or the translation put a comic emphasis on it, every night the audience erupted in loud guffaws. We were warned there might be no applause at the end, but quite the contrary happened: their thunderous relish was long and loud. I had no idea what to make of it, beyond a kind of exhilarated dissatisfaction.

We did three performances in Shanghai and five in Peking. One curiosity of the visit was that Toby and I were not allowed to travel in the coach from hotel to theatre or for sightseeing.

When we boarded it for the first time officials told us to get off and explained: 'You are the leading actor and director – there is a car for you.' This was communism. Toby and I as leaders had to fulfil the functions of notable visitors, and became casualties of the Chinese warm hospitality.

It was only three years after Chairman Mao had died, and the thaw after the Cultural Revolution was beginning, so they were thrilled to try out their English on us. One teenager came up to me in the street saying, 'How now, brown cow,' and then ran away giggling. Our typically rebellious young company also had to show off, and in the old Soviet-built hotel in Peking just before we left a group demonstrated against the Stalag-like atmosphere by knotting sheets together and shinning down from the first floor humming music from *Stalag 17*. By the end we were so tired we slept all the way to Australia, yet we had successfully brought for the first time ever a production of Shakespeare in English to the country with the biggest population in the world.

We were in Peking when we received news of the sackings, and our generous hosts couldn't understand how we artists and director of the prestigious Old Vic Company could be treated like this. At home the production at the Old Vic of the Scottish play with O'Toole in the title role was about to open, directed by Bryan Forbes.

Peter had last been on the stage seventeen years before (in that flamboyantly exposed *Hamlet* when I played Laertes). Meantime preparations for the Scottish play were like a gigantic travesty. It was pure farce, as O'Toole called the play 'Harry Lauder', and Tim West pleaded with Forbes to make changes to avert total disaster. Before the curtain rose on the first night Forbes went into Peter's dressing room and found him stark naked except for the Gauloise in his mouth.

219

'Can't wear them, darling, they're hopeless,' he said of his costume, and proceeded on in jogging trousers and gym shoes.

Next day the disaster was front page news, and one critic called Peter's performances 'deranged', another – just slightly more politely – a 'milestone in the history of coarse acting'.

'How are the houses?' Richard Burton later asked Peter, who rather gloried in all this madness.

'Packed,' he answered.

And Katharine Hepburn told him, 'If you're going to have a disaster, have a big one.'

In one cartoon Peter, dressed as Macbeth, is in the wings about to go on with the black-tied impresario telling him: 'Get on a camel – a few lines from *Lawrence of Arabia* and this could run forever!'

Tim West dissociated himself from the production entirely, but even so it was a sell-out. I refused to get involved. The wonderful office and production staff at the Old Vic, who were busy planning the next season, were given the push. So this was the sad demise of Prospect, although we were still on tour with *Hamlet* and had a long final leg in Australia to fulfil, where quite unexpectedly I was to meet my nemesis.

AGE VI
A WORLD
TOO WIDE

35

ULTIMATE NIGHTMARE

Jonathan Miller had directed Sir as Shylock in the production of *The Merchant of Venice* in which I played Gratiano. It was during the run that for the first time I became aware of Sir's stage fright. It filtered through after the play had opened, for naturally he never spoke about it during rehearsals or run-throughs, or on the first night.

I was standing in the wings one night and I could see in that rather strange light emanating from somewhere else, which you can experience from the darkness of the wings, that on his face suddenly there was an expression of shocked horror, beads of sweat and his eyes were staring as if behind a mask. It was just a hesitation: I could detect nothing more, but the flash, a fragment of a second, can seem to the victim like an age.

Then, at one point on stage, I had to scream and shout at him in character as Gratiano, and after this he took me to one side and requested that I didn't look him in the eye when I did so, but focused on his forehead or chin. After this we heard he had confessed he had a host of these abysmal, shattering lapses in which he forgot his words and the earth stood still.

One night he even forgot the list of things that a Jew has, the unforgettable 'Hath not a Jew eyes?' while he found himself wanting to say, or attempting to say, 'Hath not a Jew elbows?' Another time it happened to him when he gave a particularly brilliant performance as Othello, so amazing that afterwards he was applauded off stage by the rest of the company. But he was in such a state he brushed everyone off and headed straight back to his dressing room, where someone visited him to congratulate him, and found his eyes, just as I had, full of alarm and fear.

'But that was a fantastic performance,' his visitor told him, unnerved by what he saw.

'Yes, yes,' Sir replied, 'but how did I do it?'

It had been – and this is what terrified him – panic and auto-pilot taking over.

My nightmare arrived after we left China, and when we had already played Melbourne and Adelaide on what was now the last leg of the tour. One matinée I was in the wings in Sydney just after the interval, and about to go on and deliver 'To be or not to be'.

I was reflecting on this famous line, and the tangible silence that invariably follows as it hangs in the air, and was wondering what would happen if the actor 'dried'. I went on, began the speech, said three lines and I dried.

I was catatonic, gripped by sheer terror. I had done the play about 376 times, but my mind went completely blank and I started to sweat until I was wet through. I did not know what was coming next, but forced my mouth open to go on, and somehow the words came out on automatic pilot.

I had never questioned my ability or desire to act before, not once till now, at the age of forty-one. The panic caused a horrific worm of doubt to enter my brain, and once I started to ask 'how' and 'why' I stopped being able to do it at all. It was as though I had crossed Niagara on a tightrope 250 times and on the 251st crossing – vertigo. I was convinced I couldn't move across the stage without falling over. I would go rigid from the knees down.

After that first time it happened in *Hamlet*, the panic began to grip me more and more. When I was on stage I became so giddy that my feet and toes felt like talons, digging into the floor to stop me falling over. It was not the sort of fear I could use in my performance. It was gut-wrenching terror.

I decided to quit the theatre, my first love, at once, and concentrate on films and television. I made several of these, playing the magisterial and wholly evil archdeacon who lusts after Esmeralda in *The Hunchback of Notre Dame* as well as a gruesome figure in *Skin*, one of Roald Dahl's *Tales of the Unexpected*, who has a portrait of his unfaithful wife painted and burned into his back as a tattoo by her lover. But it was still only marginally better.

I recorded, too, *Richard II* and *Hamlet* for BBC television at Shepherds Bush. Doing these plays scene by scene I thought might be easier, but I now felt I had this concrete and permanent yoke around my shoulders. You could say this was fine for *Richard II*, for he says, 'These external manners and lament/ Are merely shadows to the unseen grief/ That swells with silence in the tortured soul.' I understood – or thought I did – what that meant. But I would never confess that I was that deeply sad and disturbed person. Before I ever did that it would be the neck and shoulders which seized up first. Whereas if I could let it all hang out and risk five minutes of unpleasantness (which I cannot do) I would be better. I do not like making waves or confrontations. I suffer a stiff neck instead.

For the television *Hamlet* I was on my third Gertrude. Barbara Jefford had been very much the Queen; Brenda Bruce, who played her on the second tour, was very much the mother; while Claire Bloom was now very much the lover. I had to change to accommodate each, because they asked for different things from me, and as a result I had to change my thoughts and intentions. This may not be noticed, as an actor can attach great importance to a couple of seconds' worth of his performance, which to an audience means nothing.

In Shanghai, earlier when we had been on tour, a Chinese professor, who had come to see *Hamlet*, said he enjoyed it very much and sent me his thesis, about fifteen pages of very closely reasoned argument about the famous line, 'Oh that this too, too solid flesh would melt,' arguing why it should be 'sullied flesh', not 'solid flesh'. It was very learned and I became convinced that of course it should be 'sullied'. When he saw the play again – and this time I had said 'sullied' – he came around afterwards and said, 'Of course, in performance it doesn't matter. It's only a word and it's gone like that.'

That was a great revelation to him, whereas what he wrote in his thesis was a great revelation to me. I realised I didn't have any one particular approach to Hamlet, yet on the other hand there was only one way I could play him: my way, coming from my personality. Doing the part on television I discovered I could kick it around, I could almost reverse what I had done before, and still believe in what I was doing, because it was such a malleable play. I thought I would have to scale down my performance for television, but not one bit of it. They insisted – the powers that be – that I played 'To be or not to be' direct to camera, and not to Ophelia, as I had on stage.

The panic attacks during these two years gradually enveloped my whole life until I became terrified even of crossing the road. Richard and I had moved from Stockwell into the house I bought in Hampstead. There were all the usual concerns with a new property – damp, potential subsidence, building works and decorating. For both of us this was a very tense time. I became quite distant, and tend anyway to keep things very close to my chest. Panic attacks were private worries. I went to the doctor who gave me some little blue pills, but I told no one.

Had I played too many Hamlets? Had the part so eaten into me that my native and natural hue of resolution had become completely sickly'd over with thought? Had I repressed so much in my life inside me in the unremitting dedication to my work that now it was payback time for what I had buried along the way? Or was it simply that boring cliché – the midlife crisis?

Whatever it was, I was never quite the same again. This crisis had a permanent effect on my personality, so I became more timid than I was before, and more vulnerable, and was much more flustered by events. In short I turned into a permanent worrier and would start to panic immediately when something unexpected happened – in a word very 'uncool'. For from now on stage fright was ever-present, that ogre that reaches into the core of your being, and even tells you that you must not go on stage, let alone have anxiety or nerve attacks. Once it is there it is always there, an almost random bomb of frailness and non-confidence. I would never know where or when it would explode. You could say the veil which I wore was now split and irreparably in shreds.

Now I felt I needed to avoid the theatre like the plague, and for two years I did so. Then after two years of this purgatory – and it really was purgatory, for I was being put through all those exposures of vulnerability, self-pity, speechlessness and self-doubt that I have portrayed in so many of the characters I played – I was invited to join the Royal Shakespeare Company at Stratford to play several leading roles. I had just done Hitler in the film *Inside the Third Reich*, when the call from the RSC came.

I had caught up with that hurtful earlier rejection by Peter Hall and Co. – it had taken twenty-two years, just under one for each mile from Birmingham to Stratford. But now, if I did not have control over my memory and nerve, how could I be certain that my lapse of both would not once again strike when I least expected it?

What had caused my stage fright I shall never know: the shock of Mum's death; the accumulation of fatigue from years of unremitting toil; the delayed effect of the débâcle with Cynthia? But true to my deep and jealously guarded sense of intimacy and privacy, I refused any suggestion of therapy.

36

THE RSC

I had loved playing the Old Vic, for it is a theatre with a soul; it had been so well lived in that with the end of Prospect it was a deep sorrow to part after so many years. The theatre itself lets you know if it likes the performance. I can feel approval or disdain oozing down the walls.

The Barbican, which was to be my next London port of call, where the Royal Shakespeare Company had its base, is early Mussolini-style. Here we rehearsed part of the time, the rest of the time at Stratford. The rehearsal areas are below sea level, so we spent the day under fluorescent lights, breathing recycled air. The canteen was down there as well, so there was no escape from the Stygian blackness. There are so many doors in this underworld that opening and closing them we would suffer from what was termed 'Barbican elbow'.

The first of my RSC plays was *Much Ado* in which I was Benedick, to be followed by *Cyrano*, *Peer Gynt* and *The Tempest*. It is a very curious thing about the Benedick and Beatrice plot, for it is the Claudio/Hero one which is supposed to be the principal plot of the play, but it never feels like that. The audience first of all wants to know the outcome of the relationship between Beatrice and Benedick.

I love the play, particularly in the production Terry Hands set out to stage, for its blatant romanticism. It has glamour, beautiful music, laughter and tears – and it is not just a frivolous comedy, but has depth. It has, too, a very black side, and that black contrasts with the other colours. It is not just a piece of tinsel – there is a touch of 'hell hath no fury' in Beatrice's character. There has been a kind of tradition recently to play the couple as though they are well on the shelf, finding each other almost at the last possible moment, with Beatrice in particular as a real old maid. That is a plausible interpretation, but it is not exclusive.

Sinéad Cusack and I set out to play the lovers as being somewhat younger, so it would become believable that during the play they experience a very violent attraction to each other. At the outset the real attraction is on the side of Beatrice. That she is not married is not because she could not get a decent fellow, it is that for her none of the possible suitors has matched up to Benedick. He has the same problems about the possibility of marriage which she seems to have.

The second approach, which we explored during rehearsals, was that as Benedick begins to catalogue all these virtues it gradually begins to dawn on him that he is describing someone he knows and that when he gets to the colour of her hair he realises it is Beatrice. As in all performances and indeed rehearsals, we were on a journey, and we emerged different in many ways and far more mature. So it is a comedy of growing up. I discovered it was very personal to me. I had just lost my nerve. My mother had died. Not very long before I had moved into a wonderful house where I would probably be living for the rest of my life. And I had found on the threshold of forty a couple of years before a partner with whom the wish and intention was to become permanent.

In rehearsal, the tart-tongued sceptic, the emotionally reticent Benedick, demanded from me a personality performance where I had to find and call on areas of rage, anger and fierceness. Before my stage fright my performances had been purely instinctive and intuitive, but now I had become more self-aware. These deep emotions may not have been part of my surface personality but

I now knew they lay beneath it, so that – and this was rather daunting when I confronted it – I knew I was playing a version of myself.

I could use my advanced or sophisticated sense of humour, or rather Benedick's advanced sense of humour, to hide my real feelings, for I did – and still do – experience myself as a bachelor in a world of couples, an adolescent court jester in a world of grown-up people, who is more at home in the world of the imagination than in the real world. It is my capacity for dreamy wonderment, combined with a terrible insecurity about who I am, where I am going and why and how, that gives me a craving, an absolute need to act.

I was to be in command again, much more than in real life, because I knew who I was supposed to be and what was supposed to happen. On stage I can somehow be noble about all the sad, distressing things that happened to me in my life. My mother's death several years before was hugely traumatic for me. And yet on stage, if I can recall what it did to me at the time, it became no longer hurtful inside. The process is a kind of purging.

We were still in rehearsal when I discovered all this. I was looking forward so much to going on stage again, for extraordinary things happen there.

Rehearsals of *Much Ado* were very productive, but before the first night, would *terror* – that stage fright – come back and hit me with a vengeance?

It did.

———

I have never been so frightened in all my life as on the first night of *Much Ado About Nothing* at Stratford. It had taken me twenty-two years to make the 23 miles from Birmingham to Stratford. The triumph was entwined with mortal fear and disaster, for as in the Kipling verses I had to confront the twin impostors just the same. To return to the stage was something I longed to do,

230

and I realised that if I did not accept their offer of four leading roles I would never go on the stage again. I just had to face it.

My terror was so extreme, so gut-rotting, that I even thought at first that I would fall over.

We were on a glass stage in Ralph Koltai's set; a glass, raked stage, with my high-heeled shoes. I was wearing shot silk, dull pinkish shot silk, and I had been on stage less than a minute and it was *black* with sweat. Every pore in my body opened up. The terror was awful! I would look down at my feet and see my whole reflection mocking me.

Fortunately no one else noticed the terror and self-doubt I was going through. It was not the impression I gave to others. I am like that: I can un-inhabit myself at will, as I did over my stage fright. Even Sinéad Cusack, who played Beatrice, saw nothing of my state, for she remembers me mainly sitting in rehearsal reading the *Daily Telegraph* and doing the crossword.

I had to do some serious thinking about memory. Up to this moment I had taken it for granted that it was there: I was a quick study, my memory was instinctual and, as I have said, virtually photographic. But over the period I had this stage fright this all changed.

People ask these questions, and I now had to ask them of myself: 'How do I learn? Why do I learn? How can I learn?'

For the first time I had to make a conscious effort to feel sure it was there – that I would remember all my lines, to put it bluntly, and to shift for ever that concrete yoke, and that is what I did – painstakingly. Only one director I worked with at this time saw it: Marvin Chomsky, who directed me as Hitler in *Inside the Third Reich*. He could tell in my eyes that I was frightened, what was going on in my mind, and guessed it was a killer: very gently he helped me to find my feet in it. But it was up to me. No longer would I ever be able to rely on my performance being a self-oblivious, magical process.

Gradually I got back my life on stage through *Much Ado* and the three productions that followed. It took a long time before the panic wore off. Every day I still dreaded the thought of having to do it, of having to go on stage. I had this terrible disease, and the cure anyway, I was told, would be to actually face it head on. I had to get back on the stage and do a whole series of make-or-break parts. It was tough, and only by creating momentum did I have a chance of blasting my way out of difficulty.

———◦◦◦◦———

This was the beginning of my and Sinéad's three years together; we both grew old in the service of Beatrice, and we went after Stratford to London, Paris, Berlin and Vienna, New York, Washington and Los Angeles. Beatrice attacks Benedick because she feels love, but cannot admit to the possibility that she loved him previously, when she had a closeness to him, and now feels furious about the way he treated her by going off to war. So there is a strong implication that he has hurt her and this motivates our relationship: we have had a past together. If the relationship was shallow and superficial, both actors and audience would have got bored very quickly.

Knowing this and playing this was the reason neither of us ever became tired, for our roles changed and grew more complex and more nuanced, the performances changed in every country we visited according to the way audiences influenced us. For instance, in New York Beatrice's hurt and fury registered strongly in that very matriarchal society. Here on St Patrick's Day morning I opened the hotel window to watch the Macy's Day Parade and the giant Woody Woodpecker balloon when I slipped and cracked two ribs on the radiator. The understudy Ken Bones took over. Cynthia's business partner Dale, one of the producers of *Much Ado*, rather naughtily invited me that evening to Sondheim's *Pacific Overtures*, where a member of the audience angrily demanded why I was there, and not on stage.

As I settled down everyone came to love Benedick. Truly he was purifying and reshaping my soul. And here again it was laughter, the audience's laughter through my contact with it, that was a strong healing agent. This was such a crucial stage to pass through in my journey. I had to filter Benedick through the force that was in me, otherwise I would be playing a creature with no heart and no insides.

So to see *Much Ado* as a play about the difficulty and danger of growing up, in which Benedick often plays the underdog, my voice full of wheeling and impotently exasperated inflections, often playing the mock innocent with farcically prolonged vowels, then hardening into firm masculinity as love replaces self-regard – well, what can I say, other than this was just me!

37

PROBOSCIS MAGNIFICA

There would be no ambiguity of intention or identity about my next role, which had two gigantic, even insuperable aspects: the huge nose was the first, the second a huge lung capacity.

For Cyrano de Bergerac, the lung capacity and memory demand apart, there was one body accessory that had to be fabricated, the 2¾ inch bumpy latex beak – what the hero calls 'the protuberance that precedes me by a quarter of an hour'. Christopher Tucker, the make-up artist who once trained as an opera singer, had worked on me before to design and make the older Claudius. Now he had the job of sculpting this monstrous protuberance on a plaster cast of my head.

We had to make fifteen noses for the nine-week US run, because of the wear and tear that occurred post performance. Breaking the spirit gum was deeply unpleasant, although I could not wait to rip it off, but the worst moment was putting it on in the first place. Once it was on I could not take it off, blow my nose or scratch it, but what would happen if it were to fall off? If this were to happen there would only be one way to show true panache. I planned to sweep down, snatch it up, and eat it!

The laughs in Cyrano come from somewhere else, deeper than his nose, which is why this is such a great play. We all have that thing about 'People don't like me because of this one thing.' Or, 'This one thing is just ruining my life.' Usually it is not true, and it was not true in Cyrano's case, as you find out at the end. The nose is merely a symptom of something else.

Ralph Richardson, who played the role in the illustrious post-war Old Vic seasons which he ran with Olivier, told me just before he died, 'I have only one word of advice for you, dear boy. Wear two noses. One for the first two acts, and a smaller one for the last three. Because the first two acts are about a nose, and the last three aren't.'

While we decided it would be better to have one nose for all seasons, Richardson was right about the play. By the end the audience has forgotten the nose.

Cyrano was the fulfilment of a dream thirty years before: I had been struck dumb by the José Ferrer film as a schoolboy. Anthony Burgess's adaptation of Edmund Rostand's extravagant and heroic comedy – a new version suggested by my friend John Tydeman – is perhaps one of Burgess's best examples of flamboyant wordplay. He took out some of the original archaisms and preciosities of previous translations: for example a kiss is no longer 'the red dot over the "i" in loving', but 'the very O of "love" in the expectant lips!'

When we began work Terry Hands asked if I knew how it felt to be ugly. This reminded me once again of my acne-ridden teenage years, when I used to stare people out when I walked towards them in the street. Terry also helped by putting obstacles in my way. When Cyrano starts his speech about all the different kinds of noses, he made me stand with my back to the audience. It was hard, but it made me work. He told me to forget all the success I had with Benedick.

'If you blow Cyrano,' he told me, 'your career goes back five years.'

But one big obstacle, which took time to overcome, was the way Sineád was passed over to play Roxanne. Sinéad, like me, had not been to drama school. She had been to University College Dublin, during which she acted at the Abbey Theatre in the evening. She would rehearse in the morning, have a tutorial in the afternoon, and play in the evening. In her early twenties she came to London and acted for Michael Croft at the Shaw Theatre. She played Juliet, with Simon Ward as Romeo, then Desdemona at Ludlow. She took over Lisa Harrow's part in *Wild Oats* at the National, in which Jeremy Irons, her husband, acted. But she was now to be cruelly disappointed.

When Terry Hands announced we were going to do *Cyrano* Sinéad took it for granted that she would be Roxanne. She asked Terry, 'Can I play Roxanne?' and was absolutely shattered when he told her, 'You're far too old, and you're not a lady.' Terry cast Alice Krige instead, but after a while, actually quite a time, Terry came back to Sinéad one day and said, 'You're going to play in *Cyrano*.'

'I am a year older and you told me I was too old a year ago,' Sinéad replied to Terry, whom she considered very gnomic.

'You're the right age now,' said Terry.

Sinéad was truly wonderful as Roxanne, and as with *Much Ado* we had the best time possible: with no other actress have I so much adored acting.

'My route through Roxanne was that she had the same passionate, romantic, beautiful nature as Cyrano,' she says, 'but she was the reverse side of the coin, and her journey was from flibbertigibbet to mature woman.'

———

We opened on Broadway at the Gershwin Theatre, which seated 2,000, and they wanted to give us microphones.

'Over my dead body,' Terry said. 'No mikes.'

We played there two months, and soon began to lose our voices, and here they brought in Clyde Vinson to help me, the only voice teacher who had an immediate practical impact on my voice.

Clyde applied the Alexander relaxation technique to the voice. He would roll me out like a pancake until every bit of my body was touching the floor, then start on the voice. He had one technique and it was such a simple thing:

'Take your thumb, push your thumb against the roof of your mouth for about twenty seconds, take it away: you can feel where your thumb has been. Now just hit that with your breath.'

I thought of the palate and the roof of my mouth, and it worked. It stopped my voice getting caught on the way up. Even if I was suffering a bit of a cold or something else, I could speak above the cold, because I was really thinking about the resonance in my head. And I was not thinking about 'down here' in the chest or throat, or here or here, I was just thinking about up here. All those earlier voice lessons, trying to think of breathing through my bum or a hole in my back – or through my balls – had never made one iota of difference – but now I had this!

When I won the Tony for Benedict on Broadway (which should, to my mind, have been for Cyrano), I gave it all to Clyde. A 6-foot Texan, Clyde Vinson died of AIDS at the age of sixty-four. I owe him so much!

───◦◦◦───

One night when I was up on the chandelier in the first scene of *Cyrano*, something instructive happened: I failed to notice that the ladder – up which I had climbed – had disappeared!

How was I going to get down? Now unless somebody down there worked out a system to get me down I couldn't get off this thing. How would the show go on? At the end of my speech, were we going to have the stage manager come out and say, 'Ladies and gentlemen, there's been a technical problem. We'll bring the curtain down while Mr Jacobi gets off his chandelier?' What actually happened was the actors, bless them, formed a human ladder to take me down.

During the performance I still stayed Cyrano, but I was Cyrano thinking, 'How the fuck am I going to get off this chandelier in a purely technical way as an actor?' It didn't take away from my commitment to the role, my absorption in the role, but there's got to be a third eye. There are no safety nets in theatre, as there are in movies and television (or in 'live' sitcoms with audiences). I can't stop and go back and do it again. I've got to create my own safety nets, and one of those safety nets requires me, as the actor, not to lose myself.

I may have to get a fellow actor out of a terrible dry, or anything, but I've got to be alive enough to do that. I've got to be aware. So if I'm there doing what I'd call wanking away, saying, 'I'm in my part, I'm in my part: I'm totally oblivious to anything else,' this will result in a blank, infertile exercise.

'Are actors intellectuals?' is a question often asked. I believe the actor is an intellectual in that he has to think what will work, what will fail. He rationalises his risks. He also has to imagine himself in a part – in performance. He imagines his way along – and acting is about pretending, so it's artificial in that sense. An actor has to be absorbed in the part, not withholding anything, yet – and this is tricky – he must also project an eye, or double of himself, into the auditorium, which will constantly monitor his actions. So as an actor I must act and watch myself acting simultaneously. I split myself in two. I put myself in the position of the audience, think what they'll think. After all, that's who I'm doing it for.

It's so important to care for the audience, to keep in mind that they'll be thinking of you: a two-way process. Otherwise the actor may just as well be masturbating. The actor is showing off, shaking about, moaning and groaning. Oooaahh! It's lovely! It's gorgeous! But he's really just wanking away, completely solitary, doing zero for anybody else. There are, of course, actors who cavort in this way: actors who go on stage to talk to themselves and exhibit their egos and massage their big personalities. And a voyeuristic public exists for them, too. There's always a market for great masturbators!

This is what Cyrano taught me, and on stage I never stop learning. For the final curtain call in New York all the girls dressed up as Gascony cadets, the boys all dressed as nuns; the front row produced champagne and, as at the close of car races, they sprayed us. I grew so excited I ripped off my nose and threw it into the audience.

38

THE JACOBI CADETS

There are some women, proper English women ranging in age from nineteen to sixty-one, who would travel 3,000 miles to see an actor perform in a role they have seen as many as sixty times or more. This even happened in those far-off, mid-Eighties years, before general hysteria in the treatment of pop and media idols set in and became endemic.

We were doing the end of *Cyrano* at the Barbican when the only four plays left in the repertoire for the last three weeks were the four plays I was in. They used to have knock-down price tickets on sale at eight o'clock in the morning for that night's performance, and so people stayed all night in their sleeping bags, when it was miserable and snowing outside, to snap up the tickets from the box office first thing in the morning.

On this occasion these single or unattached ladies, who had seen each other at other performances, were sleeping rough, waiting for seats, and formed a group, and during the night one of them wrote an 'epic' poem. A big presence in *Cyrano* are the Gascony Cadets, and she called her poem 'The Jacobi Cadets'. They all read it and the idea caught on. They sent me a card with two of the lines:

We've queued so long without regrets
That we've become the Jacobi Cadets.

This group, in whom I seemed to inspire a rather wonderful form of chaste and undemonstrative devotion, numbered a dozen or more, and among them was one American. The first thing I knew about it was coming out of the stage door one night after the performance to be confronted with them, all with 'I am a Jacobi Cadet' on their T-shirts. Those that are still alive and well enough still stand outside the stage door, and there are three of them at least who go back as far as 1983. They see everything I do many times, watch all the films, so it must cost them a fortune. I can't imagine why, but I seem to have some kind of sex appeal for them.

When I did *Breaking the Code* in New York, ten of them flew to New York; they stayed at the YWCA, and came several times to the show; I hired a stretch limo and took them out to Joe Allen's for supper. The press got to hear about the 'Jacobi Cadets', and put them on a coast-to-coast chat show, so they went on the telly, and they were so thrilled. By now I knew each of them by name, but they have never tried to meet up socially with me, and were a bit shocked at the idea.

'No, no, not at all,' they answered almost in unison when asked. 'We don't want to push, you know. We feel he's ours at the stage door. Not any more than that!'

One night one of them was mugged, and the mugger took her money and all her theatre tickets. When I heard this I replaced them, so it was love from then on; it really became devotion of the highest quality. Over the years I have owed them so much and here profess my thanks and devotion.

There is to this day in America, or so I'm told, a female fan club and website dedicated to me. When I heard about it, I was surprised as I never exactly fitted the mould of romantic hero. I was told these women call themselves 'The Oestrogen Club', which does not sound very romantic. The rule for members is that when my name is mentioned they must know six good responses to comments such as 'Who?' and 'Isn't he a bit old?'

The adoration of fans has a dark side. There were two women in America who seriously wanted to have a child by me, who wanted to have my genes while having nothing to do with me. And for a time there was another woman who stalked me: she found out where I lived in Stockwell, and one night when I was playing Hamlet she was there waiting at the door for me to arrive home. She was small and dark, but not attractive at all.

She wanted to come into the house but I managed to prevent this and keep her on the doorstep. 'I'm not attractive enough for you, am I?' she kept saying, and I then had to talk my way out of that one. Eventually she went away, but she was threatening.

The other occasion with this particular devotee was much nastier. She found out where my parents lived in Leytonstone, and one Sunday at lunchtime she arrived on their doorstep.

'There was a knock on the door,' Dad told me. He went to investigate who it was and found this woman standing there with a parcel. There was a taxi waiting, just beyond the gate, with the engine running. She thrust this parcel at Dad and told him, 'This is what your son has done to me!' She then climbed into the taxi and left.

Dad called Mum and explained what had happened, and obviously they decided to open the parcel. It contained a nightdress that had been torn and covered in semen. This was extraordinary – and, needless to say, it put them off their Sunday lunch.

That was her last visit. I had a feeling she was from Manchester, as I received letters from her some time later with that postmark.

'Why have you broken my teapot?' said one letter. 'What have I done to you that you broke my teapot? Are you going to buy me a new one?'

Along with the fans, with fame come the awards.

'You've got to get over to New York!' Terry Hands was on the phone, and I was on the island of Sark where I was filming *Mr Pye*. 'You have this invitation to the Tony Awards, and the RSC will foot the bill.'

I had been doing *Much Ado* and *Cyrano* in New York before *Mr Pye* came along, and I had been nominated for a Tony award.

'You've got to go, you've got to go!' the RSC and Terry said.

'I can't,' I said. 'I'm in Sark, I'm working.'

'Well, you just go for twenty-four hours, you've got to be there, you've got to be there!'

Sark was beautiful, the flowers were extraordinary everywhere: it was summer, and you know the lines:

I know a bank whereon the wild thyme blows,
Where oxlips and the nodding violet grows
Quite over-canopied with luscious woodbine,
With sweet musk roses and with eglantine ...

This was Sark where I went to live for three months while we recorded the three parts of Mervyn Peake's *Mr Pye*, which had been dramatised for television. No cars were allowed on the island, but there were tractors, bicycles and carts.

We became friendly with the rulers of Sark, the seigneur, Michael Beaumont and his wife, who had a fief from Elizabeth I, with their own special laws including the banning of all automobiles. Stocks Hotel was where I stayed and had wonderful food. The locals always humorously referred to themselves, the people of Sark, as '500 drunks clinging to a rock'. Everyone did drink a great deal, but the landlady who managed the nearest pub to us ran her establishment with a rod of iron. If she liked you, it was fine.

'Going down the Dixcart': this meant whenever you went to a particular beach on Sark you had to go down a gulley, known as the Dixcart Valley, and halfway down was an area called 'The Cucumber Patch' where the lesbian fraternity lived!

I put this prospect of the most extraordinary journey – to America and back – to the producers, and they agreed: 'Go with our blessing,' they said.

———○○○○———

I left the hotel in Sark, and a tractor took me and my overnight case down to the harbour, where a boat brought me to Guernsey, where a four-seater plane flew me to Heathrow, where Concorde took me to JFK, where a helicopter flew me to the 34th Street terminal, where a stretch limo drove me to the Plaza Hotel, where there was a strike, and where all the chambermaids, porters and everyone were out, and where there was a picket line. I had to walk through it, and here they were throwing tin cans and bricks at people like me, and it all became rather violent. It was like the Burl Ives song, 'I know an old lady who swallowed a fly' – the spider, the fly and so on until 'And she's dead of course!' The final line was my arrival.

I got to my room, and there was no room service, no nothing. A stretch limo collected me and I arrived at the theatre. There I won the Tony, surprisingly for Benedick, not for Cyrano. Next morning everything happened in reverse: stretch limo to 34th Street, helicopter to JFK, Concorde to Heathrow, but here the four-seater plane took me, because of fog, not to Guernsey but diverted me to Jersey, where they said: 'Well, all we can do is to get you to Sark by boat.' We started out by boat, but it was too foggy, we couldn't reach Sark, so we had to turn back, and I had to spend the night in Jersey.

Because they had heard on television that I had won the Tony, during the day the whole population of Sark had congregated on the beach where I was supposed to land. They had written 'Welcome Mr Pye' in the sand: but such a welcome had to be aborted as I didn't arrive.

Next morning a hydrofoil brought me over to Guernsey where the boat brought me back to Sark. They turned out again, a large number of them, and were waiting in the harbour waving little flags, with 'Mr Pye' on the flags! I disembarked from the boat and climbed into a pony and trap decorated with flowers, which took me up the slope to the main square and Stocks Hotel.

It was the most incredible journey, and it lasted forty-eight hours! But even more extraordinary was this unexpected fêting of Mr Pye, which I considered to be as much for Mervyn Peake, who had lived on Sark and died tragically young, relatively obscure and unrecognised.

Mr Pye was beautifully cast, with Judy Parfitt as Mr Pye's foil and ultimate disciple, the marvellous Betty Marsden as the fat lady, and Patricia Hayes (who'd been Edna in *Edna the Inebriate Woman*) as the hilarious Romanian cook in the boarding house. But sadly the isolation and special circumstances of Sark haven't stopped the island being taken over by property developers, the Barclay Brothers, who put up a castle on Alderney.

Later came three months for five consecutive years filming *Cadfael* in Budapest; locations were turning into second homes. I had been in Budapest in 1980 where I made my first starring film role in a very strange film. Called *The Man Who Went Up in Smoke*, it was based on a series famous in Sweden about a Swedish detective called Martin Beck. They had made a film of it before with Walter Matthau (in which the character was called Jake Martin), but they decided to make another with a younger actor playing the detective, shot in Stockholm and Budapest, and this was in 1980, when Budapest was still under communist rule.

During the making of *The Man Who Went Up in Smoke* I met an ex-burglar who had become an actor, and he would entertain the cast with tales of his burglaries. Years before I had a gold ring given to me by my dresser, which once belonged to the great John Barrymore, and sadly this was stolen from my Stockwell home. The thieves ripped my curtains down, left a disgusting mess on my bed, and wrecked the place. What especially hurt was the loss of personal effects, such as this ring, which was of enormous sentimental value. The burglars were never caught, but even so I doubt that locking them up would have reformed them. The only punishment to make them realise the devastation of their actions would have been to have them suffer the same sense of violation as one of their victims.

Everyone thought this ex-burglar on the set in Budapest was 'a lovely fella', but I couldn't get on with him because of this aspect of his character, which glorified his crimes and expressed no regret. I didn't confront him – the usual pattern. Most of the cast was Swedish, but they all spoke perfect English. We stayed in a very famous hotel called the Gellert, which has a fantastic swimming pool and thermal baths underneath in the basement. During the war it was the Gestapo headquarters, so it had quite a history behind it, and not always a pleasant one. Even then in the 1980s the vestibule was full of prostitutes.

I was back in Budapest for *Cadfael* in the Nineties after the 1989 revolution. For the monk they made me have a tonsure, 2½ inches in diameter: it wasn't that big, but I did feel a bit mutilated when that razor came out and suddenly I had this bald hole on the top of my head. One of the ideas is that there was nothing between a monk's thoughts and God – and God could see straight into them. Heaven forbid! Some of the young kids who came along to play monks were given the full magnum tonsure, but we were supplied with toupées for our social life.

I would get back to my hotel and stick my toupée on before going out to eat. One night I did this, and then set out to a local Chinese restaurant. I was dining alone so I took my book along, sat down and ordered my meal. When it came I put my book down to eat and for some reason scratched my head, then realised that my toupée was standing on end, sticking up. It had been very windy that evening and I looked like one of the Jedward twins from *The X Factor*. Everyone must have noticed, including the waitress taking my order. But not a word was said. Sweating and embarrassed, I relived the last half hour of my life with this thing sticking up on my head. I ripped it off, put it in my pocket and got stuck into my chop suey!

⟶∘∘∘⟵

I loved the filming of *Cadfael*. They built the set early on for the first episode in the Marfilm Studios, about thirty minutes outside Budapest; the set and the costumes looked terribly new and too highly coloured, but as time went by the set weathered.

Years later I was watching on television a new Robin Hood series, and there was *our* set. I'm not a great horseman, but I did have to ride on horseback, unconvincingly, and not easily in those flowing monk's habits, but for the most part they gave me a donkey to ride – named Daisy like my mother. It was very sweet and suited my temperament. I didn't feel drawn into the medieval Catholic world playing Cadfael, but I developed enormous affection for the character who lived in those violent and uncomfortable times. He had got a hinterland, a whole other life, because in a world of contemplation and discipline he'd spent two-thirds of his life out in the big wide world killing people. The way he dealt with violence was pre-forensic science and pre-car chases. To chase someone he had to get on a horse or run. All his detection was done by smell and touch and intuition and knowledge: not only of the world and of the human character, but also of plants, animals and nature. That is how he solved the murders.

Cadfael was a lovely character to play, but the Carlton TV people never really sold the series properly, as they never had much faith in it. I know at one point early on, the second episode I think it was, a directive came from on high that all the monks had to wear boots, not sandals, because they were frightened it was beginning to look too girlie, with our long frocks and open-toed sandals, so they decreed the monks should butch up a bit and wear hob-nailed boots.

This did us a great favour, for there were times when we were working in the Hungarian winter and it grew very cold indeed. After fifteen or so episodes, when there were more to come, they pulled the plug. They transmitted the series in mid-August, the time of year when people were not watching television. A series like that cried out for cold outside, a log fire, all toasty inside. They produced a DVD, and then it was a big success in America, where they advertised it with a huge poster, a cartoon picture of Cadfael, with a typically American message written across the top: 'Cadfael: serves God – solves crime'. They took it very seriously over there because it made money.

39

TWO BROKEN CODES FOR THE PRICE OF ONE

Hugh Whitemore became interested in writing a play about Alan Turing, the mathematician who cracked the Enigma Code in World War Two. Having read a biography of the physicist and mathematician by Alan Hodges in the *New York Review of Books*, he wrote an outline which contained much maths and logic, and showed it to me. Also involved was the impresario Michael Redington, and Clifford Williams, who had directed Whitemore's *Pack of Lies*. Nothing happened for two years and I, who was keen on the idea, kept phoning Whitemore: 'I bet you haven't finished yet' – and it was true, he hadn't.

I had lived not far from Bletchley as an evacuee, where Turing broke the German Enigma code and became one of the most important individuals of World War Two, as Winston Churchill said, in bringing about Hitler's defeat. Yet inside Turing was the child, which I, from my fortunate childhood, could at once identify with.

'As a child,' says Turing, 'my friends were numbers.'

Hugh Whitemore rang one day with the exciting news that he had a script of *Code* ready to read. I had doubts when I read the draft script. We went out to dinner at L'Escargot in Dean Street where I came straight to the point.

'It's not going to work – there is too much maths, it's too cerebral – impossible.'

'Derek,' he replied, 'remember the way you were obsessed with Roxanne in *Cyrano*?' This was not surprising because of the romantic, appealing way she was played by Sinéad. 'For the same total passion read mathematics. This is what will be sexy and exciting about Turing, the passion you put into your interest in mathematics.'

Yes, I thought, maybe Hugh has put his finger on it. I took it on when he gave me the revised script. I left with it on holiday to France and when I came back I was word perfect. I know I ought to explain what it means to have a photographic memory – which people tell me I have – but all I can say is that Turing was undoubtedly a long and complicated role to master and I managed it.

Whitemore tried to question a number of people in MI5 about the background of spying and there were, he said, 'quite a lot of people who wouldn't talk. They either said all were killed or had disappeared.' This was a danger for us, but the ticklish problem was Turing's homosexuality, the reason he was persecuted and arrested. In the play the apple he dies from eating, with echoes of the Garden of Eden, was impregnated with poison and self-administered. It was a symbol of how society viewed being gay as evil. Yet there was doubt over Turing's death: it could have been an accident, it could have been judicial murder.

The text was very wordy and throughout rehearsals Hugh was obsessively rewriting and cutting. When you think about it, a play about a gay mathematician hardly sounds like a big crowd-pleaser. But we realised that mathematics was the real sex interest in the story, not the boys Turing pursued. The key to the character was to project the excitement of his intellect with conviction, his enthusiasm and passion for his subject. We had the big speech at Bletchley, the long account about Bertrand Russell and scientific certainty, as the climax.

We were to open at the Haymarket, Nash's Majestic Theatre Royal, the brown marble and gold palace with its canopied façade on the other side of the road from *The Phantom of the Opera*. The rival attractions glared at one another – 'Derek Jacobi in the ring with Michael Crawford'. As we found out, we were to get Michael Crawford's fans when they couldn't get returns.

The theatre was steeped in such history that at one time Judi Dench thought it should be the National Theatre. The star dressing room I lived in was pure Noël Coward and it had been John Gielgud's favourite mirror station. Jack Lemmon had only lately moved out. But I dislike any after-show entertaining, which was what the suite lent itself to. Some actors give a performance on stage, then go to their dressing rooms to receive the fans and give another kind of performance. I like to wash off the make-up and go home, or at most go to a pub or restaurant. Before we opened I was shitting every colour and size of brick about being in the commercial West End: this was my first experience of it, while I had now been acting on stages just about everywhere for well over thirty years! I couldn't even bear to walk past the front-of-house. I parked my car and crept into the building at the back. I was embarrassed by those huge photos. They were of a usurper!

Although it might seem extraordinary at this stage in my theatrical career, for the first time I was having to lead a non-company, commercial venture. I was going to be the figurehead, with all the responsibilities this entailed. I was paranoid that it was all down to *me*. If the public stopped coming, it would be *my* fault; if a performance went badly, or slowly or wasn't effective, *I* was to blame – *I* had cocked it up. Worse, it was the same play over and over again. In a repertory company the variety of roles can be stimulating; you chop and change. Benedick on Monday, Prospero on Tuesday, Cyrano on Wednesday, Peer Gynt on Thursday. I would miss that; for now I had to be Alan Turing eight times a week.

By the first night we were rather dreading the public and critics' response and I don't exactly know how I managed all the different scenes: the stage set was a bizarre contrast to the theatre façade, purposefully styled so it could suggest the different locations of the seventeen different scenes: Forties aircraft hangar, high walls of early computer technology, transformers' dials, tubes, cable wires everywhere. It was like the inside of Turing's head. The play could well have been a dream, for scenes are duologues between Turing and another, and it was sometimes almost a one-man show. Men and women wander in and out of Turing's consciousness.

As with Claudius, I was in and out of Turing's younger self, and made him a non-stop fidget who bit his nails and nervously coughed and stammered. Tragically, with his uncouth appearance, in his moth-eaten tank tops and stained tweed suit, Turing had a brilliant mind, but a body which cheerfully rebelled against him with pederastic desires, wanting to pick up a bit of lovely rough over a pint.

Every night I had to go on and work incredibly hard to convince a new audience all over again of his existence. In every performance I was on trial. When I was young I could be daring, take big risks, huge, enormous, crazy risks, but when I was slightly more established I did start being taken for granted. It was expected that I was a favourite in the race and so I had to work and work, just to keep ahead, to justify being the favourite. Though it may be increasingly hard to surprise people, as an actor *surprise* I must.

When I first read the play I said this is hardly theatre, this is a lecture. Hugh and the director Clifford Williams proved me wrong: it was the scientific certainty scene which is the high point. This is where we share in Turing's own discoveries. It worked, and surprisingly turned out to be a great success on both sides of the Atlantic, while we later made it into a film which Herbie Wise directed, and Harold Pinter played the sinister Foreign Office inquisitor.

During the run of *Code*, and passing from the lofty ceilings and chandelier glitter of the Haymarket to my earthy suburban past, I had a bizarre visit. Michael Masters, my cousin, son of Mum's brother Alf who had fled some thirty years before to Australia, phoned me up, and asked if he could come and stay the night. Michael, who was the same age as me, had become very successful down under and was now on a world tour to celebrate. I said, 'Of course, do come and stay.' As soon as he came I could see he'd turned into a heavy drinker and smoker. We all retired to bed, but in the middle of the night my bedroom door burst open and a naked man blundered through saying drunkenly, 'I'm looking for the toilet!' Michael had smuggled in a one-night stand!

This made me wonder: there had always been something quite camp although understated in Dad's manner, and I remembered that with Alf, his brother-in-law, he'd always got on well. Perhaps too well!

Hugh, Dad and I went to Guildford later on to celebrate a blue plaque which was raised there in memory of Turing. I left to be photographed and Dad stayed with Hugh sitting at a table in a restaurant; he said later he didn't know what to say to Dad. There were some flowers on the table, and Hugh asked or mentioned the name of the flowers, upon which Dad, who had been very silent, suddenly grew astonishingly enthusiastic, saying, 'I can tell you all about them!' This gave Hugh a completely different perspective on my father, and I was moved when Hugh told me later that Dad took him by the hand and said, 'Thanks for all you have done for my boy.'

As Hugh had launched me into this memorable rite of passage, so too did I have the opportunity to return the favour when he married his new partner Rowan and asked me to be his best man. Hugh couldn't swim, and so one summer when I invited them to stay in France with us, I said that Richard and I would teach him.

In my best man speech at the wedding I made fun of this. Normally one is expected to lace the address on such occasions with innuendoes and seaside postcard humour, but I can never remember dirty jokes. What I did say was that I had known Ro and Hugh for many years, during which time I'd come to know some of their foibles, their fears, their fantasies, and that I would like to share an interesting fact about Hugh. He was the only person I knew, I said, out of the fairly large circle of friends and acquaintances I had, who suffered from a rare and – in certain circumstances – highly dangerous deficiency. He was totally unable to float.

I tried to teach him how to swim in France – an agonising experience, because it's not possible to make a swimmer out of a non-floater. I spent hours trying to get even just his head underwater, with endless gentle lifting of the legs at the water's edge, only to see them drift hopelessly and lifelessly down to the bottom again. A look of impotent frustration would cloud Hugh's normally benign face.

But the miracle occurred that day when Hugh, the non-floater, was now having a third helping of the matrimonial pudding – when such an over-indulgence might well have added to his sinking propensities. But here he found the infallible cure, the much-loved, much-needed rubber ring, the essential pair of water wings of the inflatable mermaid floating across the pool to support him! So now he'd be able to play in the water as in his legitimate element, confident that she would never let him down.

They would float off into the sunset of their lives, with all of us wishing them calm waters, warm breezes, gentle passage. But in order that the mermaid should stay inflated, Hugh would always need to carry a good strong pump!

40

LIFE AMONG THE
GREAT AND GOOD

We dined at the Savoy Grill. I was sitting next to her: she was a wonderful conversationalist, she was witty, she was quite a sexy lady actually, and she was a very nice companion. A fellow Libran, whose birthday falls nine days earlier than mine, I am told her Sagittarius influence could prompt her to be more out-spoken and less tactful (and more able to be decisive) than your average Libran like me.

At one point Margaret Thatcher turned to me: 'You know there are many ways in which what you do, and what I do, are the same. But there is one very interesting thing in which we are *very* different,' she said.

This was one night I was playing the Haymarket when she came along to see Jean Anouilh's *Becket*, in which Robert Lindsay played Henry II and I the turbulent priest. Bob and I were invited to dinner with her afterwards with Duncan Weldon, the producer, but Robert wouldn't go, because he was very anti-Thatcher, and couldn't bear the thought of actually having dinner with the Iron Lady.

'Oh yes, Prime Minister?' I answered, meeting her glance. 'And what is that?'

She looked at me evenly with those piercing blue eyes. 'You require a darkened auditorium,' she said, 'but I need light. I need to see their *eyes*!'

The hairs on my neck stood up – 'I need to see their *eyes!*' It was just the way she said it, very calm, that completely spooked me: 'I need to see their *eyes!*'

Until recently I couldn't understand why Bob would not go. Because I had thought, 'You know, she's part of history, even if you don't agree with her.' I did not understand why Bob refused, but I do understand it now that we have had Tony Blair. If I were asked out to dinner with Blair, I probably wouldn't go. I don't think I could sit next to Tony Blair. But I am glad I went and had that dinner.

I met John Major, too; he and his wife Norma came to see quite a number of plays I was in. He saw *Don Carlos* and was very enthusiastic, and he seemed to enjoy coming back stage. As for the royal family, I met Prince Philip, but only in passing. Every year at the end of Ascot week they have a show in Windsor Castle.

Prince Charles, who was quite close to Kenneth Branagh, asked him to put on a little Shakespeare presentation for them called 'Shakespeare's Stuff' in the Crimson Drawing Room. This was on 16 June 1982. Ken was very busy, so he asked me to do it instead, with Emma Thompson and Judi Dench. The three of us duly arrived at Windsor Castle. We were fed below stairs in the Star Chamber, while the court grandees dined upstairs, and at one point Charles came down and said, 'Is everything all right? Are they treating you OK?'

'Yes, Sir, thank you,' we said. 'Everything is fine.'

'How long is the show?' Charles asked.

'Thirty-five minutes.'

'Oh, dear – I say, you couldn't possibly make it forty-five minutes, could you?'

'Well, yes, but can someone find us a complete Shakespeare?'

They scoured Windsor Castle and couldn't find us a complete Shakespeare! Our reigning monarch didn't have a copy! Between us we dredged up sonnets from memory, and as we were also singing 'Brush up your Shakespeare' we sang it twice, once at the beginning, once at the end. Thus we stretched the entertainment out to forty-five minutes. Afterwards there was a reception, and this was the first time I met Prince Philip, who was a bit brusque. They were tired after their day at the races, so they just sat there, the Queen in lemon yellow, and Fergie, who laughed a great deal.

I retain great affection for the wholly good and worthy character of Arthur Clennam in a two-part, six-hour film of *Little Dorrit*. The novel is about altruistic, almost spiritual love, something that appeals powerfully to me, and in many ways it is Dickens's greatest novel. It is important that Amy Dorrit's attraction for Arthur is not erotic or sexual, but comes from his own inner self. In this it (and my performance) was completely unlike the recent television adaptation.

Before the director Christine Edzard started filming in Rotherhithe in 1987 she built a set down the road in a warehouse leased from the local council; she already had a permanent set for our nine months of filming at her own studios in St Mary Church Street, so this was a very East End production. Almost from the start the company became very close, as we lived there for virtually nine months. I had a room in the building where I used to stay overnight.

The first part followed the story from Arthur's point of view, the second from Little Dorrit's. One day we would film his story, the next day hers.

Under Christine's guidance I set out in my performance to switch between the perspectives, and achieve Arthur's ambivalence of character. Clennam would shift from being Amy Dorrit's hero to his own view of himself, and the placing of scenes from the two perspectives side-by-side achieved both a moving and a striking effect. In no way did Edzard treat Dickens's dialogue as sentimental, which I completely agreed with.

257

She encouraged me to bring out of the part an almost Jimmy Stewart quality, and I enjoyed showing how adaptable I could make Clennam (he must have been the typical, labile Libran!). Christine's guidance brought out of me that extraordinary quality of being able to see and show in his face the other's point of view, as well as revealing transparently his own feelings. Take a look at the coffee scene in Part One for an example.

None of the cast wore any make-up at all, and we rather objected to having our hair gelled up, to make our greasy locks look appropriate to the period. Because we filmed all the scenes in the same place on permanent sets, we became very familiar with one another, so it was like a theatrical company playing night after night, but of course with different scenes in the same characters. Organising the shooting was a logistical masterpiece.

There were some merry moments between Alec Guinness as old Dorrit, the Father of the Marshalsea, and Cyril Cusack who played his brother Frederick. These two veterans would play little games of one-upmanship or even upstaging, even though it was a film. In one scene they were sitting on a bed together, Alec in front and Cyril behind, and Alec became so tetchy about what Cyril was up to behind his back while he was speaking that at one moment he turned and asked out of character what he was doing.

'Oh, Alec, I'm ... I'm just ... thinking ...' said Cyril innocently.

'Well, fine!' Alec said. 'But then be sure you do it quietly!'

During the shooting Alec threw a rather grand dinner for twelve or fourteen people. At first we talked to the guests on either side, but there came a point when the conversation spread to take in the whole table, and the subject came up of horror films. Inevitably this meant Boris Karloff, and I expressed my view that he wasn't much of an actor, was a very strange looker, and he had a speech impediment. A hand quickly came down on my arm:

'I think you ought to stop there. I'm his widow.'

I'd dug myself such a hole and disappeared into it!

The company that made *Little Dorrit* received a mountain of fan letters for me. They held an exhibition of the costumes and photographs in the Museum of London. My white shirt was pinned up, and by the end it had turned black with the fingering by many fans. There was some eccentric Swiss woman who wrote long letters and kept pictures of me as Arthur beside her bed, so I'm told!

———

I have played a great many leaders, and that way I got to meet a lot of leaders – as well, of course, as their stage and screen counterparts. When I played Stanley Baldwin, my main scene – MacDonald's quarrel with Churchill, with Albert Finney as Churchill – was in a gentleman's urinal. In 2012 I had scenes with Winston in a twelve-part series on the building of the *Titanic*, which we filmed in Belfast in autumn 2011. I played Lord Pirie, the head of Harland & Wolff.

In the roll-call of villains I have played Hitler, President Augusto Pinochet of Chile and Philip II of Spain. The critic Nicholas de Jongh had once been heard to say at a dinner party that he wouldn't consider me for a good review until I came out of the closet. True to his promise to punish me he wrote of my Pope Hadrian VII that I acted 'as if he was in a foul mood all his life', and that he 'does not so much wear his bleeding heart on his sleeve as let it drip extravagantly over his divine white costume ... speed is this actor's addiction'. Tut, tut, Nicholas. He wrote the play *Plague Over England*, a travesty of the life of my great friend Gielgud: need I say more?

I did *Macbeth* for the RSC, directed by Adrian Noble, which was on the road for twelve weeks in a huge, cumbrous set with cantilevered platforms, which were never going to work. De Jongh summarily executed my Macbeth as an 'example of high-risk flirting and clear miscasting'. He implicated Noble, too, in the deed, saying 'he hardly helps'. Duncan Weldon, who co-produced this with the RSC, defended my Macbeth, claiming I had 'been neglected', while pointing out it was Adrian's third attempt at the Scottish play, and that his actress wife, Joanna, had just had a baby, so his mind might have been elsewhere. I'm not sure this was relevant: perhaps more to the point were the sleep-suit costumes which made us all look like moon astronauts.

Macbeth was in 1994, the same year I was accorded my knighthood, and it may be that de Jongh was even more irked by this fact, for now I still was not going to shout I was gay from the rooftops, while I still didn't care if anyone knew or not. At my Buckingham Palace Investiture the Coldstream Guards Band was playing above on the balcony, and as I came forward to receive the honour they struck up the Perry Como number 'It's Impossible': just perfect, I thought. The Queen, who had hurt her shoulder in a riding accident, dubbed me with the sword but couldn't put the gong over my head, which was done by someone else.

She spoke of the visit I had made to Windsor Castle over ten years before, which she had remembered, and asked what I was doing now. There was an even earlier encounter with her in 1972. I was performing in *Richard III* at the MacRobert Centre, Stirling University, with Dickie Briers, and on the day she visited the university there were violent student riots. Protesters had taken over the lifts and closed various exits from the building. The Queen was forced to leave by a different route, and had to pass by where I was standing: with reference to our play she remarked, 'Some things never change!'

Over in the States I was awarded a prestigious Shakespeare prize, the Folger Prize, given for services to Shakespeare, which consisted of a very large golden quill which I keep upstairs: the only award given in the name of John Gielgud. In recognition the White House invited me to breakfast to meet the President, where about 200 people were present. At the last moment Clinton couldn't attend because he was urgently called away to Atlanta, but Hillary, a study in sexiness and power if ever there was one, was the hostess, and made a brilliant speech.

In London the Queen Mother came infrequently to my shows, while Princess Margaret frequently. I grew quite pally with her, but I definitely did not like her, for she was actually rather rude. When she saw *Richard II* at the Phoenix, word came round that 'Princess Margaret would like to see you afterwards. Would you remain on stage at the end of the performance?'

I did, and she kept me waiting: she had gone into hospitality, had a couple of whiskies, and then tottered through to say hello on stage half an hour later. At another time I was invited after my show to dine with her and some ballet friends at Joe Allen's. I arrived, I sat down, where I was seated next to her. We were chatting away and she was relating something about her mum and her sister; we were getting on very well indeed. All the time she was smoking, and when the food came she would put down the cigarette, still alight on the ashtray; it would smoulder away while she had some soup or hors d'oeuvre, then take another puff, then put it back on the ashtray.

At one point she snapped open her cigarette case and selected another cigarette, and the lighter was there on the table. I picked up the lighter and was just about to light the cigarette for her. She snatched it out of my hand and gave it to David Wall, one of her ballet friends, for him to light her cigarette.

I had overstepped the mark. She had led me on to think we were chummy, but no, not a bit of it! 'You don't light my cigarette, dear, oh no, you're not that close!' This was so unnecessary. I was there at her invitation, and she made me feel very small.

Another royal encounter happened when Queen Margrethe of Denmark was on a state visit here. There was a state banquet thrown for her with 300 guests at Windosr Castle. My Danish knighthood medallion was very discreet, and I found that to wear. But I couldn't find the medal of my English knighthood, which is quite a modest pendant you wear round your neck. I could only find the elaborate decoration with the long ribbon, so I had to wear that. I felt it was very *lèse majesté*: I looked like the fairy on top of the Christmas tree!

We sat down to eat. I had a seat at a very long table: that night I dined in royal company. There were flunkeys everywhere with white gloves, and there were these gold plates which were put down before each of us, and then another plate was placed on top with food. I had navigated the soup, and that was cleared away, and then the waiter came and placed this gold plate too close to me, so I pushed it away more onto the table.

As I did this my fingers stuck because it was molten hot, and I couldn't pull my fingers off. I saw blisters forming down the side of my index finger and thumb. It was agony! Eventually the lady-in-waiting next to me understood what had happened and said, 'We'll get you some ice.'

They brought me a tumbler full of ice into which I plunged my thumb and fingers. Every time I took them out it was so painful I had to put them back in.

'Please, can I go and see a nurse or the St John's Ambulance man?' I asked her.

'No, no,' she said firmly, 'you can't leave till after the speeches.'

People round us were beginning to notice that someone was sitting there with his fingers in a tumbler of ice. Two places down sat Princess Michael of Kent who was heard to say, rather loudly to the table, 'Oh, take no notice, he's an actor. He's just showing off!'

I sat there while the darling lady-in-waiting cut up my food because I couldn't use my hand.

The Queen rose and made her speech, and by now the blisters were forming even more. The Danish Queen made her contribution to the formality of the occasion. I turned to the lady-in-waiting and said, 'Can I leave?'

At that moment the doors opened and three pipers from the Coldstream Guards entered, piped their way down the table, round the table, up the table, and I still couldn't get out. They did it again, the fuckers; they did a second circuit, but then they were out. But I still had to wait for the Queens to leave the company. Then I rushed to a nurse who put this gel on my finger and thumb.

Like Cinderella I fled from the palace: I couldn't bear to stay a moment longer. That was my big night out at Windsor Castle.

AGE VII
STRANGE
EVENTFUL
HISTORY

41

MY NEW FAMILY

After Mum's death, and after the fall-out from Cynthia, Dad became a part of my and Richard's life: we saw much more of him. He was my only living relative, my only claim to having a family. Only Raymond's son, the adoptee of Hilda, carried the name of Jacobi, but not my direct line.

Richard and I were more together now, as we have been ever since. He is more thoughtful, more aware of people's private atmospheres, what affects them and what their problems are, than I am. Richard wades in, does something about it, and remembers a week later to ring up and say, is it still all right? This is thoughtfulness, for sure, but I cannot think of quite the right word for it, for he is not saintly, but basically he is good.

To return to the age of thirty-nine, while still living in my house at Stockwell, and while I had been on my own for so many years, I had at last found someone with whom to share my life, as Mum and Dad had so fruitfully shared their life together. In Stockwell, Richard was the one who wanted to move. He wanted a bigger, grander place, and he likes the style in which we live now.

For years he had wanted a housekeeper, it is part of his background, and for him it is absolutely normal. I still feel a bit self-conscious when given my lunch by Beverley, our indispensable and much-loved housekeeper, and it doesn't feel totally natural. If something goes wrong, Richard is onto it and he doesn't make me feel guilty, or feel obliged to him, except when we have a row. Richard to an extent has taken the place of my parents for he gets everything done, and he does it for me and I have abrogated my responsibilities. I say, 'Richard would do that, I'll get Richard to do that' – and he does, but he wants recognition for doing it.

He is a brilliant cook and a great do-it-yourselfer, both of which I am not; he is a shopaholic, which I am not, so, as there are always things that we need, they appear because he loves going out to buy them. All that he can do to make life easier for me he does, and he does not do it for me to be grateful. He does it absolutely naturally because he enjoys it. I couldn't quite believe my solitude could, and would, be at last broken, but I became completely happy that it was.

Even so, I still sometimes revert or regress to the mindset of a loner, and find myself, as I did unkindly in an interview in 2007, being niggardly and a tetchy beast, saying, 'I remained single because I'm just not the marrying kind. Nor have I ever wanted my own children, although I adore other people's and have four godchildren. I am a bit of a loner, not in a sad way, but in that I am content in my own company. My only concession to sharing my home is my Irish terrier, Bella.' I hope Richard never saw this: it was a mood that passed.

When we first acquired Bella as a puppy Richard slept on the floor on an improvised bed, while she was locked in behind electric fences. She howled all night, and he spent the night with her: I couldn't bear the howling. I loathe social gatherings, and can't stand the thought of making small talk with a drink in one hand and eating things off sticks with the other. This is not very complimentary to Richard, who is more gregarious and loves people.

Richard is a typical Gemini – he is two people and there are two sides to him. He is very lovable and people respond to him in a lovable way. He is very outgoing, but the other side, the darker personality, is that he is very much into himself. I have known him in the past sink into depression. When he was down, he was under the floorboards. He would be much less tolerant of me and my work. He would speak, but there wouldn't be a smile. Usually jokey and playful, all that disappeared. He had to go and see somebody, and now he takes happy pills. All our circle of friends do, and generally most of the people we know have a little help, either counselling or taking happy pills. God knows what would happen if he didn't: when he first started the dose was much bigger, but now, just to be on the safe side, he is on the minimum.

It is a mark of who and what he is that I have probably become a little more dependent on him than is healthy, in that he is the leader on the private domestic front. Whenever we have a row – and we don't have that many because I'm non-confrontational – I will just scream for a second and walk away. But the one thing he says is: 'You're not supporting me – support me, support me!' I feel I am supporting, I do support him, but maybe, because he is such a supporter himself, my efforts do not actually register or measure up to his as a supportive person. He needs constant reassurance.

He has been a remarkable son to his parents, a son that neither of them really deserved or appreciated – and when they have needed him in their later years he is unfailingly there for them.

My great bugbear is that he tends to put me down and send me up before others, and I have heard, and I am sure they say, 'Look at the way he is treating Derek!' They believe I should be treated with respect because of my age and acclaim. I receive so much acclaim, so many pats on the back, and fans saying I am wonderful, perhaps he feels that I can afford the brickbats.

Sometimes we have spats about that for it does rile me, and when we are back home I say I don't like to be talked about in that way. But that competitive thing is never vicious between us. He has to fight his corner, and while in a sense it has faded over the years it is still vestigially there.

But by now I have well overstepped the mark: it is Richard's turn.

Richard: 'Older as Derek was, he has had a very stabilising effect on me. Derek has no insecurity about who he is, although he may worry and fuss and be anxious about details. I was very mixed up when I first met him, unsure of my direction in so many ways. The fact that he was such a settling factor for me increased his attraction, particularly seeing the way his parents loved and supported him. People like Derek coming from such a secure background just have a different aura. I would joke with him because I was feeling so jealous of his background: "Why don't I have parents like yours?"

'He is so easily able to immerse himself in any role he plays because he had such a support system in his parents, and this enables him, also, to be deeply generous on stage to others, which is a sign of how secure you are in yourself. He has an innate understanding of character. He spends most of the day preparing for his performance in the evening, and he hates all the paraphernalia and bullshit of stardom. He leads by example, but he has no idea of his power as an actor and as a leader of a company.

'We have an idyllic time together, but I am the more volatile of the two. He likes praise and public acclaim, and is determined to avoid conflict at any cost. Derek always claims he is a typical Libran, while I am a Gemini, a two-faced bastard, a difficult sign they say, but it is best for a Gemini to avoid unwise whims and fancies, for he or she fluctuates between the yin and yang. Libra and Gemini can make a good partnership all the way around. Mentally and artistically these two can "make the scene work", with just enough contrast to make life interesting, and little combat expected.

'So we were, from that time on, a permanent couple and so we have remained, but not without, as all couples, our ups and downs. For instance ...'

42

THE SUMMONS

The theatre was always – and still is – my first love and commands my greatest loyalty. I was working so hard now that I had approached the 200 mark of roles played.

Someone pointed out the other day they had seen a headline, 'Derek is one of life's great constants,' and I wondered, 'What on earth can that be about? It doesn't sound a bit like me.' It didn't refer to any appearances I made, but to what was called an 'under-fives thing' on CBeebies Television called *In the Night Garden*, for which I have simply been the constant narrator for over 100 episodes. I became known as Igglepiggle!

Night Garden is made by the team that created *Teletubbies*. For those who don't have small children, it is about bizarre little creatures who live and play in a gentle summer woodland that can be reached only in the night. Its success is sensational, not only for those between one and five, but with the parents, too, and it has won a BAFTA: it is absolutely sweet. Constant, too, have been the scores, nay hundreds, of sound recordings I have made over the years, beginning, the very first time I received cash for them, with the Marlowe Society at Cambridge.

Role after role came and went in the accelerating pace of television appearances. For instance, in *Nanny McPhee* I did a double act with Patrick Barlow, but most of our stuff ended up on the cutting-room floor; we worked out lots of gags but it all went: bits of us remain, that's all.

———————

Mum and Dad were always my greatest fans. When I lived in Stockwell they'd come round every week; they'd wash and polish my car, fill my freezer, worry about washing my clothes, sensing I could do without trivial things and just concentrate on my work.

Then one day came the summons. Dad had not been very well for some time.

We celebrated my father's ninetieth birthday in the year 2000, here in the Hampstead garden with a party among the flowers he absolutely adored. He used to come here and plant pink busy lizzies and begonias, not Richard's favourites. I was on tour and I had a week off. I used to ring him constantly, and once when I rang him he told me, 'I'm a bit breathless, son, I'm a bit breathless ...'

'Look,' I told Dad. 'You are ninety, you live on your own in Essex Road.'

'I'll go to the doctor's,' he said, so he went to see the doctor. The doctor said, 'I think you should go into the hospital for them to do some tests that I can't do.' He went into hospital, they did a test and they said, 'We think you ought to stay in overnight.'

So, still a driver, he drove back home, put the car, his pride and joy Rover, symbolic of his status, in the garage, packed a bag, called a taxi, and went back to the hospital. He was taken straight into Casualty, and it was then that I was told it was only a matter of time before he would go. I went in to see him every day and I was with him all the time, constantly by his side.

Dad was very smooth-skinned and pink-faced. In a sense it was a good thing it was so quick. They diagnosed that he had galloping leukaemia; you can have chronic and acute leukaemia, and he had the second: it was the really dangerous one which he had. And it got him very quickly.

Four days later the end came. He was not in pain, but in great distress. He kept saying to me, 'I want to go home,' to which I would reply, 'It'll be all right, I'll take you home.'

The nurse who had joined us said to me, 'He's asking you to give him permission to go.'

Somehow Dad picked this up, and now started saying, 'I want to go, I want to go.'

All I could say to this was, 'Dad, I love you very much, but if you want to go, then you must go.'

Dad just looked at me and then he died ...

This all came back to me with poignant power and force when I played the father in John Mortimer's *Voyage Round My Father* at the Donmar. It was just as if it happened yesterday. I felt I could try to recreate for the father the feelings I had for Dad, and get the audience to share them with me. And most importantly of all there was the deathbed scene. I have never witnessed anybody die before, and it was the manner of his passing I tried to convey when I came to do the play. I had to die on stage in a wheelchair: this in the Donmar, so people were very close. I thought this has got to be as real as possible.

For Thea Sharrock, who directed the Mortimer play, it set the tone of rehearsals straight away:

'Playing the blind father Derek had studied beautifully the actions and characteristics of a blind man, and of course deline- ated perfectly the compensatory gifts the blindness gave him, such as the strong memory. Everyone pretended that he wasn't blind. The way he senses through his long delicate fingers and the piercing blue eyes which see nothing was very moving.

'He made the whole part of the father especially moving in a sense that it was part of his soul, and based on his memory of his own father. For the section when he dies he says he recalls the death of his father, and the breathing, too, especially the sound of his dad's last breath; he recalled this, and this very soulful moment came into his performance. He was always alert to the rhythm and pattern of the timing, especially in this death with the breath, the memory of his own father's death, and the fine honing of the detail.'

Thea's generosity apart, in the back of my head I am saying to Dad, 'I hope you won't mind my using you as an example,' and then telling myself, 'Of course he won't mind.' So I was reproducing how he went, and people really did think, I believe, it was as real as it could possibly be, while some of the audience thought it was too realistic. I repeated it again in 2010 for Lear when at the end he dies.

After he was dead I missed Dad hugely. Right up to that week he had been fine. I don't think he was in pain when he died, but he was in distress and discomfort. One of the hardest things for me was the selling of the house in Essex Road, because it held so many memories.

43

WALKS ON THE
DARK SIDE

'Champagne for my real friends! Real pain to my sham friends!'
This was Francis Bacon's great toast, his champagne toast, that
he always gave to the company as they raised their glasses.

It was John Maybury's title, *Love is the Devil* – he wrote it and
directed it – that brought me to play the artist. What the title
actually meant is summed up by what Francis Bacon the painter
was: a physical masochist, a spiritual sadist. He liked to receive
pain physically, but he liked to give it mentally, inflict mental
sadism on others. Life he would refer to as 'a spasm of consciousness between two voids' – not a happy bunny by any means. We
couldn't have been greater opposites.

I knew the paintings. I wasn't particularly enamoured of them,
but I had to get to know them better to play him. We weren't
allowed to use any of them, for the Marlborough Fine Art gallery,
representing the Bacon Estate, wouldn't allow them to be shown
on film. John reacted to that by making every frame, in the way
he shot it, in the way he lit it particularly, like a Bacon painting.
So actually he benefited by their saying 'You can't use them.'

Francis was never to be seen painting, for John said, 'In every
biopic of a great artist the moment you start seeing the actor
painting you lose belief.' If you see I have a paint brush in
my hand, then the canvas isn't in the same shot. The only time
the two are together, when you see me put paint on a canvas,

275

is when I place a dustbin lid on the canvas and with a brush circle round the lid.

We filmed it fairly quickly, over several weeks, and some was shot in the Colony Club, then recreated in the studios, and elsewhere we filmed in the streets of London. All the extras were Francis's friends, the real thing, which was very daunting for me. Coming on the set at ten o'clock one morning, with Tilda Swinton playing Muriel Belcher, the foul-mouthed manageress who would sit in a corner and call everyone 'Cunty' – she used to shout 'Hello Cunty!' – there was one lady, one flame-haired lady who threw herself on me, saying, 'Oh Francis, Francis!'

She was pissed out of her mind but she really did think I was Francis, which helped enormously. Dan Farson was another one close to Francis, who had written a book called *The Gilded Gutter Life of Francis Bacon*, and who had a pub on the Isle of Dogs: he was very encouraging, too. I relished playing Bacon – having the cigarettes stubbed out on me was wonderful!

Bacon wasn't the handsomest of men ever, and although I don't consider myself that either, the speed with which they made me look like him in the make-up chair in all of ten minutes rather frightened me. I think it had to do mainly with the eyes. I have always had bags under my eyes, and I think mainly they emphasised these, and of course they dyed my hair. I looked like Francis Bacon pretty much within minutes, which depressed me.

Love is the Devil does very well in DVD sales: this is because George, my boyfriend, is played by Daniel Craig. There are several scenes where Daniel is bollock-naked, so all the girls want to see what 007 has got to show!

I have done many more TV or film roles than I describe at any length, or even at all – for instance Lord Fawn in *The Pallisers*, and Klaus Wenzer in *The Odessa File* with Jon Voigt, who disappointed me greatly when he dried on a line, blaming me, saying, 'Oh, Derek gave me the letter with the wrong hand,' a typical actor trick.

The highly unsympathetic (I am being polite) Otto Preminger miscast me as the spy Davis in *The Human Factor*, with Robert Morley. Robert loved his gambling to the point of compulsion. We had a three-hour wait in the middle of one night when filming, so he took me to his club, the Scaramouche, placed £200 cash in my hand and said, 'This is for you, it's a present; if you win anything you can keep it.'

I won and did keep it. We didn't get paid for this film because the production money ran out, and Otto wouldn't dip into his huge personal fortune to pay his artists: only John Gielgud received his fee in cash, on the very day it was due. But I benefited from Robert's generosity and kept my winnings.

Otto was a monster, disgraceful, dictatorial, and vile with the crew. With Robert, who played the doctor who poisoned my character, he was little better. Robert had to handle a doctor's bag and find things in it. He wasn't good with props, for he would drop them or get tangled and panic, so he said to Otto: 'Don't shout at me or I shall get fussed, darling.'

Otto instantly screamed out: '*Don't call me darling!*' whereupon Robert completely went to pieces. Nicol Williamson, who was also in the film, used to come up behind us unseen and boom out in Otto's voice to frighten the hell out of us. *The Human Factor* was great preparation for when I came to play Guy Burgess in *Philby, Burgess, Maclean*, a part I adored.

My first opportunity to go to the States had been during the National Theatre years, when we were playing the Ahmanson

Theatre in Los Angeles with *Three Sisters*, and I was Baron Tuzenbach. Maggie Smith had been nominated for her Oscar for *The Prime of Miss Joan Brodie*, which she later won, and the English company was invited to a reception at the Dorothy Chandler Pavilion. It was a sit-down affair after the performance, with four to a table, and my partner was Louise Purnell. An old man came over and sat down at our table, and we had no idea who he was until he introduced himself as George Cukor.

Every star of that era you could think of was in the Pavilion and seated for dinner – I'd be telling Mum and Dad all about it – but we still had not got our lady. At last at the door appeared this glamorous creature with mounds of Titian hair. She had long drop emerald earrings, a long coat-like dress, and it was like the Queen arriving. She sailed in straight to her table – our table. It was Greer Garson, and what an extraordinary and stunning entrance she made! The excitement I had as a child in the presence of a great star was as vivid as ever.

The company had slept in an apartment hotel in the Wilshire Boulevard. I shared with Charlie Kay. Just off the plane with jet lag, Charlie and I couldn't sleep and both of us went for a walk across the local park, which we didn't know was the notorious MacArthur Park. When we reached the other side we were taken for drug dealers and pulled over by a police car, for we hadn't realised this was a seriously dangerous neck of the woods.

'Terribly sorry, officer, we're British actors belonging to the English National Theatre!' – spoken in our plummiest accents.

Moved on, Charlie and I wandered into the Alvarado Street red-light district where every other building was a porno cinema. I'd never been to one, but Charlie was keen: he said, 'Come on, we have to go and have this experience!'

It was called *These Boots Were Made for Licking*. A few minutes into the viewing and we were falling about in hysterics – they booted us out!

As for my real-life walks on the dark side, there have been few.

I have always had a problem with hateful and evil characters. Sir Laurence rehearsed in early 1967, while still acting Othello, the part of Edgar, the Captain in Strindberg's *The Dance of Death*. This is the extraordinary account the Swede gives of love and hate in a marriage, a part which, as Larry said, was nine-tenths hate. I could never have played it, and never did, yet for Olivier it was a supreme role. He identified with Edgar, saying, 'There's hardly a thing I haven't been guilty of saying or feeling towards some or other marriage partner ... the power to wound became the obsession.'

He gave more than 100 performances, and watching Sir made me, as it did many of my friends, speechless with admiration. Yet there was a moment of great tenderness in this performance. This is when Sir picks up and cuddles a cat, and he is so tender it was extraordinary. It reaffirmed my belief that what made Sir a great actor was the choices he made: to pick up and cuddle a cat at that moment was an extraordinary choice.

I was never capable of hatred, or feel I identify personally with it – and hardly ever see my own life in the characters I play on stage (one exception was *A Voyage Around My Father*). In my own estimation, at least, I have very gentle eyes (and so I have been told) which makes it difficult to convey malevolence. The aggression does not come naturally in the way the vulnerability does.

In *Dead Again*, made in Hollywood, which Ken Branagh directed with me and Emma Thompson in the leads, I played the murderous hypnotist Madson. My work before with Ken had been entirely classical. When still a schoolboy many years before, he had come to see my *Hamlet* when we opened at Oxford. He brought his girlfriend whom he wanted to impress and it wasn't, he said, the most obvious evening's entertainment for a young suburban couple. He was obviously bowled over by the tremendous pace and excitement of the production, and my acting excited his ambition, so he wrote me a lovely note about his enthusiasm, and how he wanted to be an actor.

A couple of years later, when he was studying at RADA, he contacted me when I was still doing Hamlet and asked if he could come and interview me for the Royal Academy magazine. He was very personable and ambitious, and immediately quite at home talking to me, and he told me how much he hungered to play Hamlet in the future. I didn't much remember him except his name, but was really surprised when only about eighteen months later I saw that he'd made a hit with Rupert Everett in *Another Country*, and become a star almost overnight.

Then, when I was doing the four plays for the RSC, Ken was by now in the other half of the company, and we got together and talked again about *Hamlet*, which now he wanted me to direct. He struck out on his own, forming, at the astonishingly young age of twenty-six, his own Renaissance Theatre Company, and adopted the role I loved and applauded, that of the old actor-manager – as such a tonic and an inspiration in a theatre world dominated by Oxbridge directors. Here was someone at last with the breadth and energy and the multitasking skills of Sir Laurence who could carry these values into a new epoch, so I fell in, although with misgivings, with his ambition to have me direct him as Hamlet.

Remember, this was the first time I ever directed, and although I held nothing back and put at his disposal all my experience, and helped him achieve a truly remarkable and acclaimed performance, it was not something I found, on reflection afterwards, I ever wanted to do again. I was tremendously happy to offer him all the advice I could, about pacing in the long scenes and speeches, when to rest, how to shape the overall structure of the part. Although Ken kept reassuring me in my hesitancy in telling him what to do, with comments such as 'You are taking to directing as a duck to water,' I knew at heart it wasn't me. Gladly and lovingly I could give to Ken all the tricks and expertise, the instincts the years had built up in me and endowed me with, but I knew this was a one-off: I really needed to keep them in future *all* for me.

Thankfully this was by no means the end of Ken and me working together, for I played the Chorus in his magnificent film, with his stupendous blood-curdling performance of *Henry V*, and I then played Claudius in his film of *Hamlet*. In the former I did have, as Ken joked, scrambled Shakespeare whirring through my brain, because I was just about to open as Richard II, and was rehearsing Richard III. But what greater and more stirring depictions of scene and atmosphere are there than those five Chorus speeches?

Then, having directed Ken as Hamlet, I was thrilled to play Claudius, for me the perfect villain because he smiles and smiles, and behaves in such a courtly and plausible way. I loved him. So with Ken I have been truly in my element.

Now he'd brought me to Hollywood to play Franklin Madson, whose surname conveys exactly what he was. Donald Sutherland had been originally hired to play Madson, but Sutherland and Ken didn't hit it off. English-born, by profession an antique dealer, Madson was to provide the encounter with Hollywood which enrolled me in the list of notable villains. Branagh made the most of my looks. 'OK, we'll take what we've got and we'll use that' was his attitude.

Acting on screen is particularly to do with thinking. And the eyes, being the windows of the soul, are where the thoughts come through. This film was shot mostly in black and white, which can give the actor a sculpture he does not normally possess.

Sweeping through the gates of Paramount on my first day for *Dead Again* in a stretch limo seemed to have fulfilled a fantasy of mine. But Ken, Emma and I were far from the usual run of stars. During shooting, things went badly wrong in Ken's caravan: there was no hot water. Ken arrived back after filming, and there was no hot water running in the tap. He let it be known and they immediately went into panic mode, but Ken said,

'Don't worry – I'll move into Emma's caravan.' Your usual Hollywood star would have thrown 10,000 tempers.

One detail provided something for me that had become recognisable from *I, Claudius*: Madson suddenly develops again the stammer which hypnosis had cured when he was a boy. I told Ken it would look like a professional in-joke, and asked him to cut it. But Ken insisted on keeping it. He pointed out that it was there in the script, long before I was cast for the part, but he also said, 'You've got to stammer on one line, it *is* an in-joke.' More seriously the Association for Stammerers took exception to the film's implication that the disability can be cured by hypnosis. I thought it was quite right to protest, saying, 'It might give a lot of people false hope,' and I endorsed a round-robin letter for the British press.

Research for the part consisted largely of bringing a personal experience to bear: the visit I made to a hypnotist in 1979 to stop smoking. The hypnotist had a soporific, melodic, sleeping-pill sort of voice, very relaxing and comforting. That is what I recreated in the film. But I wasn't so amused when the time came for the big fight at the end when Madson dies. We had two stuntmen for this, but when they put on our hairpieces – the blond one for me and a red one for Ken – they looked ridiculous: two wigs fighting. So it was decreed that Ken and I 'should fight to the death' ourselves.

First Ken throws me across the room and he bashes my head into that glass cabinet which shatters, so I almost knocked myself out, even though the glass was fortunately made of icing sugar. Then for the plunge onto the giant scissors, which was my *coup de grâce*, I had to run along and fall from an upper gallery to the room below – this was about 10 feet high – dive and land face downwards on mattresses and padding. Throughout the day of filming one of the stuntmen taught me by stages how to do it: to start from kneeling to throw myself forward, then from standing throw myself, then to dive from the height. Finally I did it for real and we filmed it. What a relief it was over!

Ebullient Ken, rot his soul, insisted I do it a second time. 'I really need a shot from below. We want to see the expression on your face all the way down, Derek.' So his fifty-three-year-old co-star had to do it again. I did it for Ken.

'Fine. Just one more time, Derek, just one!' My wrists and arms by now were coming off, but I did it, I did it, but I was in more than a bit of a mess! This was love of one's fellow actor, it really was!

'That's nice,' I thought when one critic said Madson alone was worth the price of an admission ticket. 'It's a success.' It became a top grossing film in the United States, but I haven't heard from Mr Spielberg yet.

Being in Hollywood was another world. My natural habitat was the theatre, and the framework of big acting companies. Ken and Emma had a house in the Hollywood Hills with an egg-shaped pool and a view over the city; I would go over for Sunday lunch. The Americans didn't know what to make of the British actors. Here was a star actor-director and an actress with no ego, no temperament, and who behaved in a completely ordinary way. They were gobsmacked.

Another evil man was the collaborator and murderer Breton in *The Tenth Man*, the World War Two Graham Greene story. I was in Los Angeles when I heard I had been nominated for an Emmy for Breton. I said, 'It's not my scene, I hate it, I'm going back to London.' When I arrived at LA airport and was in the bar having a little drink to steady my nerves before boarding the plane I saw on the screen at the back of the bar all the Hollywood glitterati walking along the red carpet for the Emmy Awards. I was so grateful I was not a part of it. I flew home to arrive at the airport, and here Richard met me. Richard said at once, 'You won! You won!'

I thought it was classy not to have gone to the awards.

I was one of the three finalists for the casting of Hannibal Lecter for *The Silence of the Lambs*: the others were Daniel Day-Lewis and Tony Hopkins. The director was Jonathan Demme, who was very sweet and gave me five minutes of his time, but I cannot have sat on my Mr Nice enough, and I knew at once this was never going to happen. They were determined to have a Brit for their villain, though, and I'm not sure what this says about us.

Goodness knows how it would have turned out if I had played the part, but I would have been malevolent in a very different way. Tony Hopkins has harder eyes than I have. He was wonderful, but the only thing about it which remains really puzzling for me is this: Lecter bites people to death, he tears out their hearts and he eats them, and there's one scene when he's transported from one place to another, and he has this extraordinary muzzle and mask on to stop him snarling, biting and tearing flesh.

So one thinks – or rather I do – why didn't they give him an injection and take his teeth out? He couldn't gum people to death!

44

RUSSELL CROWE'S BUM

In *Gladiator* with Russell Crowe, when we spent twelve weeks in Valletta, Malta, in spring 1999, I played the Roman senator Gracchus, and it was during the filming that Oliver Reed died. I had worked before with Olly in a film based on a true story at Longleat. Occasionally, if you are still awake well after midnight, it comes on television and is called *Blue Blood*, the film version of a book written by that strange man, the Marquis of Bath, in whose stately home we filmed, with all the 'wifelets' and the Kama Sutra bedroom.

Under his former name Alexander Thynne he wrote a book called *The Carry Cot*, which was about the abuse of his daughter by the nanny: the nanny was in thrall to the butler, who was a Satanist. Oliver played the butler, I played the Marquis of Bath, and Meg Wyn-Owen played the nanny. We filmed much of it at Longleat. I had bedroom scenes in the Kama Sutra room with the Marquis of Bath's wife, who was a Hungarian-born French actress called Anna Gaël. She was also the lady of Longleat.

There was a Page Three girl taking part whose name was Fiona Lewis, an actress model. For the nude bedroom scenes the mistress of Longleat, Anna Gaël, also had to be naked, and so had I. Anna was very self-conscious, clasping her dressing gown round her to make sure no one could see her bits. She would take off her gown a little at a time, get into the bed, take it off a little more under the sheets, all very coy. Meanwhile Fiona, the Page Three girl, just stripped and said, 'OK boys, there it all is, the tits, the cunt, have a good look, get over it!' And they did, and within seconds they weren't looking, whereas with Anna they all couldn't wait to see a bit more.

This was my first film with Olly, and we hit it off at once. I think he really liked me, and when he was sober he was the gentlest, kindest of fellows. When he was drunk he was very aggressive, and could be dangerous. He was very competitive, too. Once in the bar at our hotel in Longleat, where there was a barracks nearby, some soldiers came in for a drink. He was chatting to these soldiers when he suddenly came out with 'OK!' and selected three peanuts from the saucer on the bar counter and threw these three peanuts down on the floor.

'The three of us – the first to get these peanuts out of this bar, out of the hotel, across the road to the other side: with your nose! Five hundred quid for the winner!'

These soldiers got down on all fours, pushing the peanuts with their noses, and they and Olly did it. I was watching, and naturally he was winning – he had to – when they packed it in. He gave them the £500, but he had to win.

On *Gladiator*, for the insurance he had to promise not to touch a drop, and he was, as the slave dealer Proximo, being marvellous, for this was his big comeback. One weekend his wife Josephine was with him, but I think because of the death of her grandmother she had to return to Cork, leaving Olly in Valletta on his own.

He straight away got pissed in the bar at the hotel, so drunk that they cleared the bar, because nobody would go near him except for me, John Shrapnel and David Schofield, who were the three senators in the film. We sat there in the Forum in end-less shots like the three monkeys – see no evil, hear no evil, speak no evil – and we calmed him down.

His wife flew back to Malta and it was the following Sunday. They went out together to a pub and he was still hitting the booze. A boat had just docked so the pub was full of sailors: he challenged them – this was at two o'clock in the afternoon – and fell off his stool. Soon after that he was dead. We found out later he had downed three bottles of rum the previous night. Next day, being a Monday, they carried on filming, and the cast and crew held a minute's silence on the Colosseum set. It was very moving. By the afternoon they had already found a lookalike, and when you stared across the Colosseum there was Olly – except that it wasn't Olly: it was a doppelgänger. This was eerie, it was bizarre, but this is how the movies work.

They had shot most of the film, but the ending was to have been a big scene for Olly. The last shot should have shown him as Proximo returning to the arena where Russell Crowe is lying dead, so they had to change the ending. My character Gracchus was due to be stoned to death, and I am in prison, but because of Olly's death I was upped and reinstated, and let out. So when Russell Crowe is lying dead in the middle of the arena, instead of Olly as Proximo, it is Gracchus who comes forward and says, 'Who will help me lift Marcus?'

All these giant gladiators, with legs up to their armpits, step forward and between us we pick up Russell Crowe and hoist him on our shoulders. This was done in long shot. We pick him up, but he is way up high above me, for with these giants he is out of my reach. I am not touching him at all, but in long shot it looks as if he is on all our shoulders, including mine.

We fast forward to the stage door of the Vaudeville Theatre where I am performing *God Only Knows*, Hugh Whitemore's play about the Resurrection of Jesus Christ, claiming it was a fake and had never taken place. It had not been a great success, for, as Duncan Weldon said, any play with God in the title does not go down well. One night I am leaving the stage door when a woman comes forward, asks me for my autograph, and plants a kiss on my shoulder.

'What on earth was that for?' I respond.

'I'm a *Gladiator* fan,' she says, 'and that shoulder's had Russell Crowe's bum on it!'

I didn't like to tell her, 'I got nowhere near his bum, love – he was way up there out of reach!'

45

SHAKESPEARE'S
END-GAMES

When I was first asked to play Prospero I was in my forties. I thought about it very carefully and then decided it did make sense for me to play it at that age. Prospero is often played as if he were a very old man, a kind of patriarchal Magus, but there is no reason why he should be. Miranda, his daughter, is only fifteen – the text is explicit about that – and he has spent twelve years on the island. She was a child of three, he tells her, when they arrived. Later he speaks of her having been 'a third of his life', and one interpretation of the line would only make him a man in his mid-forties.

I am not sure that he is old in body, and I am trying to think not. But I do think he has grown old in his mind. His researches into magic and his working with the elements have made his brain old. His brain has been under the most tremendous pressure to learn all the secrets of magic, and he has achieved that, but it has almost burned him out. When he talks of being near death, then he is speaking the truth, but it is not a bodily illness: he is dying from the inside. He is a man who is now mortally sick in his head.

So when I speak the famous lines, beginning 'We are such stuff as dreams are made on', I emphasise the 'we' very strongly. Is Prospero in fact saying that just as the visions he has conjured up, or the characters Shakespeare has created, are figments of the human imagination, so then man himself is a Divine dream?

I think this is so. Prospero has come to believe this himself and he has found it upsetting. He has achieved this awesome power by his working in magic, yet perhaps, after all, it is not as he thought. He is most deeply disturbed.

Michael Grandage was running the Crucible Theatre in Sheffield. He heard I had done *The Tempest* at Stratford, where I had not been altogether happy with it. So with the help of Ken Branagh he got in touch with Duncan Heath, my agent, and invited me to come to Sheffield to do my second Prospero. The production transferred to London where it became the longest-running *Tempest* in the West End.

Michael claims I am the last living actor to receive the baton from Olivier direct, and the link is direct and very strong. This may be going too far, but what he does think, and I would agree, is that I have what Olivier has, or had, in *Henry V*, namely a big vocal range, which means that I can do a two-octave jump.

The productions I did for Michael over the next years at the Donmar, subsequent to the West End run of *The Tempest*, were sure going to put this to the test! Finally, when I came to perform Lear, I lost my voice twice, so maybe this should teach Michael not to make such a claim!

What began to obsess me as I played Prospero a second time was what appeared to be an almost prophetic vision of Shakespeare's, which is applicable to our own time. In that same speech where he talks of our revels being ended, he continues, saying that all they have seen has now melted into thin air, these cloud-capped towers and gorgeous palaces, 'the great globe itself./ Yea, all which it inherit, shall dissolve,/ And, like this insubstantial pageant faded,/ Leave not a rack behind.'

Why should he use such a strange word as 'dissolve', that the whole world should dissolve? Did he, in some nightmare, look and see a future before us? For if we do end this world in a nuclear war, then that is exactly what will happen. Our great globe will dissolve, we human beings will just melt. And what is a rack? A rack is a little wisp of cloud. It will all vanish like a dream, and all that will be left of man and his achievements is that tiny wisp of cloud.

For underpinning the magic and beauty of *The Tempest* is the other side of man: Caliban, the side that is evil, and that cannot be taught good. This is something Prospero recognises when he actually says, 'this thing of darkness, I acknowledge mine'. A little earlier he has said to Ariel 'we must prepare to meet with Caliban'. What a strange thing to say. We know he has been meeting Caliban all the time for fifteen years, but this time it is as if he has to force himself to confront formally just what Caliban is, that other side of man.

Caliban is always there, the thing of darkness throbbing away under the surface in man, the evil about which we appear able to do nothing. Even when Caliban says to Prospero 'you gave me language', you can feel this has been such a mixed blessing, this ability to communicate.

———

After Prospero with Michael I did three more great classical roles: Philip II, Malvolio, and finally Lear. When Michael came to cast me in *Don Carlos* as Philip II of Spain he had a problem in so far as I love to be loved, and tend to fold myself into a love affair with the part, and do all I can to resist attempts to descend to a dark, despotic place.

Michael remembers this well: 'It is as if Derek has an internal audience, and has to approve, channel that audience which love him being emotional. We had to get him into a kind of default mode or point, so as to get the audience loving him for being nasty. We had built the trust up in *The Tempest*, so how did it go in *Don Carlos*? Well, not surprisingly, it was good after we had found the technical way to release the monster by lowering Philip down in voice. Derek never gives his best on opening night, few actors I know do, and when we did *Don Carlos* we had no props or furniture, which is very demanding for the actors. Derek's worst enemy is that he likes to get louder and madder sometimes, and he loves showing off, as if to say, "Look what I can do."'

Playing King Lear, in 2010–11, has undoubtedly been the peak of my theatrical career. When with Michael we had at last fixed up to do *Lear* at the Donmar and still had plenty of time, I could begin to think seriously how to play this ultimate of Shakespearian roles. Michael and I had talked about doing it two years before, but it was only a year before, when he had to get his programme together, that he said: 'Come on, we've got to make a decision. It's now or never.'

The first performance of *Lear* which came into my mind was Scofield's. I never saw the stage performance, only the film, which was shot almost exclusively in close-up. I had no notion of what it must have been like on stage, which as I knew was quite something. I saw Olivier on television. I saw Donald Wolfit way back on stage. All I can remember of Wolfit was the bigness, the loudness of it. He had it in his repertoire with *Tamburlaine* and *Twelfth Night*, in which he played Malvolio. I felt no sympathy with his Lear, and he didn't stay with me. It was part of something I saw when I was very young, and it impressed me tremendously, but it was never the Damascene conversion.

I had not seen Gielgud perform Lear in his Gruyère cheese costume when he was seventy-six. I saw Ian Holm, and most recently I saw Ian McKellen. They both took their clothes off in the storm scenes. There is absolutely no justification in the text for this at all, as there is for the actor Edgar taking off his kit as 'naked Tom', and as he did in Peter Brook's production with Paul Scofield. I thought the sensational effect of acting knights doing a full frontal was just not for me.

As for the lines 'Blow winds and crack your cheeks', which I performed in an intense, inwards whisper with a microphone (the only time I used one), this is much more justified in the text. There is a precedent, too, for this. Charles Laughton wanted to do this speech in a whisper, and he wasn't allowed to.

We didn't do a read-through – fortunately. What Michael tends to do is to go through the play and, scene by scene, tell the cast to say it in their own words. Not to read it as Shakespeare wrote it, but to say what the lines mean in our own words. Some were better than others at this. I, because I worked it out before, was prepared, so I cheated! I had worked it out in France, the August before we opened. I went through the part line by line, writing down on the free page opposite the meaning in my own words.

Michael and I had settled on what texts we were going to use: we had both independently cut it, and then we put our cuts together. I had always wanted to be closer to Lear's age and now I was. We cut the line to suggest his age, fourscore years: 'Pray do not mock me:/ I'm a very foolish fond old man,/ Fourscore years and upwards.' I did not waste any time in rehearsals boning up on the words as I already knew them, so I could just think about how to do it.

Michael and I were very much in accord: he gave me my head, and we did not disagree over anything much. His idea was to make it as simple and accessible as possible. My input was to illuminate what I was saying emotionally and verbally, to spotlight what was coming out of my mouth, and out of my head, and from my heart. Michael's idea was not to get in the way, not to keep making theatrical coups, and to dispense entirely with furniture.

Ultimately, what I felt was so good about it was the fluidity, because there were no set changes; you had lighting changes, but one scene followed another. There were no 'director's moments'. What the director did, what the actors did, what the lighting man did, what the sound man did, were all part of the whole, and none of them had their moment: or if they did have their moment, it was shared by the whole performance. The storm was effective, it was simple, arresting, and it looked good, it sounded good. I didn't worry myself with ideas such as, 'What am I thinking in the moment? Am I guiding it?'

I find it difficult to analyse when playing Lear, but I am letting or making the audience understand what I am saying, not as a reverently produced text, but as near as I can get it to a spoken thought, the idea or thought or emotion which has suddenly occurred to me. So I say the text as I never heard it before, and hope it comes out of me in a contemporary way. The audience may not exactly understand the particular words I am using, but because of the intonation, of the way I am saying it – 'It ain't what you say, it's the way that you say it' is the catchphrase – they can understand what I mean, and what I am feeling. It upsets people, of course, who like the end-stopped line, the Shakespearean rhythms, but these rhythms have never meant a great deal to me. I prefer my own rhythms.

I stay in the wings all evening. I cannot go back to the dressing room and hear a bit on the Tannoy. If I have got a big scene coming up I think I should have gone to the loo before, but once I go on I forget about that, I totally forget. In Lear I had a costume change, and then I was not on for about thirty-five to forty minutes into the second half. I had about forty-five minutes off, so I stayed in the dressing room for about half of that, and then I went down and sat in the wings, in order to get myself back into the play.

I treat performances as if I am still rehearsing, when I see round the edge, and everybody is doing their bit, and I get up and do mine and then I go back and sit down. So when I go on stage it is that same kind of mindset I have. It is not back to the dressing room, then back to the play. I have to stay in the play all the time.

Playing Lear I lost my voice twice, once in London, once on tour, and they had to find me a voice masseur, which was helpful: he massaged the throat and the larynx. The loss of voice in Llandudno was the worst occasion. We had done eight weeks in London, eight performances a week, then for two nights I lost my voice: after London this was our first over 1,000-seater theatre, and I was out of practice vocally, although I had done my exercises. I was compensating wildly because of the bigness of the venue, and by Friday morning the voice had gone; so I had to cancel Friday and two performances on Saturday, and then the voice came back.

The next week was Belfast Opera House, a huge stage, a big auditorium where long ago I acted Charles Dyer's *Staircase* with Tim West. I had played the character with the playwright's name, while the other character, Harry C. Leeds, is an anagram of this. Tim and I had got lots of laughs doing this romp in London, but when we took it to the Opera House (and as this was in the days of Ian Paisley) the moment the audience realised it was a play about two homosexual hairdressers you could hear the seats banging up as the good populace of Belfast departed. We followed Belfast with the 1,800-seater in Salford. Then Milton Keynes, and I managed to survive better.

At the end of every performance the stage manager would place a glass of Chardonnay on my dressing table, and that was my reward: I had got through *Lear*. On the first night in Llandudno there was a reception in the front of house, to which I went, poured down the white wine, and by Friday I discovered the worst thing I could do when I came off the stage as King Lear was to pour white wine down my throat: it was like pouring down pure acid. The nightly glass had to stop. Michael didn't like me drinking: of course, he wasn't suggesting I had in any way a drink problem, but maybe he felt with Lear I might be going that way. Anyway, as a friend pointed out, Chardonnay dries out the voice, so it cannot be good for it.

My favourite *Lear* venues were Richmond and Bath, the beautiful smaller theatres. When one live performance at the Donmar was screened worldwide, the satellite signal failed in the second part. We had to go back a bit, and start again. That was a real test of patience. In New York we performed at the BAM, the Brooklyn Academy of Music, where the auditorium is Epidaurian.

During a break after London I went to a health farm, quite a harsh juxtaposition to Lear in the storm to recover in a health farm: it was all very gentle. Lear was wrapped in seaweeds and oils, and he came out smelling rather better than when he went in. I don't think it did any good, but it was a generous gift from the Donmar. I didn't need to lose weight for I had lost over a stone.

I like Lear as a person and I loved becoming him for each performance. While I am very passive, unconfrontational, Lear is the opposite, with all that rage, all that anger, which I don't have in myself. When the RSC offered me Cyrano I said, 'I don't really have his anger – during the first two acts he unleashes this stream of vitriol.'

Terry Hands said, 'If I promise to make you angry, then will you do it?' A few weeks into rehearsal he said, 'Let's run the first two acts. With all our sins and mistakes, let's go for it, run it, and see what we've got.'

Well, we finished, sat down for notes, and in front of the entire company Terry said, 'I've got it, Derek. You're a closet butch!'

With Lear's Fool the banter can be a game show, a trial of upstaging, but that was never the issue with Ron Cook, for this was a marriage made in heaven. Much of the Fool's text went, although only the passages which were very obscure. Our two characters adored each other, which really showed in the interplay between Ron and me, and my Lear joined in the jokes and clowning. 'Where is he, I need the fool.'

There is one very significant line when Lear says, 'You are a pestilent gall to me.' I said it laughing, as if Lear didn't really mean it, but that was what he really needed and he knew it.

Michael was very proud that he revived my classical status with his four productions at the Donmar. He believes Lear shows that the challenge of mankind, or rather the challenge *to* mankind, is to be big enough to forgive. Lear's is an amazing life journey, from one who has but slenderly known himself, to someone who has full understanding. I would like to think that this, too, possibly, is what has happened to me in my journey through life, through my seven ages.

Like that earlier character of mine, who is a mixture of wisdom and disability, who claims, 'I have told the truth and set the record straight for posterity,' it may be, after all, that I've had a good measure of the 'fool's luck' of Claudius.

46

AREN'T WE ALL?

I always tend to be compared with and measured alongside Ian McKellen, my Cambridge contemporary. My career and Ian's have been on an uncannily similar and parallel course, yet, except for one brief moment when we were together at the National Theatre, we have never been with substantial parts together in a play.

That has now changed – not, paradoxically, in the theatre but on television – with *Vicious*, a sitcom about two bantering old queens, played by Ian and me, along with Frances de la Tour.

The last opportunity for a collaboration between us before *Vicious* came along was when Trevor Nunn took over running the National Theatre in 1993, and Peter Shaffer declared he was writing a play for Ian and me. Peter told me over lunch when I met him in New York that this play was about Tchaikovsky and his brother Modest. I was to be the composer, and Ian his brother: Peter was so enthusiastic about what a wonderful story it was, and he had written the first two acts, but he was having a problem with the third act. He wouldn't exactly tell me what the problem was, but his great revelation was about the mystery of the composer, namely his death in 1890 – his death from cholera, and how he caught it.

Peter talked about it with me a couple of times, but it never progressed to meeting up with Ian and Trevor Nunn, although it was billed in the press as Trevor's first production for the National. Peter has never finished it. I am sure it lies in a drawer somewhere in New York, but I never saw any of it. He did tell me when we had lunch much more recently in New York, where I was appearing as Lear – and he was by now eighty-four and very frail – that he was working on something else, a play, working more slowly and not sure when he would finish it, if ever.

I find Ian very funny, he has a great sense of humour, and he is a great companion. Strangely enough he has this little turn or one-man show in which, according to Frances Barber, he mimes who I am without saying a word, but you can easily guess it is me. In an *Aladdin* pantomime at the Old Vic in 2005, in which he played Widow Twankey (and Frankie Barber Wishy-Washy), he sent me up as the marble-mouthed Shakespearian actor, saying at one point, when Aladdin rants with passion, 'What an honour working with you, Sir Derek!' He joked that the panto was 'longer than a Trevor Nunn production'; and made an agonised plea for 'no more Shakespeare directed by Peter Hall'.

After *Aladdin* I went round to the dressing room to say hello, and Ian, as we embraced, quipped, 'How about the Ugly Sisters?'

'Look what I've found in the local shop!' he exclaimed when his impish humour took a further rise out of me on an occasion when I met him at Stratford. He pulled open his coat to reveal a T-shirt with my ugly mug as Macbeth on it – not my most glorious Shakespearian role by any straw (generally reckoned my worst)!

Ian laughed when I recently reminded him of that episode: 'It was in one of those teashops in Stratford – not Washington DC as I first thought, where I was playing King Lear. Did I buy it? Ha ha ha ha – I think we're both allowed to send each other up as we both know what we are up to. The work is such a huge part of both our lives. I can't imagine you not working. Of late, we've socialised a bit more. Frankie Barber would caricature you as being on the nervous side, and me as carefree and showing off. Probably there's a touch of truth in that, I suppose. I'm much more of a self-publicist than you, Derek.'

In 2007 he came to stay with us in France. One day we were having guests to lunch and had no flowers to decorate the house. By the house was a field of sunflowers in full bloom and Ian said, 'Come on, let's cut some.'

'But we can't,' I protested. 'The farmer will be furious.'

Ian dragged me off, however, and snipped away with the secateurs, while I stood by his side gathering up a bunch. Then fear of the irate farmer got the better of me, and I scarpered, leaving Ian to face the music.

———◆———

Last Tango in Halifax has been a huge success in its first series on BBC television. The reason is that it's like a play more than a film, with big acting scenes, in some ways resembling a 1960s Armchair Theatre. It's a refreshing change from much of the constant, edgy, ever-changing and pressurised style and content of filmed television. To me it's like going back to *I, Claudius*.

And there are even the kind of provocative discussions in it that we haven't seen for a long time in TV drama, such as when my character Alan argues with Anne Reid's character Celia about her love for David Cameron and the *Daily Mail*, both of which Alan, as an old lefty, deplores.

'Oh,' he says, 'I'm going to have to watch you.'

Like Alan in *Last Tango*, I have the image of a placid, rather jovial person. Deep down I know the opposite is going on. Worry and self-doubt in particular. I can suppress them till I need them. Tap into them and not live by them. Like most who do my job I can reach inside myself and switch off the emote button at will. I can be anonymous, inscrutable, concealed behind my veil as well as revealing myself. Mysteriously there would seem to be some source or power which I can reach down inside me and find.

My greatest stroke of good fortune was to end up with Richard. It was thirty-five years ago that we met. It was not and has not been easy and plain sailing all the time, not only because of the seventeen-year gap between us, but also because of my position in the business. It was always the scripts that were coming through the door for me. But he is the strength of the relationship, the strong one.

On New Year's Eve, 2006, we were staying with Emma Thompson and her husband Greg Wise in Scotland. They have a lovely property high up in the mountains: thick, thick snow was everywhere, and the beautiful river was flowing swiftly. All of us there set off for a walk after lunch to the river and we were going to come back at about five o'clock; there was Emma's sister Sophie, and her husband Richard, Richard and I, Greg and Emma and their daughter Gaia – and of course Bella, my Irish terrier, bounding ahead.

At this point I ought to record that the dog in *Coronation Street* is named after her: Bella Sinéad. We added the second name so we could phone up Sinéad and tell her. 'We've named our bitch after you!' This came about because one of the writers, Jonathan Harvey, was round with us at Frances Barber's one day, and we had Bella with us. Later on someone in *Corrie* had a swan and they gave it the same name: just think of a swan called Bella Sinéad!

Anyway, when we arrived back at the house we found: no Bella. 'Who's seen Bella?' The answer was no one. We started looking, we looked and we looked, and went back over where we had been. The river was in full spate, so we drove down to it and along it, and by now I was crying, I was quite hysterical. We searched for two hours until it became dark or almost dark. Richard was stoical and methodical. 'We must go here, look there,' while I was hopeless and emotional. Eventually we had searched everywhere: there was nowhere else she could have gone. Total despair reigned.

But at this moment Richard said, 'Let's just go back to the place where we last saw her' – although he had been there already, and called and called. So back there we went, along the bank, Richard ten yards ahead of me, right on the water. For no reason I walked to the edge of the bank and peered over. And Bella Sinéad was there, up to her chest in the racing water, hanging on with her paws to the bank. We had passed this spot maybe ten times and she hadn't barked once.

'She's there!' I shouted, and Richard came running back. I held onto him, he reached down to pull her out, caught her, threw her up so I could catch her, at which moment I let go of him, and he slipped down into the river. Now I was getting rid of him to save the dog!

We arrived back at Emma's. We were soaked through, but what a relief! We rushed in to warm ourselves at the fire. At this point Richard broke down – howled out. But all the time up to then he had been the epitome of 'Pull yourself together!'

———

So here are Richard and I, still pulling together. We were partnered in a civil ceremony on 21 February 2007, when we gave a party at home for our nearest friends. A curious thought I had was that everyone who happened to be there was straight. And we have lasted all this time.

Sam Mendes, who directed me as Kean, said he likes to ask actors or artists, given the toil, the heartache, and the sheer hard work and disappointments, 'Why do you do it?' or more precisely 'For what or whom?' The answers he received have been many: some for money, some for a girl- or boyfriend, many for 'myself' and for celebrity.

My answer is simple. I do it because I do it, to fulfil myself, to enjoy myself and my life to the full. What I said about playing Benedick, also – it is the romantic motive, namely that it is my capacity for dreamy wonderment, combined with a terrible insecurity about who I am, where I am going and why and how, that gives me a craving, an absolute need to act.

I have always been a company man. The Cambridge Rep, the Birmingham Rep, the National, Prospect, RSC; the very institutions were responsible for success and failure. I was subsumed in the larger entity, absorbed into the family. And this is what the theatre has always been for me: my family. As such, and as in family life, I hate showing off and I do not need approval.

All these tours, first nights, long runs, short runs, with their hazards and triumphs, their heartaches and joys, have merged into one another. I have never felt at ease being applauded, in spite of Sir's admonition to me to respond to taking the solo curtain. Grandage made me do it for *Lear* because it looks ungracious if you do not, it looks rude. But I do not relish it.

Even going back to school, to the reading of the lesson, having the light put on me there, I was reluctant to stand out. I still want to be part of the crowd, part of the company, and when my fellow players come for their bow before me, then 'I come tripping out and on alone', I find very difficult. I am happiest with the idea of being in a family where we are in it together, rather than 'I am the one you really want to say thank you to.'

As a child, I don't believe I thought about anything very much, and never philosophised, so some might say I was just shallow. Or you could say, which I suppose is truer, that I have always set more store by my intuition and imagination than by analytical thinking. The only avenue I go down in any creative way is acting. I don't have any other strings to my bow. I certainly never practised the present-day trend of self-evaluation.

I agree most of all with those words of Agamemnon in Act III of *Troilus and Cressida* when he rebukes Ajax: 'He that is proud eats up himself. Pride is his own glass, his own trumpet, his own chronicle — and whatever praises itself but in the deed devours the deed in the praise.'

As an actor I had the blessing for a very long time to have a photographic memory and to be a very fast study. I like to feel

AS LUCK WOULD HAVE IT

there is some kind of unwritten contract between myself and the
public, and that it knows about me and knows what to expect,
namely that I bring to the parts I play a kind of everyman reality,
not something extreme and out of this world, so that they identify with me because, really, I'm not so special.

All the world's a stage and I'm merely a player – aren't we all?

And as for 'Sans teeth, sans eyes, sans taste, sans everything' …
well, of course, that's still to come.

AFTERWORD AND
ACKNOWLEDGEMENTS

This book has recounted the 'Seven Ages' of my life story from 'the infant, mewling' of my birth in 1938 to what I hope, in my 75th year, is still very far from 'sans everything'. While it is a story I have wanted to tell for a long time – and many people have asked me to tell it – it has only really been made possible through a fortunate collaboration with my long-time friend, the writer Garry O'Connor, to whom I have talked extensively.

During the course of preparing this book Garry has also spoken to those who know me well for their view of me. Excerpts from these interviews are intended to provide another view of me apart from my own. In all other respects the words have been mine.

We would therefore like to thank the following individuals who spared the time to talk to Garry in the preparation of this book between the years 2005 and 2012:

Anthony Arlidge, Frances Barber, Christopher Biggins, Isla Blair, Kenneth Branagh, Michael Burrell, Richard Clifford, Richard Cottrell, Sinéad Cusack, Michael Deacon, Margaret Drabble, Christine Edzard, Michael Gambon, Julian Glover, Michael Grandage, the late Roger Hammond, Terrence Hardiman, John Harrison, Charles Kay, Kevin Kelly (for his chronology and collection of memorabilia), Ian McKellen, Sam Mendes, Anthony Mott, Julian Pettifer, Siân Phillips, Ronald Pickup, Elizabeth

Proud, the late Corin Redgrave, Michael Redington, Simon Relph, Toby Robertson, David Rowe-Beddoe, Thea Sharrock, Clive Swift, Emma Thompson, John Tydeman, Hugh Walters, Duncan Weldon, David Weston, Hugh Whitemore and Herbert Wise.

Our especial thanks to Martin Noble for his sensitive and judicious editing; and to Carole Tonkinson for her enthusiastic support and suggestions at all stages; equally also our thanks to Paul Stevens and Julian Friedmann. Finally to all friends and colleagues who have encouraged me and thought *As Luck Would Have It* would be a good idea.

I have had the great good luck to be born with a talent for acting. But, in every other sense, I am in no way special – except of course in being privileged to be a human being.

Derek Jacobi
London, 2013

PICTURE CREDITS

All images are courtesy of the author, with the following exceptions: p2 (top left) © Edward Leigh; p2 (bottom) © Express & Independent Newspapers Ltd; p3 (top left and top right) © Willoughby Gullachsen; p3 (bottom left) Angus McBean Photograph © Harvard Theatre Collection, Houghton Library, Harvard University; p3 (bottom right) © Bob Johnson; p4 (middle left) © Joan Marcus; p4 (bottom right) © BBC; p5 (top left) © W. H. Wood; p5 (top right) © John Bulmer; p5 (middle left) © Christopher Davies; p5 (bottom left) © Arne Magnussen; p5 (bottom right) © Terry Fincher; p6 (top right) © Nobby Clark; p8 (lower right) © Johan Persson; p8 (bottom) © Tyne Tees Television